THE IMPORTANCE OF BEING DIFFERENT

**PECULIAR BODIES: STORIES AND HISTORIES**
Carolyn Day, Chris Mounsey, and Wendy J. Turner, Editors

# The Importance of Being Different

*Disability in Oscar Wilde's Fairy Tales*

CHRIS FOSS

UNIVERSITY OF VIRGINIA PRESS
*Charlottesville and London*

The University of Virginia Press is situated on the traditional lands of the Monacan Nation, and the Commonwealth of Virginia was and is home to many other Indigenous people. We pay our respect to all of them, past and present. We also honor the enslaved African and African American people who built the University of Virginia, and we recognize their descendants. We commit to fostering voices from these communities through our publications and to deepening our collective understanding of their histories and contributions.

University of Virginia Press
© 2025 by the Rector and Visitors of the University of Virginia
All rights reserved
Printed in the United States of America on acid-free paper

*First published 2025*

9 8 7 6 5 4 3 2 1

LIBRARY OF CONGRESS CATALOGING-IN-PUBLICATION DATA
Names: Foss, Chris, author.
Title: The importance of being different : disability in Oscar Wilde's fairy tales / Chris Foss.
Description: Charlottesville : University of Virginia Press, 2025. | Series: Peculiar bodies: stories and histories | Includes bibliographical references and index.
Identifiers: LCCN 2024048196 (print) | LCCN 2024048197 (ebook) | ISBN 9780813953007 (hardcover) | ISBN 9780813953014 (paperback) | ISBN 9780813953021 (ebook)
Subjects: LCSH: Wilde, Oscar, 1854–1900—Criticism and interpretation. | Disabilities in literature. | People with disabilities in literature. | Fairy tales—Ireland—History and criticism. | LCGFT: Literary criticism.
Classification: LCC PR5827.D57 F67 2025 (print) | LCC PR5827.D57 (ebook) | DDC 828/.809—dc23/eng/20241028
LC record available at https://lccn.loc.gov/2024048196
LC ebook record available at https://lccn.loc.gov/2024048197

*Cover art:* "The Selfish Giant," bookplate from Oscar Wilde's *The Happy Prince and Other Tales* (London: David Nutt, 1888). (Brigham Young University Libraries)
*Cover design:* Cecilia Sorochin

*In memory of*
*Caroline May Bartels Foss*
*and Karen Cameron Scanlon*

# CONTENTS

*Acknowledgments*
ix

Introduction
"But When the Children Saw Him They Were
So Frightened That They All Ran Away"
Laying the Groundwork for a Disability Studies Approach
1

1. "It Is a Pity, for He Is So Ugly That He
Might Have Made the King Smile"
"The Birthday of the Infanta" and the Spectacle of the Freakish Body
35

2. "He Remembered That the Little Mermaid
Had No Feet and Could Not Dance"
The Love of and by Extraordinary Bodies in
"The Fisherman and His Soul"
54

3. "No Pity Had He for the Poor, or for Those Who
Were Blind or Maimed or in Any Way Afflicted"
Emotional Connection and Compassionate Action in "The Star-Child"
75

4. "You Are Blind Now . . .
So I Will Stay with You Always"
"The Happy Prince" and the Disability-Aligned
Protagonist as Utopian Hero
98

Conclusion
"We Are the Zanies of Sorrow"
Reflections and Refractions in Wilde's Prison Literature
117

Notes
143

Bibliography
165

Index
173

# ACKNOWLEDGMENTS

I would like to begin by thanking my superb editor, Angie Hogan, as well as everyone else at UVA Press (particularly Clayton Butler, Carolyn Day, Chris Mounsey, Wren Myers, Ellen Satrom, and Wendy J. Turner). This labor of love has spanned many years and required multiple drafts, mostly across separate summers, given my teaching load, so without your guidance and patience and support this project surely would never have seen the light of day!

I am deeply appreciative of my home institution, the University of Mary Washington, for numerous faculty development grants in support of research and travel, but in particular for the 2015 sabbatical award that launched the first stages of this eventual book project and for the 2018–20 Waple Professorship award that enabled me to draft my prospectus and begin the manuscript completion process in earnest. Thanks also to my UMW colleagues, especially members of my department (English and Linguistics) and of our Disability Studies Initiative. A hat tip as well to my friends at Advanced Studies in England for providing me with the opportunity to take my Wilde show on the road (well, across the pond) for two separate study abroad summers in Bath (including memorable Wilde times in both London and Oxford).

Above all, thanks to my students down through the years in the now double-digit iterations of my senior seminar capstone course on Wilde; the chance to refresh my take on his *Complete Works* every couple of years has been an essential part of my ongoing professional engagement in this area. This is not just a Victorian project, though, but also a work belonging to the field of disability studies, so I further appreciate all of the many students from my Disability and Literature, Fictions of Disability, and Representations of Autism courses over the past fifteen years, plus those who have completed English or Honors individual studies with me in the area.

I trace my love of Oscar back to the legendary James G. Nelson, who so expertly and enjoyably helped contextualize Wilde's life and work within that and those of the Pre-Raphaelite Circle, but especially of the Aesthetes and Decadents. It was about a decade or so later when I presented my first conference paper on Wilde, and encouraging remarks from John Maynard relayed to me secondhand by chance ended up inspiring me to take Oscar even more seriously as a potential core focus for my life as a teacher-scholar, leading to the launch of the aforementioned senior seminar that immediately became my signature course, and motivating me to look for more professional development opportunities.

The single most transformative moment of my scholarly career followed a few years later thanks to the incomparable Joseph Bristow, who accepted me into his 2007 NEH Summer Seminar on the Wilde Archive at the Clark in Los Angeles. To bask in the glory of the place would have been more than enough in and of itself, but the opportunity to converse and work with Joe and our whole cohort (particularly my pals Loretta Clayton, Casey Jarrin, Liz Miller, and Felicia Ruff) fundamentally engaged me on a whole new level, one quite frankly which I couldn't have even imagined possible. Following up that summer with a conference at the Clark a couple years later and then eventually getting the band back together for the *Wilde Discoveries* essay collection (2013) ensured Oscar would begin truly to dominate my professional life.

There have been many others along the way who have contributed to my growth as a Wilde scholar. Chris Snodgrass was very supportive of another conference paper, one which after many years would end up being published by yet another wonderful colleague, Frederick S. Roden, in his *Critical Insights: Oscar Wilde* volume (2019). Two specific events also merit special mention: first, in fall 2017, my participation along with Rochelle Rives and Felicia Ruff in the celebrations surrounding the Oscar Wilde Temple installation sponsored by the Church of the Village in New York; second, in spring 2018, my magical trip to Sweden for the inaugural John Andrén Conference. Organized superbly by Cian Duffy and equally impressively facilitated by the excellent staff of the Ystad Public Library, this occasion allowed me to meet a remarkable set of scholars: Evrim Doğan Adanur, Tim Chandler, Sasha Dovzhyk, Sandi Leonard, Peter Raby, and Linda Zatlin. I close this paragraph with a general shout out to any and all who sat through my papers on Wilde at various LUCVS, MCBS, NCSA, NEMLA, SAMLA, VHC, and VI conferences.

On the disability studies side of this project, I owe a debt to any number of important persons as well. First and foremost, thanks to the exceptional David Bolt, who not only provided me with the amazing opportunity to present my work on "Birthday" for the Centre for Culture and Disability Studies Seminar Series at Liverpool Hope University in Spring 2017 but then published my piece on "Star-Child" in his top-flight *Journal of Literary & Cultural Disability Studies* in 2020. I would also like to express heartfelt gratitude to Essaka Joshua, who was incredibly kind and supportive throughout the whole process of getting my first published essay on this topic out there as part of her Dis/Enabling Narratives special issue for *Journal of Narrative Theory*. Otherwise, as I've already noted numerous names of those who provided community and collaboration in disability studies leading up to my 2016 co-edited essay collection *Disability in Comic Books and Graphic Narratives*, I'll just mention a baker's dozen more here, folks I admire and appreciate for enriching my life and work in this area since then: Daisy Breneman, Jay Dolmage, Elizabeth Donaldson, Chris Gabbard, Alice Hall, Allison Hobgood, David Mitchell, Diana Paulin, Julia Miele Rodas, Ralph Savarese, Sharon Snyder, Kris Weller, and Remi Yergeau.

In conclusion, my deepest gratitude goes out to my friends and family (near or far, hybrid or in-person or virtual, old or new, young or old), who have provided me with perspective and happiness during these last number of years while I have been working on what certainly feels like my scholarly swan song—above all, to my wonderful kids and to my incredible partner, Mara Scanlon, my debt to whom is absolutely impossible for me to attempt to sum up in words here.

THE IMPORTANCE OF BEING DIFFERENT

INTRODUCTION

# "But When the Children Saw Him They Were So Frightened That They All Ran Away"

*Laying the Groundwork for a Disability Studies Approach*

Oscar Wilde published two collections of fairy tales, *The Happy Prince and Other Tales* and *A House of Pomegranates*, both of which compellingly require readers consistently to consider stigmatized physical difference that today many would gloss as markers of disabled identity. Accordingly, these stories deserve an in-depth delineation both of how one might position the renderings of their numerous nonnormative characters relative to late-nineteenth-century notions of disability and also of how these Victorian literary representations might hold generative possibilities for inflecting contemporary conversations around disability, particularly where the current reconsideration of long-standing assumptions about appropriate versus inappropriate emotional responses is concerned. The extraordinary bodies Wilde's fairy tales foreground further invite readers to think intersectionally regarding how disability-aligned identity expressions and lived experiences overlap with those of other categories such as class and socioeconomic status, ethnicity and race, and gender and sexuality—thereby offering a complex contextualization of disability's place within the larger tapestry of diversity more broadly, then and now. These two truly remarkable volumes and the appealing peculiar protagonists they prominently place before their readers—especially when combined with the strong interest they hold for fans of fairy tales and connoisseurs of children's literature alike—merit more extensive examination in order to establish a fuller sense of the wonderful richness of these still too often disregarded contributions to Wilde's oeuvre.

The extent to which Wilde's fairy tales routinely present their readers with extended engagements with so many unusual bodies is quite remarkable. *The Happy Prince and Other Tales* most memorably contains two such stories, one starring a living statue (its titular character, immobile, as most statues, even living ones, tend to be) who sacrifices his sight and his physical beauty in order to relieve the poverty and suffering of others, and the other featuring an initially selfish and imposing giant who ends up welcoming into his garden all children who wish to play there. The collection's other three tales showcase a selfless man of small means with the diminutive moniker of little Hans who pays with his life for his generosity toward a wealthy friend, a small songbird who maims and ultimately kills herself in the name of love, and an insufferable firework who becomes temporarily "disabled" after dampening himself with tears of self-pity. Three of the four texts that comprise *A House of Pomegranates* provide even more sustained portrayals of anomalous bodies. These include a performing dwarf[1] and the little princess he is intended to entertain, a beautiful "star-child" whose cruel rejection of an ugly beggar woman transforms him into a hideous wretch, and a young fisherman who cuts his shadow or soul away from his body in order to live with a little mermaid under the sea. Even the only outlier in terms of this parade of physically exceptional protagonists, a young king who ultimately refuses to wear his fancy coronation attire owing to its origins in the exploitation of the poor and the enslaved, still productively may be read alongside the rest of the above disability-aligned representations and their overdetermined relationships to both love and beauty and wealth and power.[2]

In this introduction, I will begin by summarizing some of the more notable critical responses to Wilde's fairy tales, including the three equally important book-length studies to date. The short critical review will dovetail nicely into a discussion of Wilde's audience and the extent to which the figure of the child opens up avenues for articulations with Victorian infantilizations of the disabled, the foreign, and the poor. This line of thought in turn will lead to my elaborating on the profits and problems of deigning to talk about disability in reference to these texts, given the decidedly distinct conceptualization of that term during the nineteenth century, while still attending to its instructive intersectional overlaps with other contemporary identity expressions and markers. Next, I will turn to a consideration of freakery to tease out both the centrality of the figure of the freak in the

Victorian experience of unusual bodies and to further link Wilde's literary representations of nonnormative physical appearance with such disability-aligned difference. Then, after a section sketching out some possibilities regarding potential biographical influences that might have motivated Wilde's own interest in presenting readers with so many peculiar protagonists in these stories, I will wrap up my preliminary groundwork for this study with an explanation of the significance of remaining attuned to the range of emotional responses these characters engender. In an attempt to begin bringing all this together, I will conclude this introduction with a short analysis of "The Selfish Giant" as an initial example suggesting how reading the fairy tales through the lens of disability studies can offer both truly generative insights into and intriguing questions about these brilliant pieces (followed by, at the very last, the requisite brief summaries of the rest of the chapters).

While some scholars balk at what they see as an anachronistic application of the term *disability* to nineteenth-century contexts, others claim it as a valid means of illuminating both past and present in a valuable critical articulation. As should already be clear, I gravitate toward the latter approach. At the same time, I want to respect the concerns of advocates for the former, and so I will often employ the phrase *disability-aligned* to signal that I grant it is a potentially contestatory move simply just to refer to Wilde's peculiar protagonists as disabled without some sort of qualification. I certainly do not intend to use *disability-aligned* in any way that might be perceived to be sliding toward the slippery slope of the problematic notion "everyone is disabled in some way or at some point." I personally do interact with these figures as literary representations of disability; for me, their physical differences decidedly impact how they are seen, how they are treated, and how they are ushered toward their unhappy endings. But I choose to describe them as disability-aligned precisely because for me it highlights how, though there is definitely an overlap, an alignment even, between the lived experiences of Wilde's colorful cast of unconventional characters and those of at least some disabled persons today, there is also a gap, a disjunction, between them that, again, bears acknowledgment.[3]

The Happy Prince seems the least controversial character choice to read through a disability studies lens, certainly at least after he becomes blind (if he does not already invoke some aspects of mobility impairments prior to that). Wilde's Giant, Dwarf, little Mermaid, and deformed Star-Child (given their status as enfreaked figures) also for me merit analysis from various angles that disability studies offers us; even as *disabled* and *freak* obviously are not strict synonyms (and, again, some stridently insist on their distinctness, as I will discuss a bit later on in this introduction), plenty of scholars and others persuasively have argued there are enough analogous aspects to the stereotyping and stigmatization of their physical embodiments to justify considering how these two categories may be seen as related ones. Granted, there is also a decided difference between an "ugly" Dwarf and a beautiful Mermaid, and all the more so between however humane a Giant and a human Fisherman (even one who not merely allies himself with the freakish Sea-folk but arguably becomes one of them when he goes to live with them underwater after amputating his soul). Still, I see value in exploring what new frameworks the lens of disability offers these texts, even as I embrace the idea of characterizing these peculiar protagonists as *disability-aligned* so as not to conflate their different historical and literary contexts with contemporary lived experiences of disability.

I attempt to encourage a diverse view of Wilde's disability-aligned characters by employing a wide range of adjectives to refer to their exceptional appearances. Some of these descriptors are included mainly for the sake of variety, and to encourage as wide a range of potential angles on their difference as possible, but a few do carry with them special resonances, for me and surely for at least some of my readers as well. For example, every use of *extraordinary* always contains in my head a hat tip to the foundational work (in both disability studies and freak studies) of Rosemarie Garland-Thomson. Another notable case of this is my recourse to *peculiar,* an especially engaging keyword that to my mind evokes multiple appealing associations with the word *queer,* as well as serving as a shout-out to the Peculiar Bodies: Stories and Histories book series at the University of Virginia Press. I additionally appreciate how the word's original late Middle English denotation positively glossed its nouns as distinctive, even distinguished. To my mind, this etymology encourages us to celebrate rather than reject the atypicality or oddness it primarily betokens today.

*Queer* similarly invokes significant reassignings of meaning that are even more specifically relevant to Wilde studies. Often containing suggestions of dubiousness within its references to peculiarity, but also complicating those connotations by in some contexts denoting authority and leadership, the term conspicuously further links to discourses of disability and illness when intended to convey a sense of feeling unwell or out of sorts (along with the historical identification of Queer Street as the place where those in difficulties find themselves). However, it is of course the word's connection to nonnormative gender and sexual expressions and identities that so attractively attaches *queer* to Wilde while productively emphasizing the intersectionality of disability-aligned lives. It is crucial to clarify, though, as I will address again a bit later on in this introduction, that my use of *queer* to describe the bodies of Wilde's peculiar protagonists is to be read literally, as indicative that these are literary representations of characters who are interesting owing to their actual physical difference, not merely because they might seem to invite interpretation only as metaphorical stand-ins for lived experiences associated with other identity expressions and markers.

Regarding intersectionality, I understand that its fundamental purpose should be calling attention to how multiple layers of discrimination typically lead to an augmentation of the precarities attached to any single experience of oppression, and so how it is potentially problematic to such a purpose when one of those experiences is perceived not to be indisputably present but only indistinctly evoked. I do not wish to dismiss this concern. Many scholars, though, have applied a queer studies lens to Wilde's life and work even as they had to acknowledge that understandings of what it means to be queer were not only not yet (fully) formed at the time Wilde was writing but also that these contemporary conceptualizations in fact are informed by his infamous trials themselves. As these engaging studies show, there is still value in crafting critical articulations of past and present as long as one remains attuned to the dangers of too simplistic an assumption of an equivalent presence rather than a seemingly more indistinct evocation. Along the lines of the sort of reparative reading practiced by Talia Schaffer in her *Communities of Care*,[4] I position my own utilization of a disability studies approach to the fairy tales as a hopeful exploration of the many ways in which reading Wilde's peculiar protagonists as disability-aligned characters allows for important new conversations around the anomalous body, then and now.

*The Importance of Being Different* is the first-ever book-length study of any of Wilde's works from a disability studies perspective. Attention to this angle on the author overall has been scant. In his notable monograph *Disability, Representation and the Body in Irish Writing*, Mark Mossman devotes part of his first chapter to a creative rendering relative to disability studies of Wilde's legendary appearance at the Grosvenor Gallery in his cello coat,[5] but Mossman's brushstrokes are broad and make no reference to Wilde's writings other than a single one-line quotation from his notorious gothic novel *The Picture of Dorian Gray*. David Bolt, an eminent figure in disability studies, also references this novel in his powerful piece "Aesthetic Blindness," though only in a few sentences, as a brief framing of its main argument on Maurice Maeterlinck's *The Blind*. Michael Davidson, another bona fide superstar in the field, discusses Wilde's aforementioned novel (along with the fairy tale "The Birthday of the Infanta") in a four-paragraph section in his suggestive article "The Rage of Caliban," but the bulk of the essay concentrates on Diego Velázquez's painting *Las Meninas* and Alexander von Zemlinsky's opera *Der Zwerg*. Otherwise, the dearth of disability studies work even briefly referencing Wilde is disappointing, as such a focus might refreshingly extend appreciation of both the writer and his writing beyond such standard lenses as aestheticism, nationality, and sexuality. Given the preponderance of unusual bodies across the fairy tale genre in general, this lack of attention is particularly surprising when disability, freakery, or the two together not only maintain a significant presence across both volumes but actually serve in those narratives as a crucial component informing his aesthetic choices and the sociopolitical agenda most readers see as allied with his aesthetics in these texts.

In addition to encouraging new conversations around its critical articulation of Wilde and disability studies, *The Importance of Being Different* aims to extend the still comparatively limited scholarly attention to Wilde's fairy tales. According to Jessica Straley, these texts seem something of a "critical conundrum" to many, who wonder why such an ardent advocate of aestheticism would choose to work in a traditionally bourgeois genre concerned with inculcating moral lessons in support of the status quo.[6] For Straley, that the author of works such as "The Decay of Lying" might try his hand at such stories is less surprising if one sees the genre as fundamentally one "whose assault on truthfulness was hotly discussed and debated in the nineteenth century" itself.[7] Wilde's aesthetic allegiances to artificiality in fact do lead in his fairy tales to artful and complex texts that undermine middle-class moralizing, stories which (if they gesture toward any lessons at all) leave readers puzzling over whether to gloss them as ambiguous, ambivalent, ironic, sarcastic, or sincere. After all, only one of his nine tales ("The Devoted Friend") offers anything in the way of an explicit moral, and in typical Wildean fashion, its lesson perversely appears to be that it is a very dangerous thing to tell a story with a moral.

When approaching Wilde's fairy tales, then, one needs to be prepared to read them as decided departures from the standard fare of the genre, and in particular as deliberate revisions of the era's dominant figure in the area, Hans Christian Andersen. Thus, while Maria Tatar sees Wilde as following Andersen in effecting a pronounced "literary turn," she also views the Irishman as deconstructing the Dane's bourgeois version of a "cult of beauty."[8] Anne Markey agrees, insisting Wilde "refracts, rather than reflects," the approach of his famous forebear.[9] Further, according to Jack Zipes, Andersen's happy endings do not challenge but rely upon a conventional "belief in the existing power structure that meant domination and exploitation of the lower classes," while Wilde on the other hand cultivates an "art of subversion" that exposes precisely such domination and exploitation through largely pessimistic plot outcomes.[10] Wilde's fairy tales, then, show he was very much invested in contesting the sentimentalism Andersen promulgated—and it is my contention his sympathetic interest in anomalous bodies offered him one consistent means by which to do so. Vivian Yenika-Agbaw has criticized Andersen for employing disabled characters "as objects of amusement and/or pity."[11] Wilde's own stories certainly contain their own problematic aspects where their representations of disability are concerned, but they also evince numerous progressive elements as well, moving beyond Andersen's ableism in any number of important ways, including through daring depictions that invite not just compassion for but identification with his exceptional protagonists, blurring the boundaries between "us" and "them."

Wilde's fairy tales, then, offer deft deconstructions of the sort of didacticism associated with Andersen.[12] Indeed, according to Lorraine Janzen Kooistra, he is so successful at this that he influences the development of a radical utopian branch of the genre during the next two decades.[13] At the same time, a chorus of critical voices caution against any attempt to pinpoint Wilde's purpose with these tales. Perry Nodelman notes that these works are "inherently slippery, inherently ambivalent," insisting they leave one only with "an irony that undermines irony itself."[14] Markey advises us to be prepared for "polyphonic textual spaces" ultimately characterized by their resistance to "definitive interpretation."[15] Further, Tatar testifies that the tales deliver dialectics that "bewilder" rather than "clarify," in the form of "games that feign legibility but tender opacity."[16] Still, while granting that any assertions about such slippery and bewildering texts must be put forward with caution and qualification, especially where authorial intentions are concerned, there are nevertheless numerous rewards awaiting those willing to offer more substantial treatments of these truly fascinating stories.

Three important books have blazed the trail in terms of foregrounding these underappreciated works. Jarlath Killeen's *The Fairy Tales of Oscar Wilde* was their first full-length study. Believing these stories had been overlooked because readers did not know quite how to reconcile their sense of Wilde as a "subversive writer" with "a didactic and conservative form" like children's literature, he argues that "re-situating these fairy tales in the complex nexus of theological, political, social and national concerns of late nineteenth-century Ireland" helps to resolve such difficulties.[17] According to Killeen, Wilde's tales both undermine mainstream English morality and reinforce a more properly Irish conservative tradition,[18] so "recognising the Irishness of these tales and their folk-Catholic elements helps to banish some of the critical mystery that has adhered to them."[19] He devotes a full chapter to each individual tale, and his discussions are impressively developed, ensuring his book remains the starting point for all projects in the area.

Markey's monograph *Oscar Wilde's Fairy Tales* builds off of Killeen's while attempting to provide a broader situating of the stories relative to European and Irish folklore and to the literary fairy tale. Her introduction includes a phenomenally thorough catalog of the shorter pieces of scholarship devoted to these texts up to that point in time, in part to demonstrate the extent to which "existing criticism has been limited by its tendency to approach the fairy tales from a single critical perspective: Wilde's nationality, sexuality or relationship to market forces, for example."[20] She devotes only one chapter apiece to each of the two volumes, but her discussions of the individual works within these chapters are nonetheless quite considerable. Her study represents essential reading for its meticulous and truly expert contextualization of every one of the tales in relation to folkloric traditions and the literary fairy tale.

Joseph Bristow's essay collection *Oscar Wilde and the Cultures of Childhood* features several significant chapters already referenced above (by Hollander, Kooistra, Nodelman, Straley, and Tatar). Overall, it offers an even broader sweep than Markey (connecting the tales to aesthetic memoirs, modern adaptations, and photography, as well as Wilde's immediate fairy tale successors). As the title might suggest, Bristow's book above all is notable for its emphasis on an obviously related but nonetheless distinct focus: childhood culture, and its subsets children's literature and the child reader. For Bristow, "Wilde's connections with the cultures of childhood brought about corresponding transformations, in his place as a children's writer, in the public understanding of him as a loving father, in his position as a political reformer, and in his experience as an inmate who learned what it meant to be a child in the eyes of God."[21] When a scholar as brilliant as Bristow endorses the importance of addressing how Victorian cultures of childhood inflect these tales, all those who follow in his footsteps are advised to do so as well.

Given that Wilde's intentions remain for many opaque and irresoluble, it perhaps comes as no surprise these complex conundrums are decidedly difficult to parse when it comes to audience. That Wilde referred to these texts variously as fairy tales, short stories, and studies in prose[22] in and of itself suggests the potential for contradictory construals. Indeed, he once asserted of *The Happy Prince and Other Tales* that it was "meant partly for children, and partly for those who have kept the childlike faculties of wonder and joy, and who find in simplicity a subtle strangeness," but some months later claimed that it was written "not for children, but for childlike people from eighteen to eighty."[23] Then, when *A House of Pomegranates* was questioned by a reviewer regarding if it could even be enjoyed by children, Wilde replied, in the *Pall Mall Gazette*, "I had about as much intention of pleasing the British child as I had of pleasing the British public."[24] How, then, are we to categorize these texts, and how might any determinations relative to audience inform their potential correlation with disability-aligned difference?

Perhaps unsurprisingly given Wilde's own comments, critics have offered some decidedly different answers to the question of whom we should consider his envisioned readers. According to Killeen, as Wilde first conceived of the tales as entertainment for his two little kids, they absolutely should be categorized as children's literature.[25] Markey, though, asserts that while there is "enough humour and lightness of touch to attract young readers," the marketing, presentation, and themes suggest these stories primarily were written for adults.[26] Yet, as Margaret D. Stetz documents in another excellent Bristow chapter, their republications, right on down through the most recent contemporary adaptations, overwhelmingly aim toward child audiences. Nodelman also emphasizes how publishers consistently have pitched these pieces as children's literature and helpfully suggests that the disagreements over audience have formed largely because "our most common generalizations about childhood are all about the limitations of people younger than ourselves, about how they are less than" adults.[27] For him, Wilde instead evinces "a healthy degree of respect for the tale's implied child readers,"[28] and Killeen concurs: "Wilde didn't write down to children—he challenged them."[29]

As fairy tales traditionally have explored liminality through a whole host of binaries, including that between children and adults, it makes sense that Wilde's texts might "belong uneasily to both" sides "and yet to neither."[30] Regardless, my aim here is not to attempt to resolve the matter of Wilde's intended audience for these stories but rather merely to explore the extent to which the figure of the child offers a fertile opportunity for fitting together this focus with Wilde's attraction both to odd and to small bodies. According to Killeen, Wilde was aware of evangelical attempts to dismiss Catholicism as "a religion fit only for children and other under-developed people," and Wilde's antipathy to the related infantilization of the Irish led him to employ such discourse with an oppositional purpose.[31] That not merely Victorian prejudice but also Victorian science constructed stigmatizing definitions of "under-developed" difference, of infantilized lives seen as "less than" through categories like colonized, ethnic and racial, immigrant, and working-class others, has been well documented. Disability studies scholars working on the nineteenth century see disability as inextricably intertwined with these constructions, and the little bodies Wilde features in his fairy tales (not just the fantastic or freakish ones) offer a superb opportunity to consider this further.

The figure of the child in fact is an entry point for realizing how much nineteenth-century discourse around class and work intersects with categories that today would fall under the umbrella of disability. Joyce L. Huff and Martha Stoddard Holmes, in the introduction to their landmark edited volume *A Cultural History of Disability in the Long Nineteenth Century*, assert, "the child/adult binary significantly underpinned the negotiation of disability and its consequent questions of who could or should have opportunities to learn and work."[32] While "discourses of education and charity focused on disabled children" and "articulated 'childhood' as a state of innocent vulnerability antithetical to participation in the workforce," "adults whose disabilities precluded activities seen as 'work' disrupted the child/adult binary" and thus were infantilized to "resolve the disruption" their "economic dependence" represented.[33] This connection between children and the disabled had been reinforced earlier on by the Poor Law Amendment Act of 1834, which for Huff and Stoddard Holmes "shored up" disability "as a category" by defining "anyone not classified as a child, sick, insane, 'defective,' or 'aged and infirm' [as] able."[34] In a culture where so many different bodies viewed as defective or otherwise "less than" were infantilized, the nexus between disability and the figure of the child is a significant one that, again, bears further investigation.

Perhaps no figure looms larger today in this regard than that of Charles Dickens's Tiny Tim. In America, at least, this is in part owing to the dominant role telethons played in the popular view of disability for so many decades, their demeaning message insisting that the "only hope" for disabled individuals "lay in medical cures or medical and vocational rehabilitation."[35] According to Paul K. Longmore, telethon culture "borrowed and Americanized the traits of the Dickens character: the disabled person as perpetual child, sweet, cheerful, and brave; the disabled person as invalid, helpless, dependent, and fundamentally different from 'normal' people; the disabled person as object of charity, grateful but hopeless and doomed unless those who are healthy and normal 'give'; the disabled person as vehicle of others' redemption, existing not for himself or herself, not as a human being in her or his own right, but to provide the occasion for nondisabled people to renew their humanity; the disabled person as sentimental entertainment, a figure whose pathetic situation or heroic striving touches the hearts of readers and viewers."[36] These traits remain important reference points for any assessment of the extent to which a disabled character, from the Victorian Era to the present day, might be construed as an ambiguous, an ambivalent, a pejorative, or a positive literary representation of disability.

Of course, one must be wary of falling into the fallacy of anachronistic analysis. As Huff and Stoddard Holmes aptly acknowledge, it is important to "[resist] the convenience of treating past perspectives as more unified or more limited than those we might encounter in our own time."[37] This is particularly imperative given Victorians rarely used the word *disability* itself, tending instead to employ a whole laundry list of distinct descriptors such as "afflicted, infirm, defective, deformed, crippled, and invalid."[38] Stoddard Holmes, though, previously has argued for the use of current terminology such as *disability* in scholarly work on the nineteenth century, because "our present theoretical moment" can at times allow one more strategically to "unpack" past literary texts.[39] Not surprisingly, then, Huff and Stoddard Holmes make a conscious choice to do the same; while granting they are "imposing [contemporary] categories" on the past, they do so "in order to frame" that past "in a manner that is meaningful to scholars in the present."[40] My own argument employs a similar approach.

This does not mean, however, that it is not important to develop an accurate sense of the various ways what we now refer to as disability was understood and represented at the time. In fact, a broad accounting of Victorian attitudes toward disability reinforces why an intersectional approach is so important. For Huff and Stoddard Holmes, "one factor that drew together a variety of people whom we now refer to as disabled was their exclusion from emerging standards that defined the healthy body" through principles of health such as wholeness, utility, and vitality.[41] In the lists that inevitably followed for sterilization programs and ugly laws, the overlap and in many cases conflation between the disabled and the poor or other marginalized groups is readily apparent: "the insane, the epileptic, the imbecile, the idiotic" are pooled with "inebriates, prostitutes, tramps, and criminals" as well as "the sexual perverts" and "the habitual pauper."[42] So pervasive was the identification of disability with disease and ugliness that as early as 1867, cities such as San Francisco sought to legally segregate the unable, the unattractive, the unhealthy, the unkempt from the rest of society: "Any person who is diseased, maimed, mutilated, or in any way deformed so as to be an unsightly or disgusting object, shall not therein or thereon expose himself or herself to public view."[43]

During the era there also were many profound intersections between the disqualification of disabled and unhealthy others and the disqualification of ethnic and racial others. An often overlooked but important instance of this involves American immigration policies. Huff and Stoddard Holmes (referencing the essential work of Douglas Baynton in this area) stress how the blatant ethnocentrism and racism of such policies were inextricably intertwined with an explicitly ableist construction of defectiveness as "an amorphous category that included conditions as diverse as 'the deaf, blind, epileptic, and mobility impaired'; those with 'flat or clubbed feet'; 'those who were unusually short or tall'; 'people with intellectual or psychiatric disabilities'; and 'hermaphrodites.'"[44] What is more, "a range of conditions were seen as symptoms of disability: 'Immorality, criminality, deviant sexuality, poverty, and political radicalism were all described as manifestations of various kinds of mental defect.'"[45] Consequently, "both disabled people and racial minorities were 'described as evolutionary laggards or throwbacks,'" and the "stigmatization of disability was deployed to fuel racist fears of miscegenation, as 'race-mixing' was said to result in 'deformity.'"[46] In the end, the lack of a precise definition of who exactly could be seen as constituting a person with a disability in the nineteenth century and the interrelation of today's markers of disabled expression or identity with other categories connected to class, ethnicity and race, and gender and sexuality (among others) require a broad understanding of how certain literary representations might usefully be approached through disability studies readings.

Again, I will be using the term *disability-aligned* both to indicate that I view a particular character through the lens of disability and to acknowledge that this character nonetheless might not be described by all contemporary readers as disabled. Overall, though, I join the many other disability studies scholars in supporting the use of *disability* in discussions of nineteenth-century texts. Yenika-Agbaw, for example, reads Andersen's Thumbelina and his Ugly Duckling through the lens of disability (the former because she is tiny and the latter because he is ugly) even though they both are "technically able-bodied."[47] Huff and Stoddard Holmes also open their introduction with a brief portrait of the Creature from Mary Shelley's *Frankenstein* as disabled, insisting that even though "the physically robust Creature's only disabilities are aesthetic," his character nonetheless may be read as the literary representation of a "disability experience of isolation, stigma, and peril."[48] Garland-Thomson offers her own expert critical justification for such moves in an article on Herman Melville's "Bartleby, the Scrivener." *Disability*, for her, "name[s] the cultural system of representation that imagines and creates the large and variegated . . . category of people whose bodily forms, functions, limitations, ambiguities, or appearances are considered to be abnormal, defective, degenerate, debilitated, deformed, ill, unfit, unhealthy, sick, obese, crippled, mad, ugly, retarded, or flawed."[49] Because "all these designations serve to pathologize, stigmatize, devalue, and exclude," even though there are significant differences in the bodies, contexts, and experiences of all those included under the term's broad umbrella, the "consequences of being judged as inferior and the exclusionary attitudes and practices directed against these people are analogous."[50] A final notable example of the productive ways in which one similarly may reenvision notable nineteenth-century fictional characters comes from Kylee-Anne Hingston, whose reading of Robert Louis Stevenson's Edward Hyde posits that "the era's pathologization and criminalization of aberrant bodies underlies the supposedly instinctual reactions to Hyde," reflecting a strong cultural "shift of corporeal and social anxieties onto disabled bodies."[51]

Hingston's work serves as a useful segue to a consideration of similarly inflected discussions of Victorian freakery, an absolutely essential context for this book's disability studies approach to Wilde's fairy tales. She dutifully acknowledges how "bodies that would perhaps not be considered disabled today could well have been so in the nineteenth century, and vice versa."[52] Significantly, though, freakish bodies evoke for her the very sort of "moments of irresolvable conflict"[53] she posits as typical of Victorian literary representations of disability. Building off of Julia Miele Rodas's suggestion that the "underlying purpose" of freak shows was not to ask with P. T. Barnum, "What is it?" but rather, "Who or what am I in relation to this other creature?" Hingston argues one may apply this dynamic more broadly to narrative in general, requiring readers to ask, "Who or what am I in relation to this character?"[54] This is certainly a crucial question that Wilde's fairy tales employ, particularly in the context of his audience's emotional response to the many freakish bodies he decides to place front and center as his stories' main protagonists. In Wilde's texts, the figure of the freak is as fundamental to his literary representations of disability-aligned difference as the figure of the child.

It is not at all surprising to find Wilde foregrounding such bodies in his fantastical fairy tales. According to Nadja Durbach, the freak show was "the primary cultural site for public and professional encounters with atypical bodies in the nineteenth century,"[55] with its "heyday" in Britain lasting between 1847 and 1914.[56] For Durbach, such performances and the "popular and professional debates these spectacles generated over how to interpret extraordinary bodies" are "central to understanding the place of the atypical body within nineteenth-century culture."[57] It should be noted she insists "'freakery' and 'disability' were radically different ways of dealing with difference that should not be collapsed."[58] Durbach's take on freakery remains an important one, however, for her rejection of any narrative of simple victimization and her insistence these shows "allowed for human diversity and celebrated bodily variation."[59] Her insistence that freaks "promoted discussion about the potential meanings attached to bodily anomalies" and "invited multiple interpretations" regarding "the boundary between the self and the other"[60] thus offers the option of a truly affirmative response to Rodas's question, an option Wilde decidedly encourages in his fairy tales in spite of the pessimistic outcomes he provides for his peculiar protagonists.

The aforementioned Garland-Thomson is a giant in the field of disability studies, and one of the first areas in which she established her now legendary fame is in fact freak studies. Opening her introduction to the foundational *Freakery* essay collection by noting, "people who are visually different have always provoked the imaginations of their fellow human beings," Garland Thomson goes on to assert how "fascination with the different body has occasioned enduring cultural icons" such as giants and dwarfs as well as "fanciful hybrids" such as mermaids[61]—all three featuring in Wilde's gallery of characters. For her, the unusual bodies showcased in freak shows "we would now call either 'physically disabled' or 'exotic ethnics,'"[62] and their appearance in these venues represents further evidence of the extent to which these persons were subjected to stigma: "By constituting the freak as an icon of generalized embodied deviance, the exhibitions also simultaneously reinscribed gender, race, sexual aberrance, ethnicity, and disability as inextricable yet particular exclusionary systems legitimated by bodily variation."[63] I see Durbach's investment in the freak's resistance to pathologization (which, again, allows one to see Wilde's own rendering of his extraordinary bodies as an affirmative embrace of their wonderful wonder-filling difference) as complementing rather than competing with Garland Thomson's equally necessary emphasis on the figure's vulnerability to exploitation and exclusion (which Wilde represents through his characters' profound pain and suffering on account of the stigma and peril they consistently meet with due to their difference).

Marlene Tromp's edited collection *Victorian Freaks* extends Garland Thomson's focus by situating freakery specifically within a British context while further emphasizing the importance of intersectionality in "contest[ing] discourses that naturalize race, gender, sexuality, and disability as categories describing bodily attributes rather than as structures that emerge from social relationships."[64] For instance, Stoddard Holmes's contribution reads the ending to Wilkie Collins's *The Law and the Lady* as "repudiat[ing] queerness and disability" but insists it at least "does so in a way that shows both the compulsoriness of the rejection and the loss it entails."[65] Along similar lines, Melissa Free's essay in the collection further establishes how even though "queer, disabled, dark bodies" typically wind up dead, their presence nonetheless "force[s] us to consider the ways in which they are 'fully human.'"[66] Again, given the fatal fates Wilde provides for his fantastic featured characters, such critical arguments are instructive approaches through which to assess his literary representations of disability in the fairy tales, allowing for more progressive possibilities than their consistently unhappy endings might seem to suggest.

Both Free and Stoddard Holmes draw on the widely influential scholarship of Robert McRuer and his critical articulation of compulsory able-bodiedness and compulsory heterosexuality.[67] Exploring the numerous registers of such intersectionality is essential work in most disability studies scholarship, and given all of the analyses that center around Wilde's sexuality, the nexus of the crip and the queer is a particularly compelling prism for reading his work through the lens of disability. At the same time, one must beware of the tendency to transform the freakish or disabled body into a mere metaphor for another register, even as there are important intersectional dimensions to explore that must not be ignored. That is, Wilde's nonnormative bodies should not be read simply as code for queer bodies, but their status as embodied abnormality needs to be understood as referencing actual physical attributes (and the conditions that shape the experience of those specific forms of physicality). Leslie Fiedler has lamented, in his archetypal study *Freaks*, how nineteenth-century literature consistently employs such difference as "metaphors for something else: the plight of the artist, the oppression of the poor, the terror of sexuality, or the illusory nature of social life."[68] Throughout *The Importance of Being Different*, I purposefully resist reducing Wilde's peculiar bodies to stand-ins for other identity markers or expressions, insisting instead that (however necessarily they are also informed by those other inextricable aspects of their lived experience) their physical diversity deserves to be read literally as a literary representation of disability-aligned difference.

Fiedler's opus provides a helpful way of thinking about our fascination with different bodies that neatly brings together the above foci on fairy tales, the figure of the child, and the figure of the freak. According to Fiedler, humanity's psychic obsession with freaks and monsters is rooted in the psychology of childhood, as even a cursory review of children's literature reveals,[69] and the "primary source" of children's "constant confusion about what really is freakish, what normal" is scale.⁷⁰ Early adolescence typically only exacerbates the child's difficulty in coming to terms with "scale, sexuality, our status as more than beasts, and our tenuous individuality,"⁷¹ which for Fiedler is why in famous Victorian nonsense works by Edward Lear and Lewis Carroll "the boundaries between animal and human, large and small, self and other, blur and dissolve," and why in Victorian fairy tales "Mermaids, Giants, and Dwarfs were kept alive for the imagination."⁷² Part of what is so striking about Wilde's renditions of these figures in his own fairy tales is not merely how sympathetic his portrayals are but further how he seems to invite readers to identify with his freakish characters (in direct opposition to the fear and repulsion many such representations consistently trade off of for their effect).

It is actually possible to identify some biographical elements that might suggest Wilde had a personal stake in his daring depictions of the deviant bodies he was so drawn to in these texts—especially those favorite freaks, giants and dwarfs. Killeen, for instance, notes how the common links of dwarfs during his day with atavism and savagery, particularly after the "discovery" of African Pygmies in the 1870s, encouraged some to (following David MacRitchie) exploit the long-standing Celtic connection to little people (such as banshees and leprechauns) to serve arguments for British racial superiority.⁷³ He even offers that Oscar had familial as well as patriotic motivations for explicitly setting out "to counter the prevalent association between dwarfs and evil," especially with predatory sexuality, given Sir William Wilde (Oscar's father, who was a short man some "labelled a dwarf") had been referred to as Dr. Quilp in the pamphlet distributed by his former patient Mary Travers to publicize her claim that Sir William had raped her while she was anesthetized.⁷⁴

There would seem to be an even larger body of evidence where the figure of the giant is concerned. Again, in the way of family connections, Killeen reports that George Bernard Shaw speculated Wilde "was probably a sufferer from gigantism," having "inherited this affliction from his mother . . . who was also 'unnaturally' huge."⁷⁵ Wilde was certainly tall (six feet and three inches), but it was more that many believed there was something (in Shaw's words) "not quite normal about his bigness," and so, according to Killeen, "if Wilde was aware of such rumors 'The Selfish Giant' could be read, from one angle, as his response."⁷⁶ On the nationalist front, Fiedler has noted the popular associations of giants with Ireland, owing to three famous real-life contenders for the title of "*the* Irish Giant" in the century leading up to Wilde's birth,[77] and Wilde very likely would have recalled the clamor over the excavation of the fossilized Irish Giant in Antrim (brought to Liverpool and Manchester for display during his time at Oxford).[78] Of course, giants play a prominent role in Ireland's mythic history too, from the Fomori to the larger-than-life figures of Cú Chulainn and Fionn mac Cumhaill (of which the World Heritage site the Giant's Causeway in Antrim, already a famous tourist destination by the end of the century, would have served as an unforgettable reminder). During Wilde's day, the figure of the giant was also employed to the detriment of the Irish in the form of frequent monstrous caricatures of Irish nationalists and Irish poor in the popular press.

It is unfortunately not within the scope of my project to conduct a sweeping survey of, say, newspaper accounts from the period to suggest what a range of real dwarfs and giants or other freaks Wilde might have been aware of himself. I humbly follow the suit of David T. Mitchell and Sharon L. Snyder's landmark *Narrative Prosthesis* in centering my attention on literary representation (through my emphasis on close-reading of the texts themselves) and strategically "not intend[ing] to provide a strictly historical study of disability."[79] I will, however, put forward that Michèle Mendelssohn's book detailing how Wilde's American experience shaped his future contains convincing evidence confirming how he would have not only become aware of the constructed nature of and the conditioned response to such difference but also potentially developed a deeply personal antipathy toward the stigmatization of enfreaked bodies. In the very first paragraph of her prologue, Mendelssohn aptly points out that it was during the Age of Barnum when "like a fairy tale" the "events of 1882 would divide his life sharply into Before and After,"[80] a year that "would transform him and deform his image."[81] Wilde had, of course, already been subject to more than his share of satiric ridicule in the pages of *Punch* and on the stages of *Patience,* both of which did, if more subtly, incorporate racist dimensions into their denigrations of Oscaresque aesthetes.[82] In the United States, however, he was routinely represented as a repulsive and threatening "negrified Paddy,"[83] quite relentlessly ridiculed in some circles even as he was almost religiously admired in others.

He immediately found himself lampooned, for example, in the cartoons of major media outlets. *Harper's Weekly* featured a monkey in aesthetic garb gazing raptly at a sunflower on its January cover, while the *Washington Post* asked, "How Far Is It from This to This?" in its caption to paired sketches of the Wild Man of Borneo and Oscar, "recalling the way in which human exhibits were often presented in popular sideshows and exhibitions," particularly the "evolutionary spectacles" Barnum exhibited in his "ethnographic shows."[84] "Overnight," Mendelssohn observes, "Wilde became an emblem of racial ambiguities that had arisen from new scientific research, as well as from old-fashioned ethnological displays and performances."[85] The *Post* argued he was "a degenerate, a sign of human regression towards the primitive,"[86] insisting Nature "never puts the brains of a man of mental brawn and vigor into a cavity faced by such a physiognomy as that of Oscar Wilde's."[87] Most infamously, the Currier and Ives lithograph entitled *The Aesthetic Craze* portrayed Wilde as a black enslaved person, with the racist caption, "What's de matter wid de Nigga? Why Oscar you's gone wild!"[88]

The attacks were widespread, across a range of media, such as the Donaldson Brothers' trade cards, which cast Wilde as an illiterate-sounding Frederick Douglass.[89] Perhaps most strikingly, Wilde was spoofed by professional imitators and minstrel shows throughout the tour, often staged as competing performances on the same nights as Wilde's lectures in the same cities, and drawing larger crowds.[90] There were multiple minstrelsy outfits exploiting this opportunity, some featuring African American actors and Irish Americans in blackface,[91] and many Americans consequently perceived Wilde to be "an odd specimen performing for profit" who "was destined for a dime museum freak show like Barnum's."[92] That Barnum himself appeared in the front row at one of Wilde's talks for Mendelssohn testifies to how the positioning of Wilde as a "spectacular showpiece" had indeed simultaneously transformed and deformed him, lifting him "from a lecturing zero to a freakish hero."[93]

Of course, as noted earlier, one always needs to be wary of playing the game of attributing authorial intention, especially on the basis of biographical details, and particularly for a writer as notoriously slippery and at times as purposefully trivial and deviously deceptive as Wilde. Further, it is certainly absolutely essential to acknowledge that if Wilde did develop an affinity for those whose different bodies rendered them more vulnerable to stigma and even more dangerous forms of peril, this affinity did not extend to all such individuals, for in spite of what he saw and heard in America, Wilde continued to hold racist attitudes and opinions when it came to African Americans.[94] Still, regardless of his intent, or even of the various possibilities these texts hold for progressive or regressive literary representations where his exceptional protagonists are concerned, Wilde's fairy tales remain a vital set of texts that invite readers to investigate the nexus of child culture and children's literature and disability studies and freak studies; to explore the intersection of disability-aligned difference with other categories and markers such as class, gender and sexuality, and race and ethnicity; as well as to embrace the recent revisiting of the role of emotional response when it comes to both Victorian and twentieth-first-century understandings of that nexus and of that difference.

As Stoddard Holmes has observed, there is a long-standing "connection between emotion and impairment," and, in the case of *A Christmas Carol*, "the emotional landscape of Tim's disability—what the characters feel, and what we feel in response—tends to obscure other questions we might have about it."[95] Within this landscape, there is no real opportunity to consider disability as a natural form of human variation and difference. One feels sorry for Tim, and this emotional response reduces his character to a plot-driven object of melodramatic pity placed in the story to enable the nondisabled protagonist's redemption. Despite his fundamental role in the renewal of Scrooge's humanity, Tim is not particularly present in the story itself, and ultimately readers know very little about him or his disability. What is more, as Davidson points out, it is hard to even attempt to excuse the manipulative individual characterization as at least some sort of stepping stone toward broader beneficial social change for disabled persons in that Dickens "does not use Tiny Tim to condemn the treatment of crippled children in Victorian society but to finesse Scrooge's awakening to charity."[96] Still, as Stoddard Holmes reminds us, "the Victorians went far beyond Tiny Tim in exploring the meaning of disability and ability and the ways in which disabled and able people might relate," and thus, analyzing literary representations from the nineteenth century "is not simply an exhumation of the past that has defined our limited ways of thinking and feeling in the present, but also an invitation to reopen our own narrative explorations of disability—to move beyond Tiny Tim ourselves."[97] Wilde's fairy tales constitute a similar opportunity to extend our contemporary conversations around disability and, in particular, to reexamine the role emotional response plays in our very framing of these discussions.

Elizabeth J. Donaldson and Catherine Prendergast's 2011 special issue of the *Journal of Literary & Cultural Disability Studies*, entitled "Representing Disability and Emotion," was a watershed "effort to recuperate emotions" such as inspiration and sympathy that "have been devalued or flagged as problematic in Disability Studies."[98] Their project decidedly was not intended to support some sort of blanket approval for any and all emotional responses to disability. For example, contributor Howard Sklar distinguishes the positive sympathy he wants to reclaim from the "simple pity"[99] he associates with hierarchy, shame, stereotype, and stigma. Similarly, Wendy L. Chrisman is careful to clarify, "I am not suggesting that the kind of inspiration associated with narratives of overcoming disability, narratives that invoke pity, or the charity/tragedy model of disability itself can or should be recuperated."[100] Given "No Pity" is a long-standing slogan of the disability rights movement and the oft-referenced title of a foundational text by Joseph P. Shapiro,[101] these moves are not surprising.

More broadly, pity has faced a long line of famous detractors, from Aristotle to Friedrich Nietzsche, even as it also has had some notable defenders, including Jean-Jacques Rousseau and Arthur Schopenhauer. On top of the many conflicting accounts of it as an alternately appropriate, deficient, or excessive form of compassion, parsing pity is challenging owing to the continued "terminological disarray" within what Kristján Kristjánsson has characterized as "the conceptual parish of fellow-feelings": empathy, sympathy, compassion, and pity.[102] It is essential never to disregard or dismiss the very real damage mainstream manifestations of pity have perpetrated upon disabled persons. Bearing that important reminder in mind, one of the ways in which Wilde's work serves as an invitation to reopen our own narrative explorations of disability is by encouraging a reevaluation of the extent to which alternative conceptions of fellow feelings (including pity) might hold the potential to shift the terms of discussion from victimization to empowerment.

For Kristjánsson, while sympathy is to be privileged over empathy in that it "includes a desire to alleviate suffering," the highest form of fellow feeling is compassionate pity, which in his framework replaces sympathy when the suffering one wishes to alleviate is "serious rather than trivial."[103] Accordingly, he adamantly insists, the "idea that pity necessarily involves a condescending holier-than-thou attitude" is "factually wrong."[104] If so, a reevaluation of the standard contemporary usage's narrow and exclusively pejorative perception of pity might be productive, especially for texts from the nineteenth century (when Nietzsche and Schopenhauer were themselves working through their competing views on the topic). Indeed, Kristjánsson's version of compassion-pity shares much in common with the revisionary work of Sklar and Chrisman. According to Sklar, it is the "recognition of another's difficulty as 'something to be alleviated'" that distinguishes true sympathy from "shallow pity."[105] For Chrisman, inspiring emotions contain within them a "recursive" quality that allows them to become a type of empowerment rather than inspiration porn.[106] Intriguingly, Chrisman views sympathy as analogous to pity, fear, and sentimentality[107]—which might seem, exasperatingly, only to confirm that determining which emotions may be productively reassessed in relation to disability ultimately comes down to personal preference and semantics, but which also reinforces the importance of careful reconsideration of disability and the emotions on a case-by-case basis.

Wilde's fairy tales offer several heretofore unexamined representations of disability that significantly feature nonnormative main characters, and as such they provide multiple new opportunities to consider the potentially progressive and problematic aspects of readers' emotional responses to their remarkable bodies and to their seemingly compulsory (if sympathetic) excision. They offer multitudinous, and at times seemingly contradictory, possibilities where the depictions of his disability-aligned protagonists are concerned. This can be true even within a single work, and all the more so is the case across all nine. "The Selfish Giant," arguably Wilde's best-known and most beloved fairy tale, is an instructive example of this, especially as it offers the opportunity to engage with both the figure of the freak and the figure of the child at the same time. Accordingly, I now turn to a close reading of this very short story in order to consolidate many of the ideas presented in the previous sections of this introduction and to look ahead to the content chapters that follow.

The story opens as its titular protagonist (after a seven-year visit with another prodigious monster, his friend the Cornish ogre) returns home to find his castle garden full of children playing.[108] Being a "very selfish" giant, he questions their presence "in a very gruff voice," which causes them all to run away.[109] Insisting he "will allow nobody to play" there but himself, Wilde's oversized Scrooge proceeds to build "a high wall all round it, and put up a notice-board" warning against trespassing.[110] "The poor children," Wilde relates, "had now nowhere to play," but there are consequences for the ogreish owner as well; when the next spring arrives "only in the garden of the Selfish Giant it was still winter."[111] For at least a year, it remains home to the Snow and the Frost, and their invited guests the North Wind and the Hail, none of whom apparently qualify as trespassers. Initially, then, Wilde's chilly colossus only seems intended to serve as the polar opposite of the innocent, vulnerable little children who irritate him.

Even through this stage in the story, though, Wilde's Giant is something of an unconventional one. Traditionally, giants were cast as terrifying monsters who would gobble up children and kill any foes at the slightest provocation. Here, however, as Hope Howell Hodgkins points out, "Wilde submerges the frightening aspects of his giant so deeply that the reader must invent the details because this giant's most overt failings consist of consorting with an ogre, 'a very gruff voice,' and a selfish, forbidding sign."[112] Still, the Giant also is far from a friendly one so far, and for most critics this is an effect of power and privilege. According to Markey, "the tale's concern with the use and abuse of private property brings Wilde's work close to his age's more immediate social concerns."[113] For Bristow, the message is "selfish property-ownership cannot lead to happiness."[114] To Killeen, the class-based critique is more specifically reflective of "the paternalist model of landlord-tenant relationship" in Ireland.[115] While the Giant's selfishness is indisputably positioned as a marker for systemic class prejudice, a disability studies lens calls attention to the extent to which the typical Victorian reader also would understand his inner ugliness as signaled by his physical monstrosity. But, of course, Wilde's Giant does not remain a selfish one, even as his outward appearance remains the same. In this, the story is not only subversive in the sociopolitical sense Zipes has attributed to all of Wilde's fairy tales (as a condemnation of the exploitation underwriting existing power structures) but further is contestatory toward his day's typical stereotyping and stigmatization of nonstandard bodies as well.

One morning, the Giant wakes to the sounds of spring and children filling the branches of his peach trees. In one far corner, though, it was still winter, and a boy "so small that he could not reach up to the branches" was weeping because he was "too tiny" to climb up into the tree there.[116] At this, we are told, "the Giant's heart melted," and acknowledging "how selfish I have been," he decides he will "put that poor little boy on the top of the tree, and then . . . knock down the wall" so the garden may become "the children's playground for ever and ever."[117] Wilde emphasizes, "he was really very sorry for what he had done."[118] When the rest of the kids see him coming, they are "so frightened" they run away, but because "his eyes were so full of tears,"[119] the littlest boy is unaware of the Giant's approach until he is already "gently in his hand"[120] and then immediately up in the tree at last. Overjoyed, he hugs the Giant's neck and kisses him—and "the other children," Wilde continues, "when they saw that the Giant was not wicked any longer," return.[121] Telling them, "it is your garden now," he demolishes the wall and ends up playing with the children every day for years, until he grows "very old and feeble," at which point he takes to sitting "in a huge armchair" while watching them.[122] Yet "the little boy whom the Giant loved was never seen again" after that first day, and his intense longing to see "his first little friend" once more never diminishes.[123]

On one hand, this part of the story more problematically employs another out-of-scale body (the child who is unable to climb into a tree on his own because he is "too tiny") seemingly to garner an emotional response in direct contrast to the disgust initially occasioned by the Giant's freakish size and his Scrooge-ish meanness—the little boy is an object of pity. But Wilde's story actually moves readers beyond both of these regular reactions as attention shifts toward the Giant's transformation, which presents a particularly progressive development for a disability-aligned character. After all, the Giant is not (as Longmore has noted to be most common) a minor character who only has secured a spot in the narrative so as to serve as the "vehicle of others' redemption," but instead his own redemption is the featured plotline. Further, his reformation testifies both to his fundamental humaneness (not selfishness) and to his worthiness of admiration (rather than any reduction or rejection of his person based on his anomalous body). The change in the Giant also is significant from a disability studies perspective in that it supports a view of his physical difference (and his moral character's relationship to that difference) as not in fact some sort of inherent defectiveness but instead as contingent. Wilde's own experience in America had highlighted for him the fabricated nature of such freakishness, framed by conditioned cultural, environmental, and social factors rather than permanently scripted by biology. This awareness informs the direction of his plot: what most at first assume to be a big scary monster turns out to be a big friendly giant.

What is more, if one hearkens back to the rest of Longmore's list, it is even clearer the Giant does not at all conform to the mold provided by the likes of Tiny Tim and his ilk. While he is certainly sweet and cheerful after his epiphany, and while one even might suggest his person comes across as childlike given he spends his days playing with kids in his garden, he is anything but helpless and dependent, or an object of charity. Rather than being depicted as the passive recipient of the kindness or pity of nondisabled others, it is this disability-aligned character who takes up the active role of benefactor in helping the littlest boy and then in gifting his garden to them all. He not only leads an independent life but enables others to enjoy more fulfilling lives and in that way at least seems integrated into his local community rather than isolated or ostracized owing to his difference. In all these ways, Wilde's Giant stands tall as a more progressive Victorian literary representation of disability compared to the pejorative roles often assigned to such figures.

In the final section of the tale, the Giant at last sees his special friend again, and he joyfully runs outside to greet him, only to have his face become "red with anger," for the little boy (who has not grown at all even though years have passed) appears to have been wounded: "on the palms of the child's hands were the prints of two nails, and the prints of two nails were on the little feet."[124] His friend quickly calms him, however, assuring him he need not seek any sort of revenge, for the marks "are the wounds of Love."[125] The Giant finds himself filling with "a strange awe" and, kneeling "before the little child," wonders out loud, "Who art thou?"[126] The reply is, "You let me play once in your garden; to-day you shall come with me to my garden, which is Paradise."[127] With that, the story concludes with one last sentence: "And when the children ran in that afternoon, they found the Giant lying dead under the tree, all covered with white blossoms."[128]

For many Wilde fans, the ending may seem a bit hard to take too seriously coming from a writer whose typical trajectory relies upon "sincere and studied triviality"[129] rather than anything even approaching earnestness. So, is Wilde in the end employing a disability-aligned character more predictably as sentimental entertainment designed to touch the hearts of nondisabled readers, thereby undermining the representation's otherwise more progressive elements? Or, is he inviting readers to chuckle over and dismiss those very sentimental qualities in a piece that has proceeded with lightness and humor up to that point? Might he be spoofing his audience for enjoying such sentimental fare? If we do take the tale at face value, is our response to the Giant merely one of charitable attachment to a figure in whose monstrosity we do not recognize ourselves? Or, is there instead a genuine sense of connection to his character that affirms a shared emotional lived experience of fellow feeling, which transcends (without erasing) physical differences?

All of these options should remain in play if we approach Wilde's fairy tales as complex conundrums that employ not only irony but bewilderment, irresolution, and opacity to contest their cooptation into yet another status-quo children's story. The polyphonic multiplicities of potential meanings, though, do not detract from the magnitude of how one of these possibilities invites readers in this story to identify with a disability-aligned freak who is good and kind, presenting us with an ultimately more selfless than selfish Giant, the title notwithstanding. One may feel sorry for him (because he misses his friend, or because he dies), but if one's interest in his character rises to the level of compassion, then Wilde's text is no longer limited to prompting an emotional response that smacks of sentimentalism. Instead, this tale arguably encourages readers to appreciate his person for the kindness he shows to the children. Indeed, Wilde's Giant actively models for us how to express compassion, how to act on it by breaking down the wall dividing self and other, mine and theirs. In the end, any potential ironic or satiric intentions on the author's part notwithstanding, it remains important in terms of the text's literary representation of disability that the literal last impressions of this peculiar protagonist are of a body celebrated by God in a beautiful cover of blossoms, his goodness (and the goodness of the life he led) affirmed by a reward of Paradise in the company of his beloved boy.

Markey interprets the ending as evidence that the "primary focus" of the story is "spiritual," not "social or sexual," enabling Wilde "to move away from overt moralizing towards covert suggestion."[130] Nodelman takes an entirely different tack, reading the Christ-child's stigmata as an image "depressingly insistent on focussing [sic] on pain in the midst of a supposed happy ending," which (coming on the heels of the Giant's "years of sad longing" for his friend) implies "only fools could possibly believe that goodness is rewarded."[131] The point of bringing a disability studies perspective to bear on the tale is not to decide between such dissimilar deductions but to divulge a distinct new focus, one where our attention refuses to pivot away from the physicality of the bodies before us. In this specific story, then, in addition to gauging how the Giant's freakish appearance does not preclude our empathy or compassion, we also need to acknowledge another notable aspect to Wilde's ending—its surprising linkage of the body of the child with that of the freak through a shared friendship between two different disability-aligned characters.

When he first appears in the garden, the littlest boy's especially small size and his inability to get himself into the tree may suggest, even as they do not actually literally represent, a view of disability that traffics in the sort of stereotypical connotations of dependency and pitifulness we associate with Tiny Tim. Arguably, however, the revelation that the Giant's special friend is the Christ-child truly transfigures the standard take on different bodies during the time, as the presence of disfiguring marks on the boy's palms and feet effects a compelling coupling of divinity with disability. Such a reading is reinforced by Nancy L. Eiesland's assertion in *The Disabled God* that Christ's stigmata provide the opportunity for peculiar bodies to "participate in the imago Dei, not in spite of [their] impairments and contingencies, but through them."[132] "In presenting his impaired hands and feet to his startled friends," Eiesland argues, "the resurrected Jesus is revealed as the disabled God," with the radical implication that resurrection and the promise, and premise, of heaven "is not about the negation or erasure of our disabled bodies in hopes of perfect images, untouched by physical disability."[133] As the disabled God exhibits "the signs of disability, not as a demonstration of failure and defect, but in affirmation of connection and strength," the stigmata require one "must reject the image of the 'perfect body' as an oppressive myth" and instead cherish "the nonconventional body . . . as sacrament."[134]

Approaching Wilde's character of the Christ-child through such a lens positions the peculiar body not only as accepted and loved by God but further as expressly reflective and representative of divinity itself. Just as our disgust toward the Giant transforms into appreciation, the initial pity associated with the little child dramatically dissipates here as the seemingly pathetically helpless boy is revealed to be the all-powerful Savior who lifts his big friend up into Paradise. Thus, rather than a sign of divine disapproval or retribution (as disability often had been interpreted for centuries), his stigmata do not require healing or (as the Giant assumes) revenge but are explicitly indicated to be "the wounds of Love." Seeing disfigurement as part of the perfection attributed to God, instead of as a flaw indicative of inferiority, encourages readers to embrace rather than reject the extraordinary body.

Tatar finds in more than one of Wilde's fairy tales a "privileging of a grotesque aesthetic over classical beauty,"[135] a notion that bears critical articulation with the above privileging of disability-aligned difference and the disabled God. Wilde's interest in stigmatized bodies offers a new angle into how he achieves a "hollowing out" of beauty "by investing its opposite with a powerful emotional and empathetic charge,"[136] particularly in such a way that the grotesque need not be associated with misery and suffering but also (or instead) with goodness and love. In this light, the final scene does not represent yet another instance in which a deity figure shows pity or charity toward an anomalous body in spite of (or because of) its difference, much less as a message that such bodies require curing or otherwise fixing. In a decided departure from the usual devaluation of the grotesque, Wilde's tale intensifies the positive associations assigned to the atypical body, by extending the attribution of such difference to God, not just the Giant.

Killeen and Markey both situate "The Selfish Giant" in their own ways within a Christian and an Irish context. Whether by drawing connections to Irish folk traditions or revealing parallels with the relationship between Protestant Irish landlords and their Catholic tenants, whether identifying restagings of the Garden of Eden or of the Crucifixion, their arguments offer the above disability studies approach crucial intersectional points of connection with important political, religious, and socioeconomic contexts. Other critics have suggested the protagonist's monstrous body reflects on a figurative level the unnatural and ugly attributes Wilde's homophobic culture ascribed to alternative sexualities.[137] Again, while not attempting to displace any of these approaches, *The Importance of Being Different* seeks to supplement the work of the scholars who have come before by providing a lens that does not reduce all of the fairy tales' queer bodies to mere metaphors for these other registers but offers its own new and equally significant register. According to Nodelman, "for many commentators, the stories Wilde tells about creatures like nightingales and objects like roses are not actually about birds and roses at all; and in reading the birds and roses as symbols of something theoretically more profound, those commentators tend to forget about the actual presence of the birds and roses."[138] Objecting to this tendency to allegorize characters and events that in fact are "a perfectly realistic possibility in a magical world of potential wonders," he bemoans how such "transformation of these enjoyable and meaningfully concrete entities into something less embodied and less magical seems, then, not more comprehensive but less."[139] A disability studies take on Wilde's fairy tales serves as a valuable counter to such allegorizing, remaining attuned as it does to both the actualities of embodiment and the wonders of magic by, most fundamentally, insisting that the importance of his disability-aligned characters resides in their physical differences, which we need to read literally.

Bristow begins and ends his introduction with the same adorable anecdote, as related by George Leveson Gower, who recalled Wilde playfully complaining about how one of his sons announced "with the utmost gravity" that he had "just met two lions and a tiger in Kensington Gardens" but then objected when Oscar replied that he himself had "seen an exquisite dwarf two feet high and a really fascinating ogress seven feet high in Hyde Park."[140] Wilde's imaginative interest in peculiar bodies is absolutely affirmed by the central place they hold in his fairy tales. This book aims to appreciate these incredibly engaging texts for what they, on a literal level, are: stories about characters whose lives (and deaths) are profoundly impacted by how their unusual physical appearance or attributes spur conditioned pejorative responses from others, who pose or posit them as "less than," as dismissible or dangerous, as different.

In the chapters that follow, I offer far more substantial discussions of how the tales together tease out numerous possibilities, both positive and negative, for reaffirming or re-visioning readers' sense of how literary representations of disability-aligned difference can contribute to current-day conversations around both intersectional disability and emotional response. I do not proceed chronologically, or even by collection, but rather curate the tales via my own particular order, which I feel best affords the most logical progression given my unique focus. Each of the four content chapters devotes itself to an extensive close reading of one of the tales that offer more extended treatments of Wilde's peculiar bodies.[141] Each chapter also will draw upon its own individually relevant Dickensian touchstone, as Dickens and Wilde not only work as two serviceable bookends to Victorian literary history (the rise of Boz and the fall of Bosie), but they also bring together significant strands in the period's depiction of freakery more particularly and disability more broadly.

The first content chapter opens with "The Birthday of the Infanta" and its death of a performing Dwarf, potentially mired in damaging stereotype and maudlin melodrama but nonetheless offering through its multilayered evocation of the freak show more progressive emotionally based possibilities for compassion, acceptance, and even identification beyond demeaning disgust or paternalistic charity. Positioning this tale as a rewriting of Dickens's

*The Old Curiosity Shop* encourages readers to interrogate the manipulative mechanisms that can press for problematic emotional responses toward such difference, and shows Wilde to be a writer fully aware of his own role as a showman who asks readers not only to recognize his own authorial complicity in the consumption of his plot's pain but further to acknowledge their own readerly complicity as spectators to the spectacle of the Dwarf's demise.

The following chapter reveals how in "The Fisherman and His Soul" Wilde expands his foray into freakery through a complex consideration of the role extraordinary bodies may play not as attractions whose interest resides in the revulsion they stir but rather as persons of interest whose attraction lies in the love for and between such bodies that they express. This longest of the fairy tales contains a fascinating trawl of entangled elements relative to its two disability-aligned protagonists, a little Mermaid (who, regardless of her beauty, is represented as an aberrant body) and a young Fisherman (who arguably inhabits a freakish form of his own after cutting away his shadow-soul from his body, as he then somehow can live and breathe underwater). It builds on "The Birthday of the Infanta," in part, by introducing a romance plotline between its two protagonists, a significant development only teased at in the first story. It further represents a movement beyond texts like Dickens's *Our Mutual Friend,* where characters such as Jenny Wren serve as auxiliary foils and sidekicks to nondisabled protagonists.

The next discussion carries forward the previous chapters' concerns regarding these tales' ability to move beyond documenting the destructive effects of the degradation and demoralization so many fantastic bodies face, toward a more optimistic sense of such individuals' ability to transform not only their interpersonal relationships but an inequitable society itself, a theme fruitfully found in Dickens's *A Tale of Two Cities* as well. "The Star-Child" tells the tale of a beautiful boy whose appearance dramatically alters, turning him into a hideous freak. His journey to find the mother he had cruelly rejected owing to her own wretched physical appearance teaches him the importance of loving-kindness and compassionate action toward others grounded in an ethic of reciprocity and mutuality. His eventual short-lived reign as a king after regaining his beauty allows him to champion social justice for all.

The final content chapter continues the book's focus on the stigmatization and devaluation of disability-aligned difference, but significantly more substantially seeks to (re)claim agency for Wilde's peculiar protagonists through its reading of "The Happy Prince." The story foregrounds the devoted friendship and the active benevolence of the Prince, a stationary statue whose lack of mobility leads him to pair up with a small Swallow in a compassionate campaign to alleviate the sufferings of the poor by giving away his gems and gold (becoming both sightless and unsightly in the bargain). Framing the story in relation to Dickens's *The Cricket on the Hearth* and its character of Blind Bertha establishes its disability-aligned dynamic duo as empowering agents of change rather than as helpless objects of charity.

The bulk of the book's conclusion takes up in detail a particular set of later texts—Wilde's prison literature—to offer one more fully developed example of how utilizing the fairy tales as a frame of reference provides a powerful further lens into Wilde's attraction to anomalous bodies, as the physical debilitation and mental distress he endures in jail arguably transforms his awareness of his own difference in much more substantial ways than did his time in America. Close readings of his last writings—"Epistola" (his prison letter more popularly known as *De Profundis*), *The Ballad of Reading Gaol,* and his letters on prison reform—reveal Wilde reconsolidating insights from the fairy tales into a robust defense of the many different bodies and minds that prejudice and stigma render at risk. Dickens's *Hard Times* provides a helpful intertextual reference point for Wilde's own emphasis on community and the role that humility and kindness play in his commitment to compassionate action.

The focus in this concluding chapter on mental as well as physical disabilities is a crucial one. The field of disability studies for a long time privileged discussions centered around the latter, often to the exclusion of the former. This imbalance still to this day has not been fully rectified, and so from the outset, I have been worried that Wilde's specific interest in remarkable bodies (rather than minds) might lead to my project seeming to contribute to this historical slight. As I will clarify, for many the two are perhaps better understood as inextricably interrelated, so it is often all the more important to carefully avoid reinforcing any sort of hard-and-fast binary between mental or cognitive disabilities and physical disabilities. In fact, there is substantial recent work by Eli Clare and Sami Schalk that takes up Margaret Price's absolutely essential call to challenge this problematic divide, in part through the generative adaptation of the term *bodymind* for disability studies as a useful way to ensure the inextricable interrelation of the mind and the body always is recognized and respected.[142]

I close my conclusion by very briefly offering some possibilities regarding how Wilde's other works might potentially be approached through a disability studies lens, but mainly by noting how the remaining tales (those not analyzed in the introduction or one of the four content chapters) potentially serve to productively complement or contradict the lines of approach delineated in my close readings. First, "The Remarkable Rocket" offers a stark contrast to any sympathy for the Dwarf, in the form of the Rocket's irredeemable selfishness, and the latter's "disablement" uncomfortably seems to be understood exclusively through the prisms of wholeness, utility, and vitality. Next, the problematic aspects of the Fisherman's association of disability with sacrifice and self-maiming may be put into dialogue with "The Nightingale and the Rose," where Wilde's small songbird willingly engages in self-injurious and ultimately self-destroying behavior. Then, "The Young King" serves as an appropriate coda to "The Star-Child" and its emphasis on social change, via its titular protagonist's realization his life of luxury is pitilessly provided for him through the exploitation of the poor and disadvantaged. Lastly, "The Devoted Friend" serves as a compelling counter to "The Happy Prince" (and "The Selfish Giant"), as selfless little Hans loses his life after being taken advantage of one too many times by his self-proclaimed benefactor, big Hugh the Miller, qualifying the longer tale's affirmation of agency by providing a stark reminder of how disability-aligned difference may be cruelly exploited in the name of benevolence and charity.

According to Jerusha McCormack, "It is from the margins of society, from the perspective of the poor, the colonised, the disreputable and dispossessed, that [Wilde's fairy tales] must be read."[143] A disability studies approach to these texts helps provide a broader sense of the full spectrum of marginalized lives these stories address. It also offers the opportunity to revisit our contemporary assessment of the complex emotional economies of disability; in the multiple possibilities these opaque, slippery texts suggest, there is ample room not only to reconsider disability's complicated affiliation with the conceptual parish of fellow feeling but further to interrogate the extent to which writer and reader alike might be implicated in the complex dynamics behind the gamut of emotions evoked. In the end, it may be impossible definitively to decide if Wilde's treatments are celebratory or cynical, progressive or problematic. Regardless, though, his very attention to so many nonnormative protagonists is notable in and of itself. While they may end up dead or discarded, perhaps even for some readers seeming the pathetic butt of a renowned jester's jokes, Wilde's disability-aligned characters remain most memorable for their empowering roles as agential actors and active benefactors, as attractive lovers and aesthetic lives. Certainly, these texts force readers to confront the stark realities of stigma and stereotype, and how, rather than inspiring appreciation and wonder, this might lead many merely to despair at the ultimate indignities of compulsory ablebodiedness. To my mind, though, while definitely displaying some signs of triviality, Wilde's fairy tales are on the contrary most remarkable for their own exceptional contributions to readers' ongoing realization of the vital Importance of Being Different.

# 1

# "It Is a Pity, for He Is So Ugly That He Might Have Made the King Smile"

## "The Birthday of the Infanta" and the Spectacle of the Freakish Body

Oscar Wilde famously (though some suggest only purportedly) pronounced, "One must have a heart of stone to read the death of Little Nell without laughing."[1] Wilde's quip takes for its target one of the true touchstones of Victorian sentimentality, the tragic turn of events at the end of Charles Dickens's *The Old Curiosity Shop*. Dickens's well-known work is the story of how Nell Trent (a very beautiful and sympathetic thirteen-year-old girl) is hounded to her grave by Daniel Quilp (a remarkably ugly and cruel dwarf). Intriguingly, Wilde's "The Birthday of the Infanta" is the story of a remarkably ugly but sympathetic dwarf whose tragic death is hastened by a very beautiful but cruel twelve-year-old girl (the Infanta).[2] Whether or not Wilde ever did serve up the sentimentality of his era with such a wonderful witticism (so equally playful and caustic), a critical articulation of the two texts offers some incredibly generative insight into Wilde's story and its compelling literary representation of disability.

As my introduction in part already suggested, Dickensian frames of reference can serve as useful nodes of comparison and contrast in assessing Wilde's own renditions of anomalous bodies. Exploring the ways in which his freakish Giant and disfigured Christ-child invert or otherwise reinvent the roles Dickens dreamed up for his selfish Scrooge and sentimental Tiny Tim offers one entry point for positing Wilde's work as a dramatic departure from the paternalistic approach of his prestigious predecessor. Not only does the Giant's frightening physical appearance ultimately refuse to endorse Victorian physiognomy's correlation of such a body with inner ugliness, but as an active benefactor toward others, he reverses the standard trajectory of disabled lives that relegates them to dependence upon charity. When this sympathetic depiction of the Giant's unusually large body is read alongside the especially tiny one of his special friend (who, again, is no object of patronizing pity like Tim but rather a deity worthy of worship, with the power to bestow the gift of a heavenly reward), the progressive potential of Wilde's literary representation of extraordinary bodies appears all the more appealing.

Bringing disability studies to bear on "The Birthday of the Infanta" extends our understanding of the extent to which Wilde offers positive if also imperfect portrayals of his disability-aligned protagonists (while also suggesting more sophisticated aspects to Dickens's own literary representations of disability). Specifically, through a framework that evokes the context of the freak show, Wilde in this tale highlights both the constructed nature of bodily spectacle that Mendelssohn suggests his American tour foregrounded for him and the conditioned disgust that Hingston argues drives so many encounters with peculiar bodies. Lillian Craton's provocative reading of *The Old Curiosity Shop* and her theorization of "a fictional space in which enjoyment and exploitation are often indistinguishable"[3] explores the extent to which a blending of "sentimental and grotesque aesthetics" through the figures of "the freak and the suffering girl" allows for "a subtle criticism of the very practice of displaying physical difference for social commentary."[4] In this chapter, I will consider how Wilde himself not only might seem to acknowledge the emotional manipulation writers often rely upon in sentimental narratives (especially those with designs on readers' pity) but further to encourage readers to confront their own enjoyment of the exploitation upon which so much of the emotional impact depends. This angle opens up new perspectives on why lines continue to be drawn between binaries such as abnormal and normal, evil and good, ugly and beautiful, child and adult—but, above all, it reveals how blurred these lines often are upon closer inspection.

Craton's approach to *The Old Curiosity Shop* casts a decidedly more positive light on Dickens's own depiction of disability (that is, as not merely limited to the sentimental messaging almost universally associated with *A Christmas Carol*). For her, while "small, suffering bodies are a hallmark of Dickens' sentimentality," they also are a means through which he "indicts selfishness and cruelty."[5] In this particular novel, Quilp embodies such selfishness and cruelty, and Nell embodies selflessness and kindness, but that these antithetical characters are both little serves to powerfully complicate the novel's portrayal of disability-aligned difference. From Craton's perspective, "Nell is not an anti-freak—not an emissary of the normal world, provided to guide us through the novel's collection of the unusual. Rather, she is the latest addition to Mrs. Jarley's wax collection, as much an oddity as any other character."[6] What is more, she insists, Nell and Quilp are linked in more disturbing ways: given the "lurid overtones" to Quilp's interest in Nell, Dickens allows his readers to "enjoy titillating revulsion" in entertaining the idea of them as coupled.[7] Overall, Dickens's showcasing of such spectacle reveals more about the writer and his readers, not some sort of "fundamental meaning contained within unusual bodies."[8] As Dickens blurs the lines between enjoyment and exploitation, "the author's manipulation and audience's consumption of human difference are interrogated alongside the more obvious social ills of child exploitation and poverty."[9] In the end, we must face "our complicity as consumers of pain," acknowledging how Nell's character engenders not empathy but rather "a collective sense of guilt about the enjoyment we took in her tormented journey."[10]

Positioning "The Birthday of the Infanta" as a rewriting of *The Old Curiosity Shop* entails that one consider how Wilde similarly might be requiring his readers to experience littleness as disability-aligned difference within the context of freak show dynamics. Like Dickens's novel, Wilde's story on its surface offers a sentimental framework that provides for a scathing indictment of "selfishness and cruelty" while simultaneously qualifying, if not directly challenging, any reduction of the text to a story with a moral. Wilde crafts a complex pairing of his two main characters, partly merely reversing the Dickensian roles, but also creating a sophisticated mixture of what are in the novel two separate and relatively straightforward categories of littleness.[11] Physically, Wilde's Dwarf is allied with Quilp, and the Infanta with Nell; but the Dwarf is also associated with the innocence and kindness of Nell, while the Infanta generally is associated with the cruelty and selfishness of Quilp. In other words, Wilde deftly layers his tale in ways that complicate any attempt to exclusively associate one character with goodness and the other with evil, one with ugliness and the other with beauty, one with abnormality and the other normalcy—even one with a childlike or childish disposition, the other a more knowing and mature nature.

Navigating the contradictions and dilemmas typical of all of Wilde's tales, which in "The Birthday of the Infanta" center around the relationship between the Dwarf and the Infanta, is thus an essential aspect of the reading experience, one made all the richer by the numerous points of intersectional connection the story raises. As in "The Selfish Giant," the figure of the child (while shifting to a focus on early adolescence) still underpins the negotiation of the extent to which physical difference is construed as "less than." "The Birthday of the Infanta" further forces many readers to confront their own uneasiness with disability and sexuality through romantic undertones to the relationship between the Dwarf and the Infanta that blur boundaries between child and adult. The intersection of class and disability only intensifies the perturbation of even the thought of so many generations of carefully plotted positive eugenics designed to preserve the purity of royal bloodlines being compromised by such an undesirable contamination. What is more, given the historical associations of dwarfs with atavism, the specter of miscegenation implicates ethnic and racial prejudices in the stigma that conditions the disgust manifested toward the Dwarf by those who are identified with the Spanish court. As a close reading of the tale reveals, Wilde exploits these tensions and intersections while foregrounding the central role the Dwarf's "deformity" plays in his rejection.

Wilde's early references to the Infanta's diminutiveness prepare readers to pair her conceptually with the Dwarf. Wilde not only calls her "the little Princess" but alludes to her "pale little face," her "little hand," and her "tiny slippers."[12] Part of the dramatic interest in her character, however, is that in spite of how her smallness evokes a much younger child, one understands she is on the threshold of sexual maturation. She has an apparent suitor in the young Count of Tierra-Nueva, who is about fourteen, and while on one level perhaps it is all just an innocent playing at romance, significantly it is staged right around the same age as the one between her parents that in short order led to her own birth. In fact, the twelve-year-old Infanta is, by the King's own account, the mirror image of his now dead queen on the day they met and were formally betrothed; while looking down on his daughter from a palace window as her birthday festivities are about to begin, "he seemed to see [the Queen] again, as he had seen her first . . . when he was but fifteen years of age, and she still younger."[13] The King, Wilde reports, still remembers vividly returning from this trip with "a little ringlet of yellow hair, and the memory of two childish lips bending down to kiss his hand."[14] These details are immediately followed by a passage deploying a double dose of disability-related descriptors, noting how "madly" the King loved the Queen and characterizing his passion as so great it was akin to a "terrible blindness."[15]

Through opaque boundaries between innocent childlike affection and sexualized adult attraction, Wilde positions the Infanta to occupy the same liminal state as her mother. While the King watches his daughter, he observes, "She had all the Queen's pretty petulance of manner, the same wilful way of tossing her head, the same proud curved beautiful mouth, the same wonderful smile . . . as she . . . stretched out her little hand for the stately Spanish gentlemen to kiss."[16] In the King's eyes, she is no longer just a little girl, but a powerful reminder of "his whole married life, with its fierce, fiery-coloured joys and the terrible agony of its sudden ending"; ultimately, the resemblance is all too much for him, and he leaves off watching her, to the Infanta's decided disappointment, as he rarely pays her any attention.[17] Luckily for the Infanta, today she has a whole morning full of entertainment to distract her.

Just as the curiosity shop and the waxworks in the Dickens novel evoke the aesthetic of the *wunderkammern,* so in Wilde's tale the birthday party program provides the context for reading not merely the Dwarf but also the Infanta through the lens of the freak show. The first event is a sham bullfight featuring some of the Infanta's little guests, starring her Count as the matador who slays the wickerwork bull. The sight of the boys prancing about on hobbyhorses resonates with historical dwarf exhibition performances but also suggests a self-conscious artificiality to the entertainment, immediately erasing the line between actors and spectators (as well as setting up a paralleling of the Count and the Dwarf as not merely rival performers but rival suitors as well). It is further apparent the Infanta and her guests understand they are on one level not merely spectators but part of the entertainment too, as Wilde describes them as having performatively "stood up upon the benches, and waved their lace handkerchiefs . . . just as sensibly as if they had been grown-up people."[18] This blurring of the lines between childhood and adulthood, between entertainers and audience, serves as essential setup for the wholesale deconstruction the Dwarf's arrival will consolidate.

The other acts trotted out are an Italian puppet show staging a tragic drama of death for love, an African juggler-illusionist, a troupe of church boys performing a rare dance, and "gipsies"[19] who feature zither players and dancers with a bear and some little Barbary apes that do a sham soldier's drill with two boys. Significantly, all of the acts materially embody the otherness of littleness, the related categories (in terms of popular constructions of freakery) of the foreign and the bestial, or some combination of the two. Upon seeing the princess, the "gipsies" feel "sure that one so lovely as she was could never be cruel to anybody,"[20] a tongue-in-cheek line all the more incongruous in that this parroting of Victorian physiognomy is attributed to Romani people who themselves were judged on the basis of both their ethnicity and their physical appearance. Wilde's irony seems to signal the shift about to take place with the entrance of the dwarf (the morning's grand finale). Indeed, as the story's main action plays itself out, the Infanta's actual cruelty (already suggested by the petulance, willfulness, and pride the King ascribes to her) ultimately will be revealed as far more repulsive than the Dwarf's physical ugliness, exposing the facade of loveliness that masks her self-absorbed life of privilege and power, in line with what Tatar more generally proposes is Wilde's interest in a grotesque aesthetics over that of classical beauty (an aesthetic Craton asserts "tends to transgress official bourgeoisie culture"[21]).

With the Dwarf's appearance, Wilde turns our attention to how this freak performer's stigmatized difference is immediately perceived as inviting ridicule. The "little Dwarf" sets off peals of laughter from the Infanta and her guests when he enters "waddling on his crooked legs and wagging his huge misshapen head,"[22] for "even at the Spanish Court, always noted for its cultivated passion for the horrible, so fantastic a little monster had never been seen."[23] Intriguingly, what makes the Dwarf the "most amusing" part of the royal freak show, what makes him "really quite irresistible," is not so much his monstrosity but "his complete unconsciousness of his own grotesque appearance."[24] He responds to all the laughter by himself laughing "as freely and as joyously as any of them," and after each dance he bows and smiles and nods at them "just as if he was really one of themselves, and not a little misshapen thing that Nature, in some humorous mood, had fashioned for others to mock at."[25] Significantly, such lines introduce the question of whether the audience reaction is unequivocally scripted by biology as a natural consequence of his "deformity" (a freak of nature) or is rather a conditioned but at bottom arbitrary response determined by cultural constructs (a freak of culture).[26] While the joke above all is on the Dwarf here (with Nature itself seeming to sanction responding to him as not even some*one* but some*thing* to be satirized for sport), that he even can imagine he might be "one of themselves" nonetheless raises for readers the possibility he could in fact be grouped with the guests. Given the earlier suggestions that the partygoers are on one level able to slot into the same role (as part of the entertainment), definitive distinctions between spectator and spectacle, the subject and object of such staring, begin to drop away. That is, the Infanta and her little friends evince a self-conscious performativity, as they have grown up understanding they are to some extent always on display and thus are required to fulfill particular roles when in public.

Not only do the Count and other boys serve as the first set of performers, but the Infanta herself is not immune to such slipperiness. One of the first things one learns about her, after all, is how she is kept isolated from the rest of the world: "On ordinary days she was only allowed to play with children of her own rank, so she had always to play alone, but her birthday was an exception."[27] A virtual orphan whose mother is dead and whose father is so consumed with sorrow he rarely sees her, she spends her days in the company of (or, perhaps, more accurately, under the control of) "the grim Duchess of Albuquerque who always accompanied her" in the role of Camerera-Mayor, the Grand Inquisitor of Granada, and the legendarily cruel Don Pedro of Aragon—the King's brother, who is rumored to have poisoned the Queen.[28] The Infanta is, perhaps, like Dickens's Nell, cast not (merely) as an antifreak but also is on some level aligned with those brought before her to provide appropriate spectacle for such a special occasion. As the Dwarf makes his entrance, then, Wilde invites his readers not only to judge the Infanta's comportment but further to see her as isolated by her position: "the Infanta herself laughed so much that the Camerera was obliged to remind her that although there were many precedents in Spain for a King's daughter weeping before her equals, there were none for a Princess of the blood royal making so merry before those who were her inferiors in birth."[29] She is an object to her handlers, a placeholder for the State more than a person, an exceptional figure who is always on display, and not merely when in public—after all, the narrative starts with an act of spectatorship as the King, Don Pedro, and the Grand Inquisitor watch the Infanta.

Since her birthday is the only day she is allowed to "play" with other children, her part in the whole pageant of the celebration is arguably a show in its own right. The Infanta's own playacting is particularly evident in her response to the Dwarf. Her gesture of, "with her sweetest smile," giving a rose to him when he finishes is thoroughly performative: "remembering how she had seen the great ladies of the Court throw bouquets to Caffarelli, the famous Italian treble," she tosses him a "beautiful white rose" from her hair, "partly for a jest and partly to tease the Camerera."[30] One of the reasons the Camerera must disapprove of the jest is precisely the impropriety of the Infanta even pretending she might in any way be paired with him romantically, given he is not only so far below her station but so ugly as to seem inhuman. Indeed, it is certainly not merely a matter of class prejudice but also founded on fears of miscegenation. As Killeen notes, particularly after Europeans first learned of the Pygmy peoples during the 1870s, by virtue of their new racist characterization as "atavistic survivals," dwarfs "came to symbolize not merely malevolent otherness, but also evil foreignness."[31] Again, the Dwarf's links as a freak to the foreign and the bestial clearly predetermine that he will be scripted into a position of diminished personhood, if not dangerous deviancy—the same prejudice that will drive the development of eugenics.

The Dwarf, though, takes the Infanta's gesture as a sign of her love, "pressing the flower to his rough coarse lips" while placing "his hand upon his heart."[32] The news he has been scheduled for an encore performance by "her own express command" only seems to him to confirm her return of his affection, and he celebrates by "kissing the white rose in an absurd ecstasy of pleasure, and making the most uncouth and clumsy gestures of delight."[33] However ridiculous the Dwarf's delusion, Wilde significantly begins to shift away from portraying the Dwarf merely as an object of ridicule, by having the Infanta retire from the story at this point, departing for a feast and then the siesta inside the palace. Readers remain instead with the Dwarf as he explores the garden (and, eventually, the palace) on his own. Over these several pages, the Dwarf's increasing humanization and depth (in spite of his ignorance regarding his difference and his naivete regarding the Infanta's feelings) eventually show him to be the true protagonist of the tale, the character with whom readers most clearly sympathize (even, perhaps, identify, as many surely may relate to his experiences of both joyous and unrequited love).

Wilde first switches into full-blown fantastic mode as the flora and fauna of the palace garden give voice to their various emotional responses to the Dwarf's presence amongst them. Since the story has been rendered thoroughly realistically so far, this shift can be as discombobulating as it is fun, intensifying the undermining of numerous aforementioned binaries that freaks such as dwarfs introduce—including the line between the human world and the (rest of the) natural world. This section decidedly works to tilt reader sympathy toward the Dwarf in a way that can make readers feel guilty for any laughter directed at him during the previous scene. The Flowers are thoroughly dismissive of the Dwarf, and absolutely disgusted by his ugliness. The arrogance of their pride and prejudice is certainly off-putting, but Wilde also clearly is playing for comic effect the exaggerated nature of their reactions, as well as nudging readers to acknowledge the dehumanizing humor they themselves may have neglected to interrogate during Wilde's description of the Dwarf's dancing. The Cactus, for instance, in elaborating on the Dwarf as "a perfect horror,"[34] offers a particularly memorable comment that furthers the blurring of the world of the palace and garden with that of the Dwarf and the forest from which he was taken. The insult ironically fits the speaker's own embodiment: "he is twisted and stumpy, and his head is completely out of proportion with his legs. Really he makes me feel prickly all over."[35] In yet another instance of conditioned disgust, the Cactus objects to the Dwarf's appearance (in spite of the similarities to his own) merely because the interloper does not belong at court and therefore represents a threat to what he sees as the natural order. This seems to be the basis for the White-Rose Tree's character assassination as well, as she calls the Dwarf out as a thief after recognizing the rose he is holding as the one she had given to the Infanta earlier.

Only the Violets even "meekly" attempt to speak for him (noting "he could not help" being "extremely plain"), but after being attacked by the Geraniums ("who did not usually give themselves airs, and were known to have a great many poor relations themselves") for even suggesting such a thing, some of the Violets have to admit "that the ugliness of the little Dwarf was almost ostentatious, and that he would have shown much better taste if he had looked sad, or at least pensive, instead of jumping about merrily, and throwing himself into such grotesque and silly attitudes."[36] The Geraniums seem to speak for all of the Flowers in their adherence to a script that supports their superiority and that defines disabled existence as a sad state, one incapable of supporting joy in such a life. "There was no reason why one should admire a person because he was incurable," they insist, and that he cannot help if he looks so off-putting is in fact his "chief defect" in their view.[37] The old Sundial reiterates the distinctions between not merely the beautiful and the ugly but between the rich and the poor that the Camerera and the Flowers insist upon remaining inviolably clear, announcing "that the children of Kings were Kings, and that the children of charcoal-burners were charcoal-burners, and that it was absurd to pretend that it wasn't so."[38] In all these ways, this scene helps to reinforce the intersectional associations of the Dwarf's body (particularly his ugliness) with immorality and poverty and racial inferiority.

Other than the Peacock, however, the Birds "somehow" like the dwarf,[39] and they offer readers the first real alternative, humanizing take on the Infanta's little monster. They "did not mind his being ugly," for they have enjoyed seeing him in the forest, "dancing about like an elf,"[40] an image of joy as opposed to buffoonery or revulsion. What is more, they testify to his kindness, reporting how he shared his meals with them and gave nuts to the squirrels. Here is the Dwarf, like the Giant, in the role of an active benefactor rather than a passive recipient of charity; this is the Dwarf the birds know, so they welcome him here in the garden, flying all around him and "just touching his cheek with their wings as they passed."[41] According to Wilde, "the little Dwarf was so pleased that he could not help showing them the beautiful white rose, and telling them that the Infanta herself had given it to him because she loved him."[42] The Dwarf's sweet romantic feelings for the Infanta are of a completely different nature than Quilp's possessive sexual designs and offer a decidedly different tack from the titillating revulsion and eugenicist fears the Flowers feel. In this light, the Dwarf is not laughable but extremely likeable. Indeed, the Lizards also have taken "an immense fancy" to him, and as he rests on the grass "they [play] and [romp] all over him, and tr[y] to amuse him"[43]—interestingly positioning him (as, arguably, also did the Birds' attentions) not as the performer providing the pleasure of entertainment but rather as the one for whom such pleasure is intended. Even their admission of his ugliness—"he is really not so ugly after all, provided, of course, that one shuts one's eyes, and does not look at him"[44]—is telling, for while it invites laughter, it also advances the idea that beauty should not be judged with one's eyes.

The Flowers, however, remain unconvinced, and in their annoyance with the Lizards' and Birds' attentions toward the Dwarf, they reveal all the more the social prejudices that underwrite their response to his peculiar body. They complain about the "vulgarising effect this incessant rushing and flying about has," insisting the Birds and Lizards "are mere vagrants like the gipsies, and should be treated in exactly the same manner"[45]—aligning the Dwarf's animal friends not just with him but with the rest of the birthday party performers as well. The tale has invited readers to acknowledge an ongoing deconstruction of any hard-and-fast binaries along the lines of court/subject or spectator/performer, but the Flowers certainly do not see things that way. Looking "very haughty," with "their noses in the air," they titter, "Look at his hunched back, and his crooked legs," as he scrambles across the terrace to go look for the Infanta in the palace.[46] Like the Infanta, the Flowers' self-importance is grounded in their sense of their own place and prettiness, and as such they immediately seize upon the Dwarf's disability-aligned difference as marking him for ridicule and rejection. Readers, though, are now prepared to refuse to let this stand.

Compellingly, Wilde at this point takes his readers directly into the Dwarf's consciousness, and they learn he is not only unaware of the Flowers' derision but in fact thinks they are "the most marvellous things in the whole world, except of course the Infanta."[47] The Dwarf's naivete is certainly troubling from a disability studies perspective, indicative as it is of the notion of simplemindedness stereotypically brought to bear on so many disabled persons, in life and literature alike. Such a construction is a decidedly precarious one for those upon whom it is foisted. Patrick McDonagh documents (in a chapter that opens with a discussion of the famous "Wild Boy," Victor of Aveyron) how "the public image of the 'idiot' was very much linked to the sentimental notion of the 'innocent,'"[48] and how such difference like other types of disability also was consistently related to sin and evil, to disease and degeneracy. According to McDonagh, the "conception of 'feeble-mindedness' is borne of degeneration theory and the pathologizing of poverty, indicating a growing anxiety about the burgeoning numbers of unemployed poor . . . as well as fears of increased criminal activity."[49] Regardless, then, of whether Wilde might have intended for readers to gloss this positively (as the sweet, pure innocence often associated with childhood), it nevertheless on another level reinforces the pernicious stereotype of disabled persons as "less than" intellectually. The potential to read his character as a simpleton rather than an innocent persists throughout the rest of the story and must not be airbrushed away, even as it is at least somewhat offset by Wilde's positioning of the Dwarf as a privileged (but also deluded) romantic dreamer over the next few pages. The Dwarf's simultaneous but conflicting roles (figure of the innocent child and figure of the true lover) remain in tension as readers continue to negotiate whether it is paternalistic pity or admiring attraction they should be feeling.

In the paragraph immediately following the Flowers' dismissal of the Dwarf, readers are privy to his fantasy of how he and the Infanta might spend their lives together—significantly, not at court but back in the forest where his skill and strength, his sensitivity and selflessness, are showcased. One learns he is in fact a talented woodsman in spite of his youth, and "very strong"[50] in spite of his small stature. He also is shown to be quite knowledgeable of his own world, if clueless regarding the Infanta's: "though he had never been in a palace before, he knew a great many wonderful things," from "the cry of every bird" and "the trail of every animal" to "all kinds of delightful tricks," such as how to "make little cages out of rushes for the grasshoppers to sing in, and fashion the long-jointed bamboo into the pipe that Pan loves to hear."[51] If she grew tired, "he would find a soft bank of moss for her, or carry her in his arms," and then at night "he would give her his own little bed" and "watch outside the window till dawn," when "they would go out and dance together all the day long."[52] In all this, Wilde shows his disability-aligned protagonist to be a caring and capable lover, the opposite of the dependency and helplessness typically attributed to disabled bodies.

With each new detail, Wilde not only validates both the Dwarf's humanity and the joys of his life in the forest but also the difference between being alone (as the Dwarf has been in the woods) and being lonely (as the Infanta has been in the palace), suggesting that the content if marginalized lot of the poor charcoal-burner's son is preferable to the pampered and privileged life of the powerful princess. In spite of this wealth of knowledge and talents, however, the Dwarf's solitude (as noted above) has preserved or rendered him an innocent regarding the world outside of his home. His naivete is clearly signaled, for example, by his description of a beautiful procession he once witnessed, which informed readers know actually to have been a group of heretics being sent to their death.[53] Nowhere is the Dwarf's ignorance more apparent, though, than when, while wandering about the palace, he sees "a little figure watching him" from across a room.[54] For a split second, both he and Wilde's readers assume he has found his beloved Infanta, for whom he is searching. As the Dwarf will realize to his horror when he moves closer, though, it is actually his own reflection in a mirrored wall. Still, this brief conflation of the two main characters is truly significant, as its explicit linkage of their bodies exposes and intensifies the comparison of and contrast between them Wilde has been encouraging throughout the tale, reinforcing the extent to which their fates appear interwoven in spite of their separate spheres.

Most immediately, however, this momentary misidentification morphs into a more mortifying possibility, when the Dwarf sees it is not the pretty princess but instead "the most grotesque monster he had ever beheld": "not properly shaped, as all other people were, but hunchbacked, and crooked-limbed, with huge lolling head and mane."[55] For an instant, the connection between the Infanta and the Dwarf is solidified in a particularly revealing way, for the Dwarf's initial reaction is strikingly similar to that of the court party toward the day's entertainment: he "laugh[s]," "ma[kes] it a mocking bow," and "shout[s] with amusement."[56] Shortly, though, his response becomes one of fear and loathing, which turns in on himself when he understands that he is the monster, that he is "misshapen and hunchbacked, foul to look at and grotesque."[57] With the epiphany that "it was at him that all the children had been laughing, and the little Princess who he had thought loved him—she too had been merely mocking at his ugliness, and making merry over his twisted limbs," he gives a "wild cry of despair."[58] In tears, he tears the white rose to pieces, falls to the floor "with a face drawn in pain," crawls "like some wounded thing, into the shadow," and remains there "moaning."[59] With this the readers' picture of the skilled woodsman and winning lover is suddenly in danger of slipping back into the more typical view of such an atypical body—pathetic victim at best, or menacing monster at worst.

At this terrible instant, Wilde foregrounds for his readers both the extent to which the writer potentially has been manipulating them through a sentimental frame during this section focused on the Dwarf while exploiting their own (in Craton's words) "complicity as consumers of pain." For, just as the Dwarf begins "beating the floor with his clenched hands, in the most fantastic and exaggerated manner," the Infanta and her companions happen upon him.[60] The children are set "off into shouts of happy laughter," and the Infanta remarks that "his acting is funnier still" than his hilarious dancing, "almost as good as the puppets, only of course not quite so natural."[61] This brilliant scene pulls readers in decidedly different directions: torn between compassion born out of their attachment to the Dwarf and an antipathy toward sentimentalism that allows them a good chuckle over a passage, they may feel they are meant to be laughing along with Wilde. This conflict is only intensified when, right after the Infanta delivers her laughable line about the puppets' naturalness and then begins to applaud what she sees as his new performance, the Dwarf gives "a curious gasp" and dies.[62]

The rest of the children punctuate the scene's almost indistinguishable experience of enjoyment and exploitation, demanding the princess's plaything get up and dance, cajoling him by exclaiming, "you are as clever as the Barbary apes, and much more ridiculous."[63] As she does not yet realize he is dead, the Infanta calls her uncle and the Chamberlain over, telling them her "funny little Dwarf is sulking" but must be made to dance for her.[64] Don Pedro approaches first, "slap[s] the Dwarf on the cheek with his embroidered glove," and remonstrates, "*petit monstre*. You must dance. The Infanta . . . wishes to be amused."[65] Upon receiving no response, he "wearily" announces he will have to send for a "whipping master,"[66] but the Chamberlain examines the little monster further and states, "*Mi bella Princesa*, your funny little Dwarf will never dance again. It is a pity, for he is so ugly that he might have made the King smile."[67] The Infanta laughs, still in her own moment of ignorance not realizing this means he has died, and asks why, to which the Chamberlain replies, "Because his heart is broken."[68] Upon hearing this, the Infanta frowns, and "her dainty rose-leaf lips [curl] in pretty disdain."[69] The next sentence is the fairy tale's last, crowning its far-from-happy ending: "'For the future let those who come to play with me have no hearts,' she cried, and she ran out into the garden."[70]

The Dwarf's death is shocking in and of itself, but its immediate aftermath strikes many as particularly disgusting. For some it powerfully transforms the sympathy (sentimentalized or not) they felt at his moment of epiphany into a profound compassion (if not also anger) that motivates them to condemn the mocking mistreatment he receives merely because he did not look "normal," much less beautiful. The climactic scene may seem to end up merely reversing the roles of Dickensian villain and victim, with readers indicting the Infanta for her own heartlessness, and therefore on the one hand they appreciate the irony in her insistence that any future playmates "have no hearts." At the same time, however, readers also may worry about the extent to which their own tolerance of the sometimes all-too-easy coexistence of enjoyment and exploitation has been equally heartless. As fellow participants in the spectacle of the Dwarf's demeaning death, readers must confront the possibility not only of their own complicity in the consumption of pain upon which the narrative relies but also of their own fundamental heartlessness as a consequence.

To complicate matters further, readers must consider what they perceive to be Wilde's intentions in maneuvering his plot toward this specific conclusion. A couple of suggestive word choices in the last lines potentially wrench readers toward an even more heightened awareness of both the author's manipulation of and their own participation in the construction and the critique of the conventional affect of pity generally associated with such endings. That is, given the already established erasure of the lines between the party attendees and the party performers, the tale actually allows for a deepening of the tragedy in a way not immediately apparent to most readers. Even though for many there is not a hint of sadness, much less remorse, on the Infanta's part (her lips curl in disdain, after all), Wilde does choose the verb *cried* for how she delivers her final pronouncement. This could simply refer to her volume, of course, but it just might indicate instead an emotional response to the tragedy belied by her words, an option potentially reinforced when she immediately runs out to the garden after issuing her irritated (or is it an anguished?) retort. What is more, Wilde parses the princess's request of the Chamberlain as pertaining to playmates, not performers. It is "let those who come to *play with* me have no hearts," not "*perform for* me" (my emphasis). This crucial distinction at least allows for the possibility that the Infanta, even if only subconsciously, did acknowledge and accept that the Dwarf was in fact "one of themselves."

Might the Infanta in fact have intuited in this moment some of the ways in which the lines between her playmates (especially the Count?) and her performers (especially the Dwarf?) can be blurred? Has she started to realize the extent to which she herself shares a number of similarities with, not just differences from, the Dwarf? Could she even have, on some level, appreciated, if not enjoyed, the Dwarf's attentions? The ending surely may function for some as final proof of her movement from innocence to experience, of her transformation from childlike princess to heartless adult (in line with all of those with whom she is forced to spend her days). Still, if she might be running away only because she is selfishly feeling sorry for herself that her fun was ruined, she also might have experienced some sort of epiphany through which she recognizes herself as a consumer of pain now faced with the guilt of her active role in the Dwarf's dehumanization and death. If so, readers need to contemplate the extent to which the Infanta is not an antifreak who has earned their scorn but, like Little Nell, is instead (or, at least, also) a tragic figure in her own right, deserving of their sympathy. Wilde allows for the pretty princess, on one level at least, to find herself affiliated with the freaks who otherwise would seem to function as mere fodder for her fun. Such a possibility seems to reinforce how Wilde might be purposefully exposing the mechanisms through which sentimental stories tend either to stigmatize or romanticize strange bodies.

Regardless of the extent to which one does or does not withhold sympathy from the Infanta, however, it is first and foremost the dead Dwarf with whom readers are concerned at story's end. Whether or not one sees the Dwarf's subjection to ridicule as leading to a death that one could characterize as apathetic or pathetic or sympathetic, depressing or enraging or entertaining, there is undeniably much that is attractive about his person—indeed, far more so than that of the beautiful Infanta. Markey in fact portrays the Dwarf as an artist figure with whom Wilde himself identifies, while Killeen posits he should be seen as a Christ figure.[71] Not all readers find the conclusion to be progressive in terms of its final message about the Dwarf, though. Betty M. Adelson, for instance, in her definitive history *The Lives of Dwarfs*, acknowledges Wilde's efforts to "stir in the reader a sympathetic response to the dwarf"[72] in her brief mention of the story. Yet, according to Adelson, because the "dwarf's self-awareness is assumed to lead inevitably to self-hatred," ultimately "Wilde offers a message carrying an implicit acceptance of traditional standards of beauty, a message that precludes any chance that his dwarf character can transcend stereotype."[73] So, while Wilde's narrative may privilege the Dwarf's inner beauty, its uncritical assumptions about the ugliness and thus the undesirability of his outward form to some extent fundamentally limit its success as an empowering rendering of disability and freakery.

Still, one also may spin this more as evidence backing Tatar's theorization of an aesthetic of the grotesque across Wilde's fairy tales, an aesthetic that would privilege the Dwarf's ugliness over the princess's prettiness. Markey offers some support here, noting how "Wilde defended the artist's right to 'find beauty in ugliness'" in his review of Whistler's "Ten O'Clock" lecture, and how Wilde referenced Baudelaire's influence on him in this regard (through a Decadent inversion valuing ugliness), from his Oxford notebook all the way down through his prison letter "Epistola" (also known as *De Profundis*).[74] In recognizing the pervasiveness of the era's disabling assumptions, in rejecting a more idealistic portrayal of a hero who is able to rise above cultural stereotype and social prejudice, Wilde's decision to opt for a tragic ending that portrays a culturally constructed freak who is ultimately unable to escape his day's destructive attitudes toward such difference is in this light illuminating. The compulsory excision of the Dwarf's nonnormative body should remain troubling and may seem to short-circuit any move away from victimization toward empowerment. As Zipes has argued, though, one of the ways Wilde cultivates an art of subversion is by opting for largely pessimistic plot outcomes that "compel readers to question why social relations do not give rise to a better world,"[75] hopefully inspiring compassionate action with a goal of righting the wrongs the Dwarf experiences by working to prevent them from continuing to constitute the predominant response to peculiar bodies and all disability-aligned difference.

What is more, both Killeen and Markey agree "The Birthday of the Infanta" refracts in progressive ways Andersen and other predecessors. The former finds in Wilde's text "a complete reversal" of "The Ugly Duckling" and its linking of "physical beauty and psychological happiness."[76] The latter similarly sees Wilde as "introducing a disjunction between the beautiful and the good that is totally lacking in Andersen's story."[77] She further offers a number of Madame d'Aulnoy's literary fairy tales as other sources Wilde draws upon primarily to react against, reversing d'Aulnoy's trope of "equat[ing] physical deformity with malevolent heartlessness."[78] Mitchell and Snyder, in their aforementioned *Narrative Prosthesis*, aim to "explain the ways in which authors, working from a variety of disability contexts, read and revise oppressive social rhetorics."[79] The Dwarf's demeaning demise reinforces Mitchell and Snyder's insistence that disability represents "the master trope of human disqualification," and supports their interest in texts that "leave the wound of disability undressed so to speak."[80] "The prosthetic function" in such works is thus "to undo the quick repair of disability in mainstream representations and beliefs" and instead to "make the prosthesis show," precisely so as to "leave the disabled body as a troubled and troubling position within culture."[81] In this way, one may posit that Wilde's tale counters traditional representations of disability through a "troubled and troubling" conclusion that subverts the classic fairy tale happily-ever-after ending.

Regardless of how one views the Dwarf's death, as a disappointing excision or a subversive critique, the ending certainly does not prevent readers from responding to his character more out of the paternalistic pity that characterizes most reactions to Tiny Tim (if not also Little Nell). For many, though, Wilde does seem to be actively soliciting not just empathy or sympathy for the Dwarf but actual appreciation of, even identification with, his person. It is precisely the sort of detailed knowledge of the Dwarf's thoughts and feelings Wilde offers that encourages a truly compassionate rather than pathetic emotional response, even if ultimately the response ends up being typified more by anger directed at how the Dwarf is degraded. If readers experience what Sklar characterizes as a recognition of the need for alleviation in the circumstances that contributed to the tragedy, and that in turn leads to the recursive motivation Chrisman identifies to not just feel but to act, then readers may in fact help enact a shift from a victimization to the empowerment of freaks and (other) disabled persons. Again, extending Zipes's focus to include an acknowledgment of the ways exclusionary systems of power and privilege marginalize disability specifically requires readers confront the fully lethal ableism that insists on and persists in condemning someone as fundamentally winning as the Dwarf to be mocked and abused so shamelessly. The indignity with which his humanity is stripped away from him in the last few paragraphs is damning, as he is successively cast not as a person—not as the smart woodsman and sensitive lover to whom Wilde has invited his readers to become attached just a few pages earlier—but as a puppet, ape, and slave. Ultimately, regardless of their response to the princess's predicament, readers' sympathy for the Dwarf should be exponentially intensified by their own guilty realization of the dialectic of enjoyment and exploitation comprising their consumption of his pain. Readers are led to understand what above all causes the unhappy conclusion here is pernicious ableism and the conditioned disgust it relies upon as our still standard response to threat of otherness, here of disability-aligned physical difference.

Wilde (his heartless joke at Little Nell's expense notwithstanding) is certainly not immune to the powerful pull of melodrama. Yet another of his authorial decisions at the end of the narrative suggests how he may be pushing readers to eschew mere sentimentality for a more egalitarian emotional response. The Chamberlain, one will recall, pronounces the Dwarf's death "a pity," not because a life has been lost but rather because the court has lost a source of entertainment, one that "might have made the King smile." By providing readers with such a self-serving summary of what has been lost, one that entirely disregards the Dwarf's humanity, Wilde stirs up readers to reject any recourse to the sort of pity Shapiro and so many others in the disability community condemn and instead to acknowledge the real tragedy as the death of a protagonist who is more attractive in his person than he has been perceived to be unattractive in his body or pathetic in his end. Capitalizing on readers' own collective sense of guilt can serve as a catalyst for a commitment to change not just the disabling cultural, environmental, and social barriers still faced by different bodies today but further to change one's own conditioned attitudes and actions. While it may in fact be impossible to make it through the story's final pages without laughing, surely it is equally true that one must have a heart of stone to read the death of the Dwarf without tearing up.

In this chapter we have seen numerous possibilities regarding how to read disability-aligned difference, any number of which provide promising leads in terms of encouraging the sort of reparative reading Schaffer endorses. As I noted in the introduction, Wilde's fairy tales are complex conundrums that do not yield clear or easy answers. How precisely to read them is for readers to decide on their own. Is the Infanta an enemy of the freaks or ultimately (even if unwittingly) allied to their cause? Is the Dwarf a sweet soul or a pathetic patsy? Either way, Wilde's attraction to peculiar bodies in this tale serves to expose the manipulative mechanisms that can employ potentially problematic emotional responses toward such difference. Overall, Wilde shows himself to be a writer fully aware of his own role as a showman of his characters, who asks readers not only to recognize his own authorial complicity in the consumption of their pain but further to acknowledge their own readerly complicity in this pain as spectators. Even though the Dwarf's tragic end may seem to foster a sense of hopelessness about the general cultural detachment from (if not actual delight in) the dehumanization of disability-aligned difference, the tale's indictment of the terrible cruelty inherent in the nondisabled abjection of the nonnormative body as an undesirable and, ultimately, a disposable "thing" stands in and of itself as an indispensable intervention.

# 2

# "He Remembered That the Little Mermaid Had No Feet and Could Not Dance"

## The Love of and by Extraordinary Bodies in "The Fisherman and His Soul"

"The Fisherman and His Soul" offers a fascinating trawl of entangled elements connected to two main disability-aligned characters (a little Mermaid and, eventually, a young Fisherman), requiring readers to confront the messy meeting of emotion, identity, power, and relationships in the story's narration of their difference. An obvious inversion of its famous forerunner, Andersen's "The Little Mermaid," the tale also builds on "The Birthday of the Infanta" by introducing a romance plotline between its two protagonists, a significant development only teased at in the previous pairing. The little Mermaid's status as a freak (again, Fiedler and Garland Thomson both list mermaids as one of the most legendary freak figures in literature) extends numerous aspects of the previous chapter's discussions while providing a more progressive reading of the desirability of peculiar bodies and of the love (not just acceptance) they deserve. What is more, with the story's extended focus on the interactions between the Fisherman and his Soul, Wilde also is able to delineate some of the dynamics that drive the conceptualization of disability as a lack, as being "less than" (along the same lines of otherings involving foreignness and bestiality). Accordingly, in this longest of his fairy tales, Wilde expands his foray into freakery through a complex consideration of the role extraordinary bodies may play, not as attractions whose interest resides in the revulsion they stir or as auxiliary characters serving as foils or sidekicks to nondisabled protagonists but rather as primary persons of interest whose very attraction lies in the love they express as and for and between such bodies.

Melissa Free's analysis of the importance of Jenny Wren to the plot of *Our Mutual Friend*, specifically to the climactic union of Lizzie Hexam and Eugene Wrayburn, provides not only an intriguing take on Dickens's novel but also a helpful entry point for exploring Wilde's representation of disability-aligned difference in "The Fisherman and His Soul."[1] Jenny is another notable Dickensian dwarf, who for Henry James is, like Nell Trent, a "pathetic" character, "a little monster" who "belongs to the troop of hunchbacks, imbeciles, and precocious children who have carried on the sentimental business in all Mr. Dickens's novels."[2] James's take on her character further reinforces the extent to which the figure of the child and the figure of the disabled other (here invoking both physical and mental disabilities by referencing hunchbacks and imbeciles) are inextricably interrelated. For Free, the Dickensian universe is one "in which impairment, deformity, slander, and queerness are grounds for abjection," yet, in spite of so many conditioned hostile reactions, "the power to transform belongs to freaks" in that "outcast figures" such as Wren serve as "critical aids to the traditional heroes and heroines whose lives they transform and save."[3]

While such a rendering potentially limits Jenny's function to serving as the vehicle of others' redemption, there are also elements of the active benefactor to her character as well. One interesting angle into Wren's role in this regard pertains to her adopted name and its allusion to the Cock Robin stories in which her avian namesake ends up widowed on her wedding day,[4] connecting her plotline to the world of nursery rhymes and folk stories. Another particularly intriguing element involves Wren's fancy of referencing fairy tales herself, especially Cinderella.[5] According to Free, "Jenny's play-acting as Cinderella" is "ironic, a temporary indulgence while Lizzie, the novel's true Cinderella, is in hiding"; in reality, Jenny plays "the part of fairy godmother, transforming the working girl into a lady and wife."[6] In this way, while Jenny may not get to star as the romantic lead, she nonetheless is portrayed as a munificent magician rather than a malevolent monster like Quilp. Wren's auxiliary role relative to Dickens's nondisabled protagonists notwithstanding, Free argues that as "a textual receptacle for nonnormative desire, race, and physicality, the freakish body matters because of rather than in spite of that which makes it different."[7] Even as their anomalous characters may become "necessarily disposable" once they "bolster the normative" by facilitating the conventional marriages with which so many Victorian storylines conclude,[8] for Free fictions such as *Our Mutual Friend* require readers to recognize that "queer, disabled, dark bodies" nonetheless are "fully human."[9]

Similar instructive intersections are present in "The Fisherman and His Soul," yet, significantly, Wilde's tale also forwards a decidedly unconventional romance plot featuring two disability-aligned protagonists rather than relegating its remarkable bodies solely to sideline support for nondisabled newlyweds. This is a marked reversal of Andersen's narrative, which follows his Little Mermaid as she falls in love with a human prince and decides to call on the help of a Sea Witch to gain his love (and herself a soul). Her pact promises her legs in exchange for her voice, but even though she attracts the attention of her prince through her entrancing dancing (which she performs only at the price of piercing pain), in the end he marries another, and the Little Mermaid dies of a broken heart. Andersen decides to avert total tragedy, though, by having her transform into a spirit of the air who just might still earn herself a soul and a life in Heaven if she can do good deeds for approximately three hundred years.

Flipping Andersen upside down, instead of depicting a mermaid willing to give up her life under the sea to gain a human soul, Wilde tells the tale of a human who is willing to give up his soul to be able to live with his mermaid beneath the waves. The story stars a Fisherman who, with the aid of a (Land?) Witch, amputates his own soul[10] (physically manifested as his shadow) for this purpose. However, after only three years, he takes back his Soul when he is unable to resist the temptation to go see a dancing girl, only later learning he cannot send his soul away a second time. As a result, the lovers can no longer be together, and in the wake of her eventual death without reunion, the Fisherman also dies of a broken heart. In his celebration of the love between the little Mermaid (who is stigmatized by the local priest as a dangerous freak) and the young Fisherman (who literally cuts his soul away from his body to join the Sea-folk) as worthy of our compassion and admiration, Wilde bolsters the aberrant body, even if ultimately both of these characters suffer the same eventual fatal fates as the Giant and the Dwarf.

Given Wilde's positioning of littleness as at least part of what might be glossed as disability-aligned difference in "The Birthday of the Infanta," his Mermaid may be approached through a similar lens as well. Andersen's Little Mermaid is fifteen years old, and while Wilde does not provide specific ages for either of his lovers, his recourse to the adjectives "little" and "young" certainly allow we are likely somewhere within the liminal (be)tween space where one is neither fully a child or fully an adult. All the more so, though, it is the Mermaid's hybrid embodiment (through which she straddles the lines supposedly separating the human and the animal, the familiar and the foreign, the blessed and the damned) that qualifies her as a freak. While her beauty might seem to identify her more with the Infanta, she more powerfully aligns with the Dwarf's peculiar body, for as a member of the Sea-folk she is grouped in the story both with fantastical creatures such as Fauns and with terrifying beasts such as sea monsters. In fact, when the young Fisherman catches her in his net in the opening scene, so conditioned is he to contextualize such difference as freakish spectacle that he believes he has "snared some dull monster that will be a marvel to men, or some thing of horror that the great Queen will desire."[11] Befitting her hybrid form, her loveliness is represented not just along the lines of stereotypical male objectification of the female body (her hair "as a wet fleece of gold" and her skin "as white ivory") but further as distinctly an attribute of a sea-creature: "Silver and pearl was her tail, and the green weeds of the sea coiled round it; and like sea-shells were her ears, and her lips were sea-coral."[12] Above all, it is the silver and pearl tail that makes hers an anomalous body, that marks her as part fish and that later serves as the locus of her lack in the eyes of her lover.

The Fisherman is "filled with wonder" upon actually examining her extraordinary body,[13] and while literally this wonder is represented as owing to how beautiful she was, the word also evokes spectators' reactions to Victorian freaks on display (as indicated by his initial recourse to "monster" and "horror"), preparing readers for the ways in which Wilde's narrative will counter the increasingly typical response to such difference as pathological error, in the name of a more positive wonder. Here, though, far from love at first sight, upon capturing her he simply wants to secure this object of amazement as a profitable prize possession. Thus, when he "drew the net close to him" and "clasped her in his arms," she experiences his touch exclusively as frightening: "she gave a cry like a startled sea-gull," "looked at him in terror," and "struggled that she might escape."[14] Tellingly, his response is not to reassure or free her, but to hold her all the more "tightly" so as to "not suffer her to depart."[15] She is his prisoner; her unusual body is his to control, to command like a creature that exists to do his bidding.

When the weeping Mermaid begs for his mercy, he strikes a bargain with her. He will let her go so long as she makes him a promise, to come whenever he calls and to sing for him—a promise he extracts from her not because he is enchanted with her voice but rather because it might make him rich: "for the fish delight to listen to the song of the Sea-folk, and so shall my nets be full."[16] Their deal hinges on an ability she possesses by virtue of her identity as a mer-creature, something that no human could replicate. Thus, in the opening scene, the relationship between the able-bodied Fisherman and the freakish Mermaid is one in which he holds all the power. For her part, the Mermaid appears truly traumatized by the encounter, as upon finally being released from his grasp she swims away "trembling with a strange fear."[17] Unlike the Dwarf, she is all too aware of the peril in which her exceptional body places her, and readers consequently can be concerned her captor's cruelty is bound to be as deadly as the Infanta's.

The little Mermaid nonetheless fulfills her bargain faithfully, and whenever he demands it, she mesmerizes the marine masses with her "marvellous" music.[18] The lyrics to her songs further reinforce how she belongs to another realm entirely, one full of many other creatures that are equally remarkable departures from the Fisherman's familiar world. She sings, among other things, "of the Tritons who have long green beards, and hairy breasts";[19] "of the Sirens who tell of such wonderful things that the merchants have to stop their ears with wax lest they . . . leap into the water and be drowned";[20] "of the nautilus who has a boat of her own that is carved out of an opal and steered with a silken sail"; "of the happy Mermen who play upon harps and can charm the great Kraken to sleep"; and "of the Mermaids who lie in the white foam and hold out their arms to the mariners."[21] Killeen, referencing Nina Auerbach, notes how "in the nineteenth-century [sic] mermaids were generally considered dangerous by male writers," as "a kind of divine and demonic figure" not merely representing gendered difference but also serving as "a particularly useful image in figuring the colonised Other."[22] Her status as an exoticized foreign body again shows Wilde to be well aware of freaks' intersectional framing in connection with other categories of marginalized people (especially those created owing to Victorian views on racial purity and deviant sexuality). At the same time, his descriptions lean more toward painting her world as one of magic and wonder, charming readers as well as the fish, and perhaps helping to work a change in the young Fisherman himself.

Her voice does bring the young Fisherman the success he had dreamed of, as "all the tunny-fish came in from the deep to listen to her," and he was able to catch them.[23] Wilde's opening undermines the usual narrative, in which dangerous mermaids trick and trap naive watermen. Yet, the power dynamic is subtly shifting, as the Fisherman finds himself increasingly captivated by her and her beautiful voice, not altogether unlike the aforementioned merchants and mariners susceptible to the allure of such difference. "Oftentimes he called to her" now, but, understandably given their initial encounter, she would "never come near him that he might touch her," and "when he sought to seize her" again she would jump "into the water as a seal might dive."[24] Eventually, as "each day the sound of her voice became sweeter to his ears," he ended up forgetting "his nets and his cunning," showing "no care of his craft" as all the tunnies "went by in shoals" while she sang.[25] Victorian readers may be worrying at this point he is headed for trouble, a victim of her "unnatural" influence, while our century's likely are screaming for her to stop her own ears with wax to deaden the sound of his surely duplicitous pleading, but Wilde instead is moving toward a different arc altogether, one promoting acceptance and love instead of manipulation and cruelty. Abandoning the confines of his own cunning, the Fisherman opens himself to an appreciation of another, opens his Self to the Other, eventually professing his love and begging her, "Take me for thy bridegroom."[26]

Surprisingly, perhaps, the Mermaid replies that she could in fact love him in return, but only if he was willing to give up his "human soul," for "the Sea-folk have no souls."[27] That the soul is explicitly identified as a human attribute would seem to only reinforce the little Mermaid's positioning as a fantastic Other; along with the associations with animality when she is compared to a seagull and a seal, casting the Sea-folk as soulless in effect further dehumanizes her.[28] Still, Wilde's story seems to privilege life and love with the likes of the little Mermaid, for the Fisherman chooses to become a part of her world of wonder rather than to retain the ostensibly superior status his soul supposedly grants him: "I will send my soul away . . . and in the depth of the sea we will dwell together, . . . and all that thou desirest I will do, nor shall our lives be divided."[29] In "The Birthday of the Infanta," readers are privy to the Dwarf's fantasy of how the Infanta's love for him might lead to their sharing a life together in his world, in the forest with his animal friends—a fantasy, of course, never to be realized, maybe even intended to be mocked as naive. Here, though, the marvelous world of the Mermaid is validated over the Fisherman's own mundane one. He chooses to join her, endorsing union over separation, even to the point of ceding the power he once held over her ("all that thou desirest I will do").

Early the next morning, the Fisherman visits his local Priest to inquire about sending away his soul, but his fantasy is emphatically frowned upon by this God-appointed guardian of human goodness. As was the Camerera, the Priest is invested in preserving the line between human and freak. Even the very idea of the Fisherman wanting to link his fate with hers for the Priest can only be associated with a diseased or dysfunctional mind, and he exclaims, "thou art mad, or hast eaten of some poisonous herb, for the soul is the noblest part of man."[30] The Fisherman's plan, the Priest categorically insists, "is a sin that may not be forgiven."[31] His position is not simply a response to the Fisherman's disregard for the soul's significance, however. Grounded in an anthropocentrism he purports is endorsed by God, but in direct contradistinction to the disabled Christ-child's tender friendship with the Giant, the Priest discards not only all nonhuman bodies as unworthy of God's love and salvation, but even the lives of any persons who dare to identify with them: "And as for the Sea-folk, they are lost, and they who would traffic with them are lost also. They are as the beasts of the field that know not good from evil, and for them the Lord has not died."[32] Isolation is the only way to avoid contamination of the two worlds, so the prospect of the Fisherman's integration into this other world unsurprisingly calls forth conditioned condemnation from the Priest, who stigmatizes difference as evil and threatens those who diverge from such a belief with the peril of eternal damnation.

The Fisherman tearfully repeats his appeal, noting how Fauns and Mermen have such happy lives, but above all asserting that the promise of his union with the little Mermaid should outweigh all other considerations, asking, "what does my soul profit me, if it stand between me and the thing that I love?"[33] Wilde is riffing here off of the Gospel of Mark, where Jesus asks his disciples, "For what shall it profit a man, if he shall gain the whole world, and lose his own soul?"[34] Christ's emphasis on self-denial and sacrifice in this passage is thus a significant reference point for readers as they sort through their emotional responses to the Fisherman and the Mermaid. Sympathy for the latter, for many immediately established by her predicament upon finding herself under the Fisherman's thumb, is only intensified by the Priest's attempts to turn her into the devil. At the same time, the Fisherman's defense of her worthiness of love in the face of the Priest's dismissal, and his willingness to sacrifice his soul to gain her whole world, begins to allay any fears she is suffering merely from Stockholm Syndrome. At this point, though, it remains undecided if his dispute with the Priest should be glossed as self-serving possessiveness or as a more selfless devotion that leads him to follow his heart and embrace rather than reject his beloved's remarkable body.

It is certainly important to note the Fisherman's use of "thing" here and to remain wary of his sense of superiority and his seeming reduction of her to only a body. It only enrages the Priest, though, to hear such a sacrilegious speech. "The love of the body is vile," he fumes, "and vile and evil are the pagan things God suffers to wander through His world. Accursed be the Fauns of the woodland, and accursed be the singers of the sea!"[35] The Priest's abjection of these fanciful hybrid creatures, the Fauns and the Sea-folk, is grounded not only in a privileging of the soul, which denigrates "the love of the body," but further in a belief that deviant bodies are degenerate soulless abominations. Fascinatingly, however, his attempt to elaborate upon why they need to be shunned hinges on his own imaginings of dangerous liaisons with them, and he unintentionally reveals his own vulnerability, even attraction, to these supposedly monstrous bodies and the illicit passions they purportedly promote: "I have heard them at night-time, and they have sought to lure me from my beads. . . . They whisper into my ears the tale of their perilous joys. They tempt me with temptations, and when I would pray they make mouths at me."[36] The Priest's unsolicited confession unconsciously grants the taboo pleasures that potentially await those willing to suffer the stigma and ostracization associated with a love of such peculiar bodies and the "connections between freakishness, queer desire, racial hybridity, and disability" Free finds in Collins and Dickens.[37] The Fisherman certainly is unwilling to suppress his own awakened attraction and submit to the sort of self-denial the Priest desperately clings to, declaring, "For her body I would give my soul, and for her love I would surrender heaven."[38]

The Father and the Fisherman offer two different paths that correspond with two orientations present in other work published by Wilde earlier the same year. In the book version of *The Picture of Dorian Gray*, Lord Henry Wotton explains to Dorian during their initial encounter how one might see both "the Hellenic ideal"[39] and the "new Hedonism"[40] he calls for as a conscious countering of the "tragic survival" of "all the maladies of mediævalism" as reflected in the "self-denial that mars our lives" when we allow ourselves to be governed by "the terror of society, which is the basis of morals," and "the terror of God, which is the secret of religion."[41] Similarly, in his prose manifesto *The Soul of Man* (out just a few months ahead of *The Picture of Dorian Gray* and *A House of Pomegranates*), Wilde points to the tension between an ideal of "joy and beauty" and the "worship of pain."[42] The latter he associates with "Mediaevalism, with its saints and martyrs, its love of self-torture, its wild passion for wounding itself, its gashing with knives, and its whipping rods."[43] The former he identifies with the Renaissance but also with a new Individualism "expressing itself through joy" and embracing pleasure as Nature's "sign of approval."[44] The Fisherman's love for the little Mermaid and his willingness to part with his soul in order to experience the marvels and joys of her underwater world, then, while decidedly holding an element of danger, also can be considered as corresponding with Wilde's privileged path toward "self-development."[45] Significantly, Wilde characterizes such self-development not as selfishness (which "always aims at creating around it an absolute uniformity of type"[46] and thus insists upon "asking others to live as one wishes to live"[47]) but rather as unselfishness (which "is letting other people's lives alone, not interfering with them," since it "recognizes infinite variety of type as a delightful thing"[48]). The above context can be crucial in establishing Wilde's endorsement of his Fisherman's choice.

Without the support of religion or society, the Fisherman turns instead to a source perhaps seeming more (un)naturally allied with what the Priest objects to as the blasphemous charms of aberrant bodies: "a certain young Witch who . . . was very cunning in her witcheries."[49] A lost figure in the Priest's eyes like the Fauns and Sea-folk, someone whom the Fishermen himself acknowledges "men call . . . evil,"[50] her life as an othered outcast "who dwelt in a cave at the head of the bay"[51] positions her in a liminal space between the soulless Sea-folk and the Priest's parish. Though the Fisherman seeks to relieve himself of something burdensome to him (his soul), the Witch assumes he needs her help acquiring something instead, calling out to him upon his approach, "What d'ye lack?"[52] Intriguingly, her first guess is that he wants "fish for [his] net," and she claims she has music through which to accomplish the trick.[53] Not just another deviant body the Priest would disparage, the Witch is immediately set up as a rival to the Mermaid, someone also with the power to give the young Fisherman what he wants, whether it be booty in the form of full fishnets or beauty in the form of fetching fairness. Indeed, the Witch appears jealous of the little Mermaid and tries to lure the Fisherman to choose her instead, insisting he dance with her at a full moon witches' sabbath to learn the secret of how to send away his soul. As will be emphatically reinforced later, her demand implicitly calls to mind what the little Mermaid lacks—feet with which to dance for, or with, her beloved.

Seemingly supporting the Priest's condemnatory association of the soulless with "the beasts of the field," the Fisherman must pass a hooting "great owl, with yellow sulphurous eyes," and a snarling black dog before he can reach the mountaintop by midnight to witness witches "flying through the air like bats."[54] As soon as his own Witch arrives, they begin their dance together and, further foregrounding the Mermaid's missing feet, "the young Witch jumped so high that he could see the scarlet heels of her shoes."[55] However briefly the moment lasts, there is a decided erotic charge to their movements: throwing "her arms about his neck," and with "her breath . . . hot upon his face," she urges him on, telling him, "Faster, faster!"[56] He continues to dance "as one snared in a spell," catching her "by the waist," and whirling her "madly round and round."[57] Indeed, he seems on the very verge of forgetting all about his Mermaid when, at the invitation to "worship" with the Witch, "a great desire to do as she besought him seized on him" and he follows where she leads.[58] Strangely, though, given his frustration with the Priest's (and, supposedly, God's) opposition to his love, he unconsciously makes "the sign of the Cross" and calls "upon the holy name," which sends all the witches away screaming "like hawks," except his dance partner.[59] She too tries to flee, but before she can escape, he "[catches] her by her wrists, and [holds] her fast," ignoring her cries of "Loose me,"[60] in a move that replicates his capture of her rival in the opening scene. Here again, in spite of the Witch's own attempts to trick and trap him, her disability-aligned freakish body is the one that is ultimately represented as the imperiled one. The Fisherman's reliance upon control and his sense of superiority that justifies it in his mind continue to give readers pause regarding if he remains more of a danger to, than a devotee of, not just the little Mermaid but any and all of the deviant bodies who are the inhabitants of the world he supposedly wants to join, the denizens of the water and the woods and the wild.

As he demands to learn from her the secret to casting away his soul, she seems truly afraid, of him and for him. Her eyes "dim with tears," she replies, "Ask me anything but that!"[61] When he just laughs and grasps her "all the more tightly,"[62] the beautiful young Witch makes one last-ditch effort to win his attention(s); "fawn[ing] on him and put[ting] her face close to his," she whispers, "Surely I am as fair as the daughters of the sea."[63] But the young Fisherman is now absolutely resolute in his purpose to abandon his soul for the little Mermaid's love. Still reeling and a bit out of control from the intensity of his testing on the mountaintop, he resorts to a threat of violence to get what he wants, forcing the Witch to comply with his wishes. Finally, she gives him a "little knife" and tells him that "what men call the shadow of the body" actually is "the body of the soul," so if he stands "on the sea-shore with [his] back to the moon, and cut[s] away from around [his] feet [his] shadow," he may send his soul away.[64]

This he then proceeds to do and, while his outward appearance remains unchanged, after severing his soul from himself, the Fisherman arguably becomes primarily defined by a lack as surely as if he had amputated a limb instead. In an admittedly unnerving transmogrification of the medieval self-mutilation Wilde believes is so destructive to self-development, the Fisherman's act does not entail diminishment, sacrifice, or victimization but rather fulfillment, gain, and optimization; that is, it constitutes a form of self-realization rather than self-flagellation. He is now arguably a freak in his own right, a soulless human able to live and breathe underwater. After promising to meet his Soul (now a separate character in the story) at that spot once a year to give the latter a chance to persuade him to restore their former union, he jumps into the sea and "the little Mermaid rose up to meet him, and put her arms around his neck and kissed him on the mouth."[65] While Andersen's witch-enabled wish-fulfillment entails torturous physical pain for his Little Mermaid, Wilde's instead offers his disability-aligned lovers not medievalism's "wild passion for wounding itself, its gashing with knives," but rather a wild passion for wooing and a gushing with kisses, to be equally enjoyed by both down below.

Their union represents a truly remarkable plotline in multiple ways. For one, the little Mermaid is not, like Jenny Wren, merely the ministrant for mainstream heteronormative romance between privileged nondisabled lovers; she is the desired beloved worth more than the young Fisherman's whole world. Also, if Wilde's peculiar bodies serve, as Free might suggest, as "textual receptacle[s] for nonnormative desire, race, and physicality," it is not in order to stigmatize her difference along expected lines, drawing her as a dangerous deviant the degeneracy of whose love smacks of the taboo of "race-mixing." The Priest may redirect his anxiety regarding the instability of his own relationship to such difference toward identifiable others, freaks like the Fauns and the Sea-folk, but the Fisherman sees the Mermaid through the lens of love and wonder rather than sin and error. What is more, the Fisherman, although not visibly "crippled" or "deformed" after cutting away his shadow, still according to the Priest is now damned for his own difference (by virtue of his vice in lacking a soul). Without a soul he technically is no longer whole, but as Markey observes, for Wilde his "unorthodox passion is redemptive rather than evil."[66]

As Durbach and Garland Thomson have established (and Free's piece on *Our Mutual Friend* supports), enfreaked bodies are more often than not imbricated with related constructions of dehumanizing animality, fanciful exoticism, queer desire, and racial hybridity. Perhaps unsurprisingly, then, in the annual meetings where the Soul attempts to tempt the Fisherman away from the Mermaid, he does so through narratives seemingly designed to appeal to the Fisherman's eye for the attractions of such difference. The first year, the Soul describes his travels with a camel caravan of Arab merchants "into the country of those who curse the Moon," where he saw marvelous things such as "the Gryphons guarding their gold on the white rocks, and the scaled Dragons sleeping in their caves."[67] As they continued on, he reports, "the Pygmies shot arrows at us . . . and at night time we heard the wild men beating on their drums."[68] He then supplies a long list of the many amazing peoples he encountered after passing through the Tower of Apes and the Tower of Serpents: the Magadae, "who are born old, and grow younger"; the Laktroi, "who say that they are the sons of tigers, and paint themselves yellow and black"; the Aurantes, "who bury their dead on the tops of trees, and themselves live in dark caverns"; the Krimnians, "who worship a crocodile"; the Agazonbae, "who are dog-faced"; and the Sibans, "who have horses' feet, and run more swiftly than horses."[69] Throughout this cataloging of his travels, the Soul foregrounds animality, exoticism, and hybridity in order to pique the Fisherman's interest in the infinite variety of type Wilde associates with beauty and joy, in the hopes he will give in (as he did not with the Witch) to other enthralling experiences that might rival the enchanting charms of the little Mermaid.

Eventually, said caravan arrived at a city where the Soul convinced a priest to take him to see their god. When he was first shown an ebony idol that was not the true god, he withered the priest's hand out of anger with the attempt to trick him, which secured another promise he would be shown the real god. In the next chamber, though, realizing its ivory idol also was not the god, the Soul blinded the priest for trying to fool him again. This portion of his tale not only perpetuates the association of unusual bodies with decadence and with danger but here also employs disability as a form of punishment in disturbing ways. In stark contrast to the Fisherman's willing self-amputation, the withering and blinding serve as significant reminders of the still-dominant pejorative associations that cast disability as undesirable and unfortunate. At the same time, though, overall, the Fisherman's welcome embrace of such difference seems the privileged response. He is happy and satisfied rather than lost and accursed, so when the Soul offers him what turned out to be the actual god (a Mirror of Wisdom that the Soul stole and secreted away in a nearby valley) in exchange for allowing them to be reunited, the Fisherman merely laughs and says, "Love is better than Wisdom . . . and the little Mermaid loves me."[70]

The second year, the Soul describes another journey through many more exotic places. In one of his exploits, posing as a Dervish on a pilgrimage to Mecca, he entered a city of which he relates, "Thou canst not think how strange a people they are. When they are glad they go to the bird-sellers and buy them a caged bird, and set it free that their joy may be greater, and when they are sad they scourge themselves with thorns that their sorrow may not grow less."[71] Here, again, exoticism and foreignness (but also with potentially fearful suggestions of captivity and self-maiming) are explicitly envisioned by the Soul as the most likely means to draw the attention of the freak-identified Fisherman. Eventually, the Soul was escorted by guards to a young Emperor's palace where, deep within a terraced garden with a nightingale singing, he is castigated for his lack of obeisance to the ruler. His punishment was to be death, but as an immortal soul he cannot be harmed, so a scimitar whizzed through him without hurt and he stopped both a lance and an arrow in midair. Promised half of the Emperor's riches from a "marvellous"[72] treasure-house if he would just leave without further trouble, he instead demanded a Ring of Riches that guarantees the world's greatest wealth. It is this ring the Soul now offers to the Fisherman, but he is completely immune not only to other wondrous worlds beyond the sea but further to the very sort of material rewards he initially sought, laughingly replying, "Love is better than Riches . . . and the little Mermaid loves me."[73]

While the Fisherman is not at all tempted by the Soul's dazzlingly decadent tales that end with promises of unlimited wealth or wisdom, the third year, he decides to leave the sea to go with his Soul to watch a veiled girl dance with bare feet. When the Soul tells him about the "marvellous" sight of her "naked" feet and how they "moved over the carpet like little white pigeons," "a great desire [comes] over" the Fisherman, as "he remembered that the little Mermaid had no feet and could not dance."[74] This single salient detail powerfully reinforces how she is not merely a deviant body that society and religion view as dangerous by virtue of her difference; even her own beloved ultimately cannot overlook what he experiences as her lack, a physical difference that, even if only unconsciously, nonetheless renders her "less than" in his eyes, at least in this respect. Thus, he becomes filled with longing for that which she does not have (she "had no feet") and for that which she cannot do (she "could not dance"). His weakness in returning, however temporarily, to the original dynamic of their relationship (where the Mermaid is merely an object, here unable to satisfy his own selfish desires) turns the tale toward tragedy.

Readers suspect something is afoot as soon as the Soul reenters the Fisherman's body, for he immediately insists, "Let us not tarry, but get hence at once, for the Sea-gods are jealous, and have monsters that do their bidding."[75] Whisking him away from the shoreside like there is not a moment to lose, accompanied by a derogatory assertion of how threatening the Seafolk are given their association with monsters, the Soul relies upon the selfsame binary the Priest uses to separate humanity from the soulless "singers of the sea" he characterizes as "vile and evil." The Soul then proceeds to lead the Fisherman to three separate cities, none of which are home to the dancer with the naked feet, and what is worse, he punishes the Fisherman for having forsaken him, by forcing the Fisherman to commit terrible acts. At the initial stop, he makes the Fisherman steal a silver cup, then the next night to beat a child "till it wept,"[76] and lastly to kill a kind merchant who had taken him into his home. When the Fisherman upbraids his Soul for manipulating him to murder, the latter simply boomerangs the blame, accosting the former for casting him out into the world without a heart. Trembling, the Fisherman responds, "Nay, but thou art evil, and hast made me forget my love, and hast tempted me with temptations, and hast set my feet in the ways of sin."[77] While he resorts to the same good/evil binary leveraged by the Priest against his love, it is here the Soul rather than the soulless Seafolk who occupies the role of treacherous tempter. The Fisherman inverts its terms so that it is his own temporary forgetting of his love, and his error in reuniting with his Soul, that have "set [his] feet in the ways of sin," not his liaison with his legless leman. Significantly, feet are no longer what he mourns as missing in the Mermaid, or his method of travel toward the pleasures of the dancer he wanted to see, but instead these attributes he once so prized now in fact are the means of his sinking into the "sin" of selling out his sweetheart by allowing lack to veil love.

The Fisherman ruefully repents of his decision to leave the little Mermaid, and he pulls out the Witch's knife to send away his Soul a second time, only to have the Soul reveal that the trick works only once. While technically whole again with his Soul's return, the Fisherman symbolically realigns himself with disability by declaring, "I will bind my hands that I may not do thy bidding, and close my lips that I may not speak thy words."[78] The Soul attempts to console him by continuing to hone in on the little Mermaid's lack: "Who is thy love that thou shouldst return to her? The world has many fairer than she is. There are the dancing-girls of Samaris who dance in the manner of all kinds of birds and beasts. Their feet are painted with henna, and in their hands they have little copper bells. They laugh while they dance, and their laughter is as clear as the laughter of water."[79] The Soul suggests that fairness itself is tied to one's ability (here, as a dancer), not one's beauty, subtly questioning the Mermaid's attractiveness, even her worth, while simultaneously evoking the happy "soulless" world the Fisherman prefers, in delineating the dancers' appeal with references to water and to nonhuman animals.

The Soul immediately offers a second example of why the Fisherman should not be perturbed over learning he cannot rejoin the Mermaid under the sea, describing another destination with a garden full of blue peacocks that also features a dancer: "And she who feeds them dances for their pleasure, and some times she dances on her hands and at other times she dances with her feet. Her . . . nostrils are shaped like the wings of a swallow. From a hook in one of her nostrils hangs a flower that is carved out of a pearl. She laughs while she dances, and the silver rings that are about her ankles tinkle like bells of silver."[80] Again, it is her talents as a dancer that provide pleasure, her allure again emphasized through delicate echoes of the denizens and domains of the (nonhuman) difference the young Fisherman remains devoted to—generally in the setting's exoticism but more particularly in laughter's connection to water from the previous proposal (with the pearl and the hook offering additional associations with the sea), and in the suggestion of birds and beasts through descriptions of her body (nostrils like swallow wings) and her dancing (on hands and feet). As he promised he would, though, the Fisherman seals his lips, binds his hands, and heads back to the bay where he met the Mermaid. Yet, while "great was the power of the love that was within him," she does not reappear when he pleads for her to do so.[81]

For two full years, he calls to her every morning and then searches for her in tidepools, water caves, and sea valleys, but she never once answers him, nor can he find any trace of her. All the while, the Soul is constantly urging him to give up his vigil, first with more evil temptations and then with good motivations (to help the poor, widows, lepers, and beggars; or to fight Famine and Plague[82]). Wilde's fairy tales often provide him a platform to advocate for social justice, in particular where poverty is concerned (as we shall see in the next two chapters), and his disability-aligned protagonists usually take the lead in this regard. Here, however, it seems readers are to privilege the Fisherman's personal duty to the little Mermaid and their interpersonal relationship over even helping the diseased and malnourished all around him. Is Wilde asking his readers to ponder, "what shall it profit someone, if one should save the whole world, but lose one's own true love?" Eventually, the Soul gives up his tricks and expresses the simple wish to reenter the Fisherman's heart, acknowledging, "thy love is stronger than I am."[83] To this the Fisherman assents, pitying the Soul's life without a heart, but the Soul reports, "I can find no place of entrance, so compassed about with love is this heart of thine."[84] Then, right as the Fisherman replies, "I would that I could help thee," at that very moment "a great cry of mourning" rises from the sea,[85] and the waves bring to shore the dead body of the Mermaid.

Unlike the Infanta, who by running away seems unwilling or unable to confront the role her mockery of the Dwarf and his monstrous body played in his death, the Fisherman remains to mark his mistake with manifestations of sorrow and affection. Weeping both "as one smitten with pain" and "as one trembling with joy" (seemingly joining the two ideals Wilde contrasted in *The Soul of Man*), he tenderly lavishes his love on her, even though as the word choice makes clear, she is not there.[86] Wilde writes, "he flung himself down beside it, and he kissed the cold red of the mouth, and toyed with the wet amber of the hair."[87] As "he held it to his breast," Wilde continues, "to the dead thing he made confession"; "into the shells of its ears he poured the harsh wine of his tale," and "bitter was his joy, and full of strange gladness was his pain."[88] The consistent recourse to "it" and "the" instead of "her" here is jarring, as all he is ironically left with is a "dead thing," precisely owing to his terrible error in seeing her only as a body rather than a person, and in particular as an anomalous body that ultimately (even if only in a moment of weakness) seemed lacking to him, "less than" for its difference.

At that precise moment, the waters rise—described, in terms again foregrounding the intersection of animality and disability, as "the white foam moaned like a leper" and "with white claws of foam the sea grabbled at the shore"—in an expression of grief at the tragic consequences of such othering, while "from the palace of the Sea-King came the cry of mourning again, and far out upon the sea the great Tritons blew hoarsely upon their horns."[89] The Soul is afraid and urges him to flee the shore, but the Fisherman replies, "Love is better than wisdom, and more precious than riches, and fairer than the feet of the daughters of men."[90] With this acknowledgment of his tragic mistake in allowing a misguided sense of the Mermaid's peculiar body as lack (rather than merely difference) to determine the final course of his relationship with her, "he knew that the end was at hand," and as "he kissed with mad lips the cold lips of the Mermaid" one last time, "through the fulness of his love his heart did break," and at last "the Soul found an entrance and entered in, and was one with him even as before."[91] With that, "the sea covered the young Fisherman with its waves."[92]

In this provocative short paragraph, Wilde pairs his young Fisherman with the young Dwarf, both of whom die of a broken heart owing to love rendered impossible by both individual attitudes and social barriers stemming equally from a form of ableism. Unlike the Dwarf, though, the Fisherman has no one to blame but himself; after all, he is not the victim of a love interest's cruel rejection but its perpetrator. At the same time, his case arguably also shows how his society's normative standards of beauty still hold sway even over one devoted to forbidden desire and blasphemous love. The seemingly insignificant description of his lips as "mad" not only recalls the Priest's use of the word to characterize the Fisherman's ungodly passion for the little Mermaid but also the Infanta's father. The King had loved his young Queen "madly" with "that terrible blindness that passion brings upon its servants," and, after her death left him "like one bereft of reason,"[93] during his monthly visits to her embalmed body, he "would clutch at the pale jewelled hands in a wild agony of grief, and try to wake by his mad kisses the cold painted face."[94] The Fisherman's own mad kisses bestowed upon the Mermaid's cold and lifeless body invite a reassigning of meaning akin to the reclamation of the word by mad studies, a privileging of his appreciation of and passion for atypical bodyminds as an explicit counter to the uniformity of type marshaled against all monstrous anomaly by medieval morals. Thus, while readers perhaps find some consolation in the reentry of the Soul into the Fisherman's heart, Wilde insists their primary focus is on the tragedy of his two disability-aligned protagonists and how (in a world that sees the relationship as an unnatural and ungodly abomination) their unconventional love is rendered as an expression of the dangerous queer desire and racial hybridity typically projected onto freakish bodies.

This tragedy represents another important opportunity to explore how Zipes's more general theorization of Wilde's art of subversion may be usefully inflected with a disability lens. Zipes argues that the Soul represents "social convention," while the Fisherman embodies "nonconformity," and Wilde's "utopian impulse" positions the latter's death as a "provocation."[95] Given that society's banishment of enfreaked others (including the little Mermaid), and then the Soul's self-interested undermining of the "healthy" relationship between the Mermaid and the Fisherman, lead to such pain and suffering for both of the disability-aligned lovers, the compassionate condemnation of the causes behind their heartbreak provides insight into the specifically ableist social pressures that subject such strange bodies to isolation, stigma, and peril. In Andersen, the Little Mermaid's tragedy ostensibly is offset by her transformation into an ethereal spirit (instead of being fated to merely disappear by dissolving into sea foam). The message for the adverting mind, especially that of the child reader, may be summed up in the suggestion of how happiness in the here and now is not finally what matters most. As long as she selflessly and consistently does good unto others, Andersen's Little Mermaid will gain an immortal soul and ascend into Heaven, and all of her suffering will have been worth it, even justified.

What is more, the children who hear the tale can help or hinder how long it takes her to complete her three-hundred-year task, depending on whether or not they listen to adults and behave.

In Wilde's world, temporal authority also attempts to assert itself over the interpretation of the outcome of his disability-aligned lovers' subversive desire to circumvent the barriers society and religion have put in place to preserve the separate spheres of human self and freakish other. When, the next morning, the Priest arrives at the shore along with "a great company" to bless the sea, upon finding the Fisherman "drowned in the surf" with his arms "clasped" around "the body of the little Mermaid," he frowns and reiterates his stance on the obscenity of all intercourse with aberrant bodies, announcing, "I will not bless the sea nor anything that is in it. Accursed be the Sea-folk, and accursed be all they who traffic with them."[96] In a final abjection of the grotesque miscegenation such traffic constitutes to his mind, he continues, "And as for him who for love's sake forsook God, and so lieth here with his leman slain by God's judgment, . . . bury them in the corner of the Field of the Fullers, and set no mark above them . . . that none may know the place of their resting."[97] The Priest would have it God does not approve of such immoral coupling, and since the crowd that follows him automatically accepts the stance he dictates to them, in their eyes too the Fisherman and the Mermaid are not lovers, persons, or even bodies, but only things: "The people did as he commanded them, and in the corner . . . where no sweet herbs grew, they dug a deep pit, and laid the dead things within it."[98]

Wilde does not give the Priest's position the last word, however. Three years later, he finds his altar "covered with strange flowers that never had been seen before," flowers "of curious beauty," a beauty that "troubled him" but that also made him feel glad somehow.[99] As he begins his sermon, he finds himself still "troubled" by the flowers' beauty: "their odour was sweet in his nostrils, and there came another word into his lips," for even though he does not himself know why, he speaks "not of the wrath of God, but of the God whose name is Love."[100] The people are so moved they all weep to hear his message, and with his own eyes "full of tears," he asks his attendants about the flowers.[101] "What flowers they are we cannot tell," is the report, "but they come from the corner of the Fullers' Field."[102] This detail from the fairy tale's final paragraph recalls the blossoms that cover the Giant (in another final paragraph) as a sign from "the God whose name is Love" (the Christ-child who bears the wounds of Love and who as the disabled

God rewards rather than rejects such peculiar bodies) that even the Priest cannot deny. In the face of this divine sanctioning of the Mermaid and her Fisherman, the Priest goes to the shore with the same large crowd to bless "the sea, and all the wild things that are in it."[103] What is more, "the Faun also he blessed, and the little things that dance in the woodland, and the bright-eyed things that peer through the leaves. All the things in God's world he blessed, and the people were filled with joy and wonder."[104] In this way, the monstrous body is reenvisioned as the marvelous body, transforming conditioned fear and disgust into unanticipated delight and amazement. Yet Wilde, even here, still insists on qualifying, if not fully questioning, the efficacy of this change of heart in the Priest and his people, for the fairy tale ends with the following deflating lines: "Yet never again in the corner of the Fullers' Field grew flowers of any kind, but the field remained barren even as before. Nor came the Sea-folk into the bay as they had been wont to do, for they went to another part of the sea."[105]

Wilde wants to ensure that readers sympathize with (again, even identify with) his little Mermaid and her young Fisherman, that they come to celebrate their love, and further that they see their odd coupling as sanctioned by God. At the same time, though, he also aims to resist a happy ending or any trite moral that might ultimately dilute the extent of the peril their difference places them in. The Fisherman and the Mermaid may seem to overcome the odds stacked against their happiness by sharing such a fulfilling life together for a few years, but, owing to a world not just insistently unaccommodating but outright antagonistic toward them, it ends in heartbreak as surely as does the Dwarf's unrequited affection for the Infanta. So, while this ending shares with that of "The Selfish Giant" a moving signal of divine approval in the form of the fantastic flowers that indicate the winningness and worth of Wilde's peculiar protagonists, here there is no physical appearance of the embodied disabled God nor any spoken promise of a well-earned place in Paradise. Readers are left merely to speculate as to whether or not the blossoms themselves might imply as much, for, after all, the soulless Mermaid would seem to have no recourse to such a redemptive reward. Indeed, the Fisherman might not either, depending on whether or not it matters if his Soul was acceptably restored right before he died. Even so, would he actually care to go to Heaven without his beloved Mermaid? In the end, this ending would seem to resonate more with that of "The Birthday of the Infanta," refusing to provide resolution in the form of any consolation for the tragic fates that befall the two disability-aligned protagonists whose life and love as a nonnormative couple fails to rise above convention.

As Free argues, freaks and other outcast figures tend to play a sacrificial role in Victorian narratives, inhabiting expendable extraordinary bodies which nonetheless powerfully push readers to acknowledge how deserving they are of dignity and love. Huff and Stoddard Holmes's insights into how inextricably ableism was woven into the fabric of common nineteenth-century economic and moral objections to nonnormative bodies are crucial here. After all, the Fisherman falls short when it comes to both utility and wholeness when he abandons his trade and cuts away his soul in order to free himself to follow his fish-girl full fathom five for a fantastic life with her family of freaks. The Mermaid and her Fisherman, even if religion and society ultimately render them disposable outcasts, still fortify Free's contention that "the power to transform belongs to the freaks" and, more crucially, these two disability-aligned protagonists and the story of their love "force us to consider the ways in which they are 'fully human,'" not monstrous.[106]

Wilde invites readers to reject both the Soul's heartlessness and the Priest's prejudice, seeing love, not loss—self-development, not self-denial—in the passion between queer bodies and the tale's ironic inversion of medieval self-wounding. "The Fisherman and His Soul" undeniably allows for an association of atypical bodies with lack, an identification of them as "less than." But it also encourages positive emotional responses to disability and freakery, undermining the stigmatized identities those in power insist upon assigning to them in an attempt to limit any new understandings of or relationships with any groups or individuals upon whose othering their authority and privilege depends. In this alternative take, readers are encouraged to celebrate Wilde's disability-aligned lovers and to endorse not just a tolerance of love *for* bodies society traditionally has devalued as deviant and discarded as dangerous but more profoundly to endorse an appreciation of the love *of* and *by* bodies embraced precisely for, rather than in spite of, their difference and diversity.

3

# "No Pity Had He for the Poor, or for Those Who Were Blind or Maimed or in Any Way Afflicted"

*Emotional Connection and Compassionate Action in "The Star-Child"*

"The Star-Child" serves as an important pivot point for this study in shifting from an emphasis on the impact of isolation, stigma, and peril as experienced within individual lives and relationships toward a broader focus on social justice. Such a focus is hinted at near the end of "The Fisherman and His Soul" when the divine sign signaling God's approval of Wilde's two extraordinary lovers leads the Priest belatedly to offer his blessing to the Sea-folk and the Fauns and all of the other fantastic bodies he had formerly forbidden his parishioners from accepting as equally worthy of love. His about-face comes too late, though, as the whole community of curious creatures already had removed themselves from the area owing to his intense antagonism. In the next two stories, Wilde's plotlines ask readers to move beyond mere empathy or sympathy (where we feel sorry about the misconceptions and mistreatment that create such unfortunate circumstances and tragic outcomes but are not necessarily moved enough to turn tears into compassionate commitment and dedicated action). While "The Star-Child" certainly continues Wilde's concern with depicting the damaging and dangerous effects of the othering of disability-aligned difference, it ultimately utilizes its peculiar protagonist's personal journey as a means of reinforcing for readers how his epiphanies about acceptance and equality require social transformation, not just individual alteration.

"The Star-Child" exposes how selfishness and cruelty drive the rejection of nonnormative bodies, and it further interrogates the treacle of readers' sentimental emotional response to the victims of such mistreatment, through its complicated rendering of the complex relationship between Kristjánsson's "conceptual parish of fellow-feelings" and disability. While, on the one hand, the story may seem to invite stereotypically pejorative responses to disability (for example, presenting ugliness as a form of punishment from God), it nonetheless also suggests more progressive possibilities through its strong stance against the stigmatization of and violence toward unusual bodies, through its significant attention to the crucial element of reciprocity underwriting the emotional connections that lead to compassionate action, and through its ending's envisioning of transformative change on both the individual and the collective level. Wilde skewers the initial egotism of the Star-Child, only to champion his later loving-kindness and egalitarian commitment grounded in a humble acknowledgment of mutuality that successfully addresses the social injustice he identifies as causing so much suffering, here and across the rest of his fairy tales. By broadening Wilde's focus, taking readers beyond the narrower frame of interpersonal relationships to consider the systemic problem of inequality (and ableism's fundamental contributions to that problem), "The Star-Child" testifies to the importance of refusing to ignore the abuse of marginalized lives and of resisting and reforming inequitable structures of prejudice and privilege.

In "The Star-Child," Wilde yet again simultaneously employs the figure of the freak and the figure of the child as a means of meditating upon the dearth and death dealt with by disability-aligned characters. Zipes sees all the pain and suffering throughout the tale and its unhappy ending as revealing how "Wilde's ideological position implicitly mocked Andersen" and how he "constantly insisted on the need to rid society of domination."[1] Markey, on the other hand, reads the ending as so pessimistic that (especially given this story's place as the final entry in the second collection) "it punctures any lingering hope that the good we do may live after us" and reinforces how Wilde's works "are not agents of social change but belong to the self-referential world of art."[2] Regardless, readers find themselves faced with irresolvable tensions, even oppositions, that productively require a careful consideration of any proposed conclusions. In the end, whether one decides to side with Zipes or Markey or one refuses to choose, the through line that nonetheless becomes clearer and clearer in opaque text after opaque text is that Wilde is consistently drawn in compelling ways to the atypical body, and that for him these exceptional characters are central to a range of interrelated concerns that (whether intentionally or not) in turn expose the role of ableism in the isolation, stigma, and peril they face, while requesting an emotional response that moves beyond empathy through a compassionate commitment that works toward beneficial social change.

With its backdrop of the French Revolution, Dickens's *A Tale of Two Cities* similarly asks its audience to confront the damage of long-standing systemic inequalities, even as its final emphasis falls upon the singular sacrifice of Sydney Carton. For many, the "far, far better thing"[3] that Carton does in giving up his own life for the happiness of Lucie Manette with Charles Darnay potentially provokes the same sort of maudlin emotional responses evoked by Tim Cratchit and Nell Trent (while simultaneously sliding him into Jenny Wren's auxiliary role where the primary heteronormative romance plot is concerned). In "Sentimental Transport and Stoic Sacrifice in *A Tale of Two Cities*," Richard Bonfiglio attempts to offer a different take. He opens by acknowledging that the novel's sentimentality has had its share of critics, from James Fitzjames Stephen's contemporary Victorian evisceration of its "grotesque and pathetic writing" (especially its "very strong dose of sentiment with caricature") on down past Georg Lukács's exposure of its "petty bourgeois humanism and idealism."[4] For many, *A Tale of Two Cities* settles for the consolation of individual reformation and redemption rather than insisting upon this being accompanied by the further transformation on a collective level that more fundamental sociopolitical change would effect. Bonfiglio, though, believes Dickens actually effectively merges the two emphases, positing "sentimental transport" as a "narratable journey" that "transforms fellow feeling into public action."[5]

While Bonfiglio's argument does not consider the relationship of disability to any potential messages about pity or activism, it nonetheless can serve as a helpful Dickensian framework through which to begin to consider Wilde's more explicit acknowledgment of the necessity of commitment to both personal and collective change in "The Star-Child." In fact, a disability studies lens significantly qualifies Bonfiglio's claim for the novel's progressive project of transforming fellow feeling into public action, by revealing Dickens's troubling recourse to a rendering of disfigurement as the embodiment of evil while simultaneously separating it from the experience of oppression. Dr. Alexandre Manette is the novel's most obvious disabled character, his long-term mental health struggles and post-traumatic stress as a result of his eighteen-year unjust imprisonment in the Bastille visibly manifested for readers in his obsessive shoemaking. Carton may also serve for some as a sympathetic disability-aligned figure, perhaps as someone living with chronic depression. In the end, though, Dickens's framing of his whole narrative seems to position disability as pitiable in the pejorative sense, as a marker of suffering or weakness at best, as an indicator of "the worst of times"[6] half of the backdrop to the story.

Interestingly, Bonfiglio at one point contrasts Madame Thérèse Defarge's "undisciplined passions" with Carton's "Stoic self-command" in order to tout how the latter "resists a transindividual experience of undifferentiated and undisciplined affect" in that "broader social forces do not push Carton to die on Darnay's behalf."[7] Dickens's villainization of her character shifts the focus away from the egregious lived experiences of the poor and disenfranchised that might justify the social change the Revolution in theory at least intended to address, encouraging Bonfiglio and others ultimately to privilege the personal over the political. What is more, it plays into Dickens's overall juxtaposition of good and evil by drawing a fundamental distinction between fairness and disfigurement. Madame Defarge is "absolutely without pity," a "tigress" whose "inveterate hatred of a class" has rendered her the most "dreaded" and "ruthless" of all the many women "upon whom the time laid a dreadfully disfiguring hand";[8] Carton, on the other hand, goes to the guillotine with the vision of his namesake (the son of Lucie and Charles) in turn honoring his own handsome golden-haired son with Carton's name and bringing him to the scene of his sacrifice, a place now "fair to look upon, with not a trace of this day's disfigurement."[9]

The mortal combat between Madame Defarge and Miss Pross at the end of the penultimate chapter powerfully reinforces the self-same binary behind the book's final staging, for in addition to the hearing loss Miss Pross suffers as a consequence of their struggle, the narrator explains, "By good fortune, too, she was naturally so peculiar in appearance as not to show disfigurement like any other woman. She needed both advantages, for the marks of gripping fingers were deep in her face, and her hair was torn."[10] In *A Tale of Two Cities,* then, odd bodies and minds still seem subject to our pity or detestation, with disfigurement only conceived of as something dreadful marking deficit, if not also wickedness. At the same time, Bonfiglio's notion of "shared suffering as a narratable journey" that "transforms fellow feeling into public action"[11] nonetheless translates quite effectively to "The Star-Child," where Wilde provides more explicit acknowledgment of the intersecting "exclusionary systems legitimated by bodily variation" Garland Thomson identifies, which limit (and, in some cases, eventually eliminate) whole populations of marginalized lives. This fairy tale offers its readers a potential redemption of both disfigurement and pity, as well as opening the possibility for parlaying the public act inspired by fellow feeling into a set of actions that move beyond personal motivations to acknowledge the larger goal of systemic change.

The story starts with two poor Woodcutters making their way home on a frigid winter night, navigating their way through a forest full of reminders of the disabling difficulties such cold can cause: Turtle-doves with "frost-bitten" feet, a "limp[ing]" Wolf complaining of the "perfectly monstrous weather," a Mountain-Torrent "hanging motionless in air," even the little twigs "the frost kept snapping."[12] Significantly, right from the outset, the story insists on an acknowledgment of the similarly disabling difficulties of poverty. Fearing for their lives after losing their way, the Woodcutters are momentarily relieved when they finally find the edge of the woods, but when they "[remember] their poverty," they begin "bewailing their misery," complaining, "Injustice has parcelled out the world, nor is there equal division of aught save of sorrow."[13] Just then, though, a beautiful star appears to fall to earth nearby, and their thoughts turn to treasure; they race toward it only to discover a sleeping child wrapped in a golden cloak. One laments, "This is a bitter ending to our hope," and then proposes, "Let us leave it here, and go our way, seeing that we are poor men."[14] The other, however, insists "it were an evil thing to leave the child to perish here in the snow," and thus "very tenderly he took up the child," his companion "marvelling much at his foolishness and softness of heart."[15]

Later, the Woodcutter will characterize this action as an instance of pity: "yet did I show thee pity when I found thee in the forest."[16] Notably, the Woodcutter does not merely feel empathy for the child's unfortunate circumstance, only to leave it behind (as his comrade does); his pity is something he actively "shows" in order to relieve, not just recognize, the Star-Child's difficulty. His pity is first and foremost a merciful act (deciding against leaving the child to die) that establishes a hierarchical relationship between a superior benefactor and a helpless recipient. But it is also a compassionate act, one that surpasses mere charitable concern in his tenderness, further foregrounded by the contrast with his wife's hardheartedness when she initially refuses to accept the child, claiming it is a "changeling" that could bring "bad fortune."[17] The Woodcutter rejects such superstition, insisting instead it is her anger and suspicion that is cause for pain or regret, not the predicament (another mouth to feed) presented by his bringing home the strange child. Eventually, his softness works a change in her, and when he brings the little one over to her, "she kisse[s] it, and [lays] it in a little bed where the youngest of their own children was lying."[18] Importantly, given the tale's trajectory, in this opening scene, Wilde positions his Star-Child as a catalyst for the valorization of fellow feeling and loving-kindness (over and against selfishness and cruelty) as the proper response to a world in which inequality and injustice entail so much sorrow and misery for so many.

There is a long history of the changeling as a stand-in for disability, but Wilde's story is not another retelling of the popular Stolen Child myth. Markey in fact is adamant the Star-Child should not be read as a changeling.[19] Yet while it may be more accurate to label him a foundling, as Lindsay Smith does, there is nonetheless still an important linkage here to the disability-aligned figure of the natural child, or wild child, that Smith more explicitly references in her reading of "The Young King," with her mention of Caspar Hauser, and then returns to in her discussion of the Dwarf in the paragraph immediately before she takes up "The Star-Child."[20] McDonagh's aforementioned opening focus on Victor, the Wild Boy of Aveyron, in his articulation of "the public image of the 'idiot'" with "the sentimental notion of the 'innocent,'"[21] only further reinforces how these strange foundlings from the woods evoked for many Victorians associations with cognitive difference. The Star-Child's potential status as a foundling certainly at the very least initially identifies his character with marginalized lives like that of his poor adoptive family in a society where lineage so powerfully determines one's lot in life. While eventually the Star-Child will see his beauty and the singular items found with him as marking him as special, at this point the baby's health and safety relies solely upon the humble Woodsman's compassion. From the outset, then, the Star-Child (as his hyphen might suggest) is something of a hybrid figure, potentially allowing him to be glossed as a disability-aligned character even before his eventual enfreakment.

Significantly, though, as he grows up, the most remarkable thing about him is his striking beauty, and thus his difference does not cause him to experience discrimination or other difficulties; rather, to his mind it embodies his superiority. According to Wilde, "every year he became more beautiful to look at, so that all those who dwelt in the village were filled with wonder, for . . . he was white and delicate as sawn ivory. . . . and his body like the narcissus of a field where the mower comes not."[22] He consequently "despised" not only the other children of the village but even his adopted siblings, all of whom he (ironically, as a foundling) looks down upon for their "mean parentage."[23] His pitiless arrogance is not limited to the playmates he commonly refers to as his "servants," though: "No pity had he for the poor, or for those who were blind or maimed or in any way afflicted, but would cast stones at them and drive them forth on to the highway."[24] "Indeed," Wilde continues, "he was as one enamoured of beauty, and would mock at the weakly and ill-favoured."[25] In this, Wilde's story aptly captures the intersectionality of class and disability, as the poor are seen as treated similarly to (if not simply lumped together with) those whose looks are judged to be inferior, even if only just not physically attractive ("ill-favoured"). These lines capture how the Victorian values of wholeness ("maimed"), utility ("blind"), and vitality ("weakly") are all intertwined so as to join together the fates of the members of such different groups, all viewed through the same lens and therefore subject to the same types of misjudgment and mistreatment. The peculiar bodies of the poor and disabled provoke only ridicule from the Star-Child, his smug sense of superiority (like the Infanta with the Dwarf) channeling his derision directly at the physical differences his conditioned disgust sees as deserving denigration. His lack of pity leads to contempt and abuse rather than equality and respect: "Yet did his beauty work him evil. For he grew proud, and cruel, and selfish."[26]

This scene also offers some important insight into Wilde's potential positioning of pity relative to disability. The Star-Child's parents, distressed by his behavior, frequently would "chide" him, saying, "We did not deal with thee as thou dealest with those who are left desolate, and have none to succour them. Wherefore are thou so cruel to all who need pity?"[27] Significantly, his parents characterize "all who need pity" as those in circumstances comparable to the Star-Child's own situation before being rescued by the Woodcutter: they have been "left desolate" and "have none to succour them." On the one hand, the sense of dependency and helplessness explicitly attributed to the poor and the disabled would seem to reinforce a hierarchical division between the fortunate and the unfortunate—a division that problematically enables a charity/tragedy model. Still, the comparison to the Star-Child's original distress is in and of itself significant. If the

Star-Child himself once was "desolate" and in need of "succour" but now clearly no longer is, then "all who need pity" do not, at least necessarily, permanently occupy an inferior position relative to others (including anyone willing to offer help)—and thus they are not "less than" in any essentialist way. Further, since the support one would provide to those such as the blind, maimed, and ill-favored would not be in the form of some sort of miracle cure, it instead might merely serve as an alleviation of their hardship in the form of better treatment and understanding, not an erasure of their physical difference.

This is reinforced by the local priest, who attempts to teach the Star-Child "the love of living things."[28] Interestingly, unlike the Priest from "The Fisherman and His Soul" (who insists all anomalous bodies are accursed), this reverend father actually favors an orientation that requires respect for all creatures great and small, including disability-aligned little animals: "God made the blind-worm and the mole, and each has its place."[29] Again, Wilde could be poking fun at such a message as trite, but he also might be advocating for acceptance of, even reverence for, all of the variety of different positions a person or any other living thing might occupy in the universe—an attitude that, instead of disregarding or degrading them, values each and every such "place." Further, that the line about "the love of living things" is placed in the sentence immediately following his parents' reference to "all who need pity" strengthens the case for the privileged response as one defined by genuine loving compassion, not self-righteous paternalism. The selfish Star-Child, however, does not listen to parents or priest, answering their pleas by "pierc[ing] with a sharp reed the dim eyes of the mole" and "cast[ing] stones at the leper."[30] The priest's expansiveness where the place of pity and succor rests relative to others (including, as he does, animals and all other living things), as well as the Star-Child's attacks against not only the disability-aligned leper but little creatures like the mole, both in their own opposite ways suggest how the boundary between human and animal (which continues to be a fundamental aspect of the dehumanization of such bodies) is in fact a flexible one that allows for an understanding of pitiable circumstances as contingent or temporary rather than essential or permanent.

The tale's turning point occurs when a "poor beggar-woman" with "bleeding" feet[31] appears in the village as a literal embodiment of the intersection between disability and poverty. When the Star-Child sees her, he proclaims, "There sitteth a foul beggar-woman.... let us drive her hence, for she is ugly and ill-favoured."[32] Wilde's use of "ill-favoured" here once again immediately identifies her as one in need of pity, and the passage as a whole also is telling in that it indicates the primary impetus behind berating the beggar woman is that she is foul-looking (like the Dwarf), not that she is so poor she needs to ask for alms. Perhaps predictably, then, the boy's response remains the same—he "threw stones at her, and mocked her," until the Woodcutter intervenes, rebuking his adopted son for being "hard of heart and know[ing] not mercy."[33] It is at this very moment the father offers the aforementioned characterization of his own original succor as an act of pity, reminding the Star-Child, "yet did I show thee pity when I found thee in the forest." This comment causes the woman to faint, and after the Woodcutter carries her into his house, they realize she is the boy's real mother; the cloak and chain found with him confirm he is her son, left to die in the woods by robbers.

Called in to meet his long-lost parent, the Star-Child laughs "scornfully," and "angrily" denounces her claim with another explicit attempt to distance himself from disability, poverty, and the nonnormative bodies he is so bent on rejecting: "Thou art mad to say so.... I am no son of thine, for thou art a beggar, and ugly, and in rags. Therefore get thee hence, and let me see thy foul face no more."[34] His prejudicial privileging of fairness and his spiteful rejection of what he sees as its opposite prevents him from responding to her with the loving compassion that moves one to act and provide support. Wilde's fairy tales present readers with numerous forms of difference that may be glossed as disability-aligned, and the Star-Child's mother inhabits one such bodymind. She is impacted both physically and psychologically by her poverty (or, as Dickens might say, literally and figuratively disfigured by it)—and then treated poorly because "she is ugly and ill-favoured." Indeed, as in his immediate response to first noticing her, it is specifically owing to her "foul face" that the Star-Child dismisses her in this scene. What is more, the idea there could be a familial connection between one so beautiful and somebody so grotesque strikes him as so ludicrous (as ludicrous, the Camerera might say, as a romantic connection between the lovely Infanta and the ugly Dwarf) that he spuriously accuses her of madness, further augmenting her character's affiliation with disability. As such, this scene constitutes a truly compelling instance of the conditioned disgust Hingston theorizes as the standard response by those who need to abject disability-aligned otherness in an attempt to disassociate themselves from it and preserve the illusion of their own normative identity.[35]

Crucially, his mother's reaction to this rejection provides further opportunity to reflect on the nature of pity as valorized here, confirming it is loving compassion and not sentiment or handouts that Wilde positions as the required response. After all, she does not ask for his charity or his mercy but rather his affection: "I have need of thy love."[36] Her use of "need" echoes that of his adoptive parents' "Wherefore art thou so cruel to all who need pity?" thus further suggesting love and pity are inextricably allied, as emotional connection is the necessary resolution she seeks, not relief of her poverty. Her son, however, remains unmoved, "shut[ting] the doors of his heart against her" and in a "hard and bitter" voice telling her she only has brought him "shame" in that he had thought he "was the child of some Star, and not a beggar's child."[37] He refuses her even a farewell kiss, asserting, "thou art too foul to look at, and rather would I kiss the adder or the toad than thee."[38] His words reveal how his pitiless inaction in withholding love stems from his loathing of her person on account of her abject physical appearance (which is owing at least in part to the disfiguring effects of poverty), an abject appearance he sees as not merely subhuman (she is fouler than the adder and the toad) but actually too disgusting even to look upon. His heartlessness shares the arrogant assumption that her difference (in appearance, health, and wealth) is shameful.

As Prendergast has observed, "the conception of 'pity' . . . is undertheorized in much disability studies," and it is therefore worthwhile to consider how the field might recirculate and refigure it.[39] Kristjánsson's delineation of the "terminological disarray" within what he has characterized as "the conceptual parish of fellow-feelings" is, as noted in the introduction, particularly instructive for any attempt to navigate these troubled waters. Again, for Kristjánsson, "empathy is a necessary condition for being able to experience sympathy, compassion, and pity, but it does not include the desire to alleviate suffering"; sympathy is also "an emotion that arises prior to both pity and compassion" but is "different from empathy in that it . . . includes a desire to alleviate suffering."[40] Kristjánsson's privileged form of fellow feeling is compassion, which in his framework replaces sympathy when "the suffering is serious rather than trivial."[41] He does not end up clarifying the difference between compassion and pity, perhaps fittingly given the same term, *Mitleid*, typically is translated into English as "pity," for Nietzsche, but "compassion," for Schopenhauer. His final point, though—that no matter the extent of terminological disarray, the "idea that pity necessarily involves a condescending holier-than-thou attitude" is "factually wrong"[42]—suggests that a reevaluation of the standard contemporary usage's narrow and exclusively pejorative perception of pity might be productive, especially for texts from the nineteenth century (when Nietzsche and Schopenhauer were themselves working through their competing views on the topic). Kristjánsson's attempt at a historical corrective to the contexts in which it might have been used in the late nineteenth century seems a significant one, for while Wilde despises altruism, charity, philanthropy, and sentimentality, he seems to valorize compassionate pity, which, as we shall see, he associates with mutuality and reciprocity rather than superiority and paternalism.

Kristjánsson ends his chapter on pity with an allusion to Rousseau, of whose alternate conception of pity John M. Warner provides a helpful accounting. For Rousseau, "from pity '*alone* flow *all* the social virtues,'" including "benevolence and even friendship."[43] Warner continues, "pity, understood aright, is not only a restraint on . . . unadulterated self-love; it is also the foundation of sympathetic social identification."[44] Given Wilde's continual engagement with selfishness in his fairy tales, and the potential for understanding sentimentalized pity and its self-serving charity as ultimately stemming from a self-centered sense of superiority (from self-love), Rousseau's positive version of pity as spawning social identification seems a crucial intervention. Indeed, "one of pity's primary functions" for Rousseau is not just "to soften the harsher expressions of self-love" but further (since "pity and the set of virtues that grow out of it remind us that we share the imperfection of the afflicted . . . party") to establish itself as "a positive catalyst of social togetherness."[45] To hearken back to Bonfiglio, conceiving of "shared suffering as a narratable journey" that "transforms fellow feeling into public action" might just be one way to begin to refigure the role of pity, to resituate its place, within disability studies.

As T. L. S. Sprigge has noted, Schopenhauer's championing of *Mitleid* in "On the Basis of Morality" draws upon Rousseau's discourse on pity. For Schopenhauer, compassion-pity represents the foundational impulse underlying morality itself: "Only insofar as an action has sprung from compassion does it have moral value; and every action resulting from any other motive has none."[46] Pity-compassion leads to an emphasis on both justice and loving-kindness, and thus entails an "active effort to relieve the sufferings of others however caused."[47] Indeed, it holds the potential to transcend "mere subjective feeling" in that "to feel compassion is to see through the apparent distinction of oneself from other people."[48] This is perhaps comparable to what Bonfiglio argues motivates Carton to trade places with Darnay, but with an added element of social aspirations and social action grounded in a sense of social togetherness. It also allows for an affirmative response to Hingston's question, "Who or what am I in relation to this character?" In any case, this sort of response is precisely what the priest and his parents have been trying to foster in the Star-Child (identification leading to compassionate action)—and ironically, given his vehement verbal response to her plea, his mother had asked even less of him, simply for his compassionate action to constitute a reciprocal return of her own affection. At this stage, however, Wilde's main character remains mired in his arrogance and self-love.

Intriguingly, right after Wilde provides a rational explanation for the boy's presence in the woods to replace the magical notion he is a Star-Child, the fairy tale veers off into the fantastical, beginning with a freakish mutation. His last words to his mother work as a curse, for when he returns to his companions, they mock him because "his face was as the face of a toad, and his body was scaled like an adder."[49] This plot development is definitely disturbing from a disability studies perspective. With this reversal, the Star-Child finds himself on the other side of the divide excluding those who find themselves disadvantaged (or, here, literally disfigured) owing to their health or looks. He is no longer the embodiment of physical perfection; instead, he effectively is enfreaked as The Toad-faced Kid or as Snake Boy. Readers likely feel it fitting that his new foul exterior matches his poisonous personality, but such a response relies on the same disabling premise through which the Star-Child justified his cruelty to others—physiognomy's damaging insistence that one's appearance reflects one's true nature. What is more, Wilde seemingly uncritically employs the age-old view of disability as not just an "evil" fate but (in the Star-Child's opinion, anyway) as a "punishment" for his "sin": "I have denied my mother, and driven her away, and been proud, and cruel to her."[50] This threatens to overshadow how there had been no suggestion previously that the afflicted and ill-favored are in any way to blame somehow for finding themselves in need of pity, be they abandoned child, mole, leper, or beggar woman. The Star-Child's adamant contention that his transformed deformed appearance represents some sort of judgment upon him is jolting and arguably reverses much of the momentum built thus far toward a more progressive acceptance of such difference as having its own natural place in the universe.

Deciding he must search out his mother for forgiveness, the Star-Child inquires of a Mole regarding her whereabouts, but the little creature cannot say where she might be, because the boy previously had "blinded [its] eyes."[51] He also asks for news about her from a Linnet who cannot fly above the treetops to look for her because he had "clipt [its] wings" and from a little Squirrel who worries the boy seeks to kill the beggar woman since he had killed the Squirrel's own parents.[52] At these reminders of his cruelty, where his arrogance had led him to maim or kill living things he deemed "less than," the Star-Child "wept and . . . prayed forgiveness of God's things,"[53] at last learning the old priest's lesson. Eventually, his reversal is complete, as he experiences the same treatment to which he had subjected beggars and lepers (and little animals) in his prideful superiority. Whenever he passed through villages, "children mocked him, and threw stones at him," and the peasants would not even allow him to sleep in their barns for fear "he might bring mildew on the stored corn, so foul was he to look at."[54] The workers "drave him away," and no matter where he went, "there was none who had pity on him."[55] After three years of wandering, his lot is much like his mother's, disfigured physically and psychologically from the impact of his profound poverty: the "sharp flints" of the roads "made his feet to bleed," and throughout the whole wide world, "there was neither love nor lovingkindness nor charity for him."[56] Here, again, the story suggests that while charitable aid can be part of the action pity requires to alleviate suffering, so too are love and kindness, the wellsprings of true compassion (which is precisely why his mother told him she was in need of his love, not of food or money or a place to shelter). Ultimately, his freakishly ugly state seems more a blessing than a punishment, as it effects an inner transformation through which he becomes humble, kind, and selfless (like the Giant)—and he begins to understand through his own need for pity how an awareness and acceptance of shared "imperfection" can break down egotistical boundaries between Self and Other.

Readers may prefer Wilde's abject enfreaked protagonist to his former self, but do they pity him—and, if so, is that a good or bad thing? Nodelman decidedly does not experience any such feelings, finding "something over-the-top about the melodrama and intensity of the suffering" where both the Dwarf and the Star-Child are concerned that strikes him as "a little funny."[57] Certainly the guards at the city the Star-Child eventually arrives at see him in this light, mocking his search for his mother by joking, "Of a truth, thy mother will not be merry when she sees thee, for thou art more ill-favoured than the toad of the marsh, or the adder that crawls in the fen."[58] Recognizing their opportunity to exploit this vulnerable freakish body, they decide to "sell the foul thing for a slave," and the boy soon finds himself in the dungeon of an "old and evil-visaged man"[59] who is revealed to be "the subtlest of the magicians of Libya."[60] Unfortunately for the Star-Child, he is not a good wizard, for his untoward appearance here actually does simplistically reflect an inner cruelty. This mean magician gives him, under threat of beating, the task of retrieving a hidden piece of white gold from a nearby wood. As he is returning empty-handed after a fruitless search, he hears "from a thicket a cry as of someone in pain," so, "forgetting his own sorrow," he runs to the rescue of "a little Hare caught in a trap."[61] Wilde explicitly characterizes the boy's emotional response as "pity," and it leads him to free the poor creature, noting, "I am myself but a slave, yet may I give thee thy freedom."[62] This compassionate act of succor to a fellow creature in need of pity reaffirms the earlier emphasis on the interchangeable roles of benefactor and recipient but takes it one step further, suggesting one may occupy both positions simultaneously.

The sequence also introduces a central component to Wilde's conceptualization of pity—namely, reciprocity. The Hare asks what it can "give [the Star-Child] in return" and takes him to find the gold.[63] The boy feels as if the creature's assistance greatly outweighs his own act of pity, insisting, "The service that I did to thee thou hast rendered back again many times over, and the kindness that I showed thee thou hast repaid a hundred-fold," but the rabbit replies, "Nay, . . . but as thou dealt with me, so I did deal with thee."[64] This exchange highlights how, if one takes the tale at face value, true pity requires action arising out of genuine emotional connection (like the love his mother asked of him) to ensure its expression is not merely a smug sentiment or performative gesture designed to make do-gooders feel better about their generosity. As the Star-Child's words suggest, it consists of not only "service" but "kindness," grounded in an ethic of reciprocity that revises, if not fully deconstructs, the hierarchical superior/inferior binary between benefactor and recipient. Again, Wilde could be teasingly lampooning charity's treacle through a cloyingly simplistic rendering of the Golden Rule, but it nonetheless also is important (in terms of potentially re-visioning some late nineteenth-century literary representations of disability-aligned difference and the emotional responses they allow for, if not encourage) to consider how "The Star-Child" and his other fairy tales offer instead a form of social critique intended to expose the many self-serving invocations of that saying, which plague the very sort of sentimentalized pity he rejects.

Indeed, this sequence in a way may represent Wilde improving upon Rousseau, for whom "one who pities another apprehends that he is both like *and* unlike the suffering other—alike insofar as he realizes that he, too, is in principle subject to whatever misfortune the aggrieved party suffers, but different insofar as he also realizes that he does not suffer *in fact*," thereby placing "limits on the forms of association that are actuated by it."[65] Wilde's scenario would seem to insist upon an acknowledgment of mutuality, since, as this particular interaction shows, all parties not only may find themselves on either side of the benefactor-recipient relationship but may even find themselves on both sides at the same time. However it may seem that certain circumstances are unlikely to change (or even cannot be changed)—one's level of comfort or health or wealth, if one is poor, for instance, but also more explicitly disability-aligned aspects of one's person such as if one is blind, maimed, ugly, or mad—such circumstances do not prevent one from filling either role, separately or simultaneously.

Even as the Star-Child's understanding and practice of pity alike seem transformed, his lesson is not yet complete. As he arrives back at the city gate, a leper calls out to him, "Give me a piece of money, or I must die of hunger. For they have thrust me out of the city, and there is no one who has pity on me."[66] This detail further reinforces this disabled character's association with poverty, not merely because he is starving to death but also in that his condition disqualifies him from being seen through the categories of wholeness, utility, and vitality. As Killeen notes, in a capitalist society, someone seen as useless—as unfit, unable, and unhealthy—represents a "threat to the economic environment," a drain on resources, if he is allowed to remain within the city walls.[67] As his cruel beautiful self, he had cast stones instead of coins at lepers, but now, even though he knows he will be beaten by the magician, "the Star-Child had pity, and gave him the piece of white gold."[68] Once again, the boy simultaneously occupies the roles of one who needs pity and one who practices it. This inflects what might otherwise seem an instance of the unhelpful Band-Aid of charitable almsgiving in such a way that it may entail the transformative necessity of fellow feeling. Following the Woodcutter's example, he does not merely feel sorry for the leper's predicament; having pity requires showing pity, and not just through action but through genuine interaction. That is, one's own need should confirm rather than remove one's obligation to respond with a humble and "healthy" respect for the mutuality that resides at the heart of these interactions.

The next day's events repeat this sequence after he is sent out to find a piece of yellow gold. The Hare leads him to the gold, and the boy asks, "How shall I thank thee? . . . for lo! this is the second time that you have succoured me," to which the rabbit replies, "Nay, but thou hadst pity on me first."[69] Upon his return, the leper is waiting and "entreat[s] him sore," so he again subjects himself to a beating in order to "ha[ve] pity" on the leper.[70] Then, for a third day in a row, the Star-Child is sent out on a similar mission, with the added caveat that the magician will set him free if he returns with the red gold but will kill him if he returns without it. Again, the Hare hears him weeping and leads him to the coin; again, the Star-Child wants to "reward" the rabbit, while the creature insists the boy's initial act of pity in responding to its cries has merited such willing continued service.[71] Their exchanges forcefully impress the fundamental equality of benefactor and recipient that allows pity to serve as a "positive catalyst" for both fellow feeling and social justice. Confronted by the leper a final time, with his life on the line, the Star-Child shows his sincere selflessness by "ha[ving] pity on him again, . . . saying, 'Thy need is greater than mine,'"[72] a compassionate gesture devoid of the trappings of duty or shame and, crucially, an acknowledgment of their shared need (even if one's is greater). Passing through the city gate to meet his fate, his transformation from pitiless cruelty to pity-full lovingkindness now complete, his body, unbeknownst to him, instantly reverts to its prior wondrous form.

To his surprise, then, "the priests and high officers of the city" surround him, proclaiming, "Thou art our lord for whom we have been waiting, and the son of our King," continuing on to tell him, "It was prophesied of old that on this day should come he who was to rule over us."[73] When he is shown his reflection in a soldier's shield, he realizes "his comeliness had come back to him," but significantly, he also observes "that in his eyes which he had not seen there before."[74] While his outward appearance now would allow him literally to lord himself over others, his eyes suggest he is changed inwardly. Those around him clamor for him to become their king, yet he refuses, saying, "I am not worthy," relating how he denied his mother and now must find her and secure her forgiveness.[75] At that very moment (this is a fairy tale, after all), he sees her among the gathering crowd and rushes over, kneeling down to kiss "the wounds on [her] feet. . . . sobbing, as one whose heart might break," and saying to her, "Mother, I denied thee in the hour of my pride. Accept me in the hour of my humility."[76] When she does not answer him, he turns to the leper, who is at her side, and begs him to intercede on his behalf; eventually, they both tell him to rise, and, lo, they are transformed from their abject states into a King and Queen, his parents.

The scene complicates further any attempt to gloss the tale as an exclusively positive literary representation of disability. One might argue it constitutes a progressive reconceptualization of disfigurement in that, ultimately, the beggar, the leper, and the freak are revealed to be essentially majestic, no matter what their outward appearance might have seemed to otherwise suggest. The Star-Child's depiction as "one whose heart might break" also aligns him with the Dwarf and the Fisherman (as well as the Mermaid?), who died from that cause, and his mother's wounds on her feet (and his own for that matter) even recall the Christ-child's stigmata and perhaps invite readers to position this scene as a revelation of the disabled God, as a testament to the divinity of disability. Yet, already allowing for the Star-Child's enfreakment to be taken as the sort of "pathetic fall into disability" Prendergast mentions in her discussion of Stephen Crane's *The Monster*, now all three characters' reverse trajectory from "degradation" to "majesty"[77] also potentially serves to reinstate the binary between those who are beautiful, fortunate, or powerful and those who are not. If this royal family only is viewed as in need of pity's charity when they are an ill-favored beggar woman, a foul leper, and an ugly freak, then is acceptance and integration only possible for them when they are back in their royal bodies? This development thus remains problematic, even if Wilde's endorsement of an active, reciprocal conception of pity, and his portrayal of a disability-aligned character as empowered to aid others while still in a pitiable abject state and in need of succor himself, are decidedly progressive.

Throughout both his collections, Wilde seems to relish frustrating traditional expectations for fairy tales, particularly when it comes to their handy morals and happy endings. Here, though, all appears headed toward a classic happily-ever-after—and not merely for the formerly peculiar protagonist and his family but for all of the people in the kingdom, and even for all the animals (from the moles to the hares). The Star-Child is crowned king, and Wilde's narrator pronounces, "Much justice and mercy did he show to all. . . . Nor would he suffer any to be cruel to bird or beast, but taught love and loving-kindness and charity, and to the poor he gave bread, and to the naked he gave raiment, and there was peace and plenty in the land."[78] Here is Bonfiglio's transformation of fellow feeling into public action. Here is Warner's Rousseauian pity as a "positive catalyst for social togetherness." But then, in the short final paragraph, the narrator matter-of-factly reports, "Yet ruled he not long, so great had been his suffering, and so bitter the fire of his testing, for after the space of three years he died. And he who came after him ruled evilly."[79] Is Wilde merely taunting his readers for allowing themselves to be manipulated into sentimentalized pity for his protagonist and for wanting to believe that a utopian happy ending is in fact possible? Or, is he inviting sincere investment in his character and the ethic of reciprocity central to his compassionate and efficacious version of pity, intending with the ending again only to forcefully reiterate how dangerous and daunting a task is the restructuring of society in such a way that it would eliminate ill treatment and inequality?

As one comes to expect from his fairy tales, the story continues to present as a slippery conundrum when it comes to sorting which answer seems more likely (or if it can be both at the same time). Some critics certainly feel strongly one way or the other. Killeen, for example, reads the Star-Child as an embodiment of "the suffering Christ"[80] (as he does the Dwarf and the Mermaid and the Happy Prince[81]), and as such he reads the boy's "elevat[ion] to kingly status" as comparable to the "broken, battered and abandoned Christ-figure ascend[ing] the throne."[82] For Killeen, one needs to understand that "the crucifixion is the centre of Wilde's theology of liberation," which posits that it is "only by being broken" that any of these characters "become salvific," revealing that for Wilde, "the sign of disgrace is a sign of victory."[83] Although he does not explicitly make the connection, such a reading complements Eiesland's notion of the disabled God and its progressive possibilities for the literary representation of disability. Contra Killeen, Markey argues that "despite Wilde's calculated evocation of a Christian framework," the story "resists restrictive interpretations which focus only on its spiritual significance."[84] She views the tale as a "complex and multi-layered"[85] exploration of the "ongoing tension between inner, spiritual and outward, physical beauty that is never completely resolved."[86] If anything, the "cautionary, deflationary ending allows a retrospective irony to temper the story's investigation of the value of individual sacrifice and the ultimate efficacy of compassion," with the implication that "kind deeds inspired by individual suffering are not enough to change the world."[87] While Killeen and Markey may seem to provide diametrically opposed takes on how one should view Wilde's conclusion, they do share an emphasis on brokenness and failure. The extent to which such an emphasis might be glossed as pessimistic or redemptive remains undecidable for many, yet arguably, regardless of which side one's scales tip toward, the work's representation of pity as a potentially revolutionary response to brokenness and failure can still be considered a central concern.

Significantly, both of the above interpretations equally allow for a revisionist take on pity, regardless of whether one finds the final stress to fall on enlightenment or inefficacy. What is clear is that the tale's particular presentation of pity is not allied to but in fact defined against its popular versions as marshaled forth in the service of altruism, charity, philanthropy, and sentimentalism (all of which Wilde deeply disapproved of, as he voiced in various other venues). Perhaps not coincidentally, between 1887 and 1890 (the years immediately preceding the 1888 appearance of *The Happy Prince* and the 1891 appearance of *A House of Pomegranates*), Wilde referenced both Rousseau and Schopenhauer in separate journalistic publications. One of these essays, "A Chinese Sage," his 1890 tribute to Chuang Tsŭ (Zhuang Zhou, or Zhuangzi), offers compelling evidence Wilde held a powerful aversion to the form of charitable pity rightfully decried for its paternalistic condescension and hypocritical sentimentality. For Wilde, Chuang Tsŭ's "caustic criticism of modern life" compellingly "combines with the passionate eloquence of a Rousseau the scientific reasoning of a Herbert Spencer."[88] As "there is nothing of the sentimentalist in him," according to Wilde, Chuang Tsŭ nostalgically idealizes "a certain Golden Age when . . . people loved each other without being conscious of charity, or writing to the newspapers about it," when "they were upright, and yet they never published books upon Altruism."[89] What is more, in Wilde's account, Chuang Tsŭ characterizes the appearance of "the Philanthropist" as "an evil moment," in part as it led to the "mischievous idea of Government," the two then working in tandem by causing "charity and duty to one's neighbour to interfere with the natural goodness of the heart of man" and "by interfering with the individual . . . [to] produce the most aggressive forms of egotism."[90] Philanthropists, then, "were a set of aggressive busybodies who caused confusion wherever they went. They were stupid enough to have principles, and unfortunate enough to act up to them. They all came to bad ends, and showed that universal altruism is as bad in its results as universal egotism. They 'tripped people up over charity, and fettered them with duties to their neighbours.'"[91]

That Wilde's admiration for Chuang Tsŭ, and along with it a potential predilection to theorize a version of compassionate pity that (hearkening back to the previous chapter) is associated with self-development and self-realization rather than self-aggrandizement or self-victimization, might be reflected in "The Star-Child" is in fact plausible. Wilde not only explicitly praises his sage's metaphysics as "intensely humorous" but also characterizes his story-telling as "charming,"[92] even remarking on the place of "talking animals . . . in Chuang Tsŭ's parables and stories," where "through myth and poetry and fancy his strange philosophy finds musical utterance."[93] Wilde has on numerous occasions seemingly praised other artists and thinkers for anticipating or reflecting his own aesthetics and politics.[94] Accordingly, Wilde might be tipping his hand here by revealing how, in his own parables and stories (equal parts "intensely humorous" and "charming"), his gallery of extraordinary bodies—remarkable children, fantastic freaks, and, yes, talking animals—are the means by which his own "strange philosophy finds musical utterance" through "myth and poetry and fancy." This potential influence on Wilde's own storytelling aside, Chuang Tsŭ indisputably represents a key figure in Wilde's critical articulation of aesthetics, metaphysics, and politics in his tour-de-force manifesto *The Soul of Man* (originally published one year after "A Chinese Sage" and during the same year as *A House of Pomegranates*). After all, for Wilde, "it is clear that Chuang Tsŭ is a very dangerous writer" precisely because "the ideal of self-culture and self-development, which is the aim of his scheme of life, and the basis of his scheme of philosophy, is an ideal somewhat needed by an age like ours, in which most people are so anxious to educate their neighbours that they have actually no time left in which to educate themselves."[95]

As this same ideal is the aim of Wilde's own scheme of life and philosophy as expressed in *The Soul of Man*, it is therefore not surprising one need only peruse the first few paragraphs of that more renowned essay to glean the extent to which in it he also strongly condemns philanthropic and governmental exacerbation of problems such as poverty. Intriguingly invoking discourses of disease, unhealthiness, and ugliness, Wilde asserts, "The majority of people spoil their lives by an unhealthy and exaggerated altruism" when "with admirable, though misdirected intentions, they very seriously and very sentimentally set themselves to the task of remedying the evils that they see. But their remedies do not cure the disease: they merely prolong it."[96] If the Star-Child's compassionate pity is of this ilk (that is, philanthropic charity founded in paternalistic condescension and hypocritical sentimentality), then Wilde might be said to join Markey in casting it as misguided and ineffectual. Singling out charity as the foremost of "altruistic impulses" we all need to "restrain," he even goes so far as to assert that "such charity degrades and demoralizes" and "creates a multitude of sins."[97] A few paragraphs later, Wilde returns to the topic, disputing the notion that "the poor are grateful for charity."[98] In Wilde's view, "charity they feel to be a ridiculously inadequate mode of partial restitution, or a sentimental dole, usually accompanied by some impertinent attempt on the part of the sentimentalist to tyrannize over their private lives."[99] Significantly, Wilde is willing to extend "pity" to the "virtuous poor" who might be "grateful for charity," but not his admiration, which he reserves for those who refuse to accept its dehumanizing terms: "Man should not be ready to show that he can live like a badly-fed animal. . . . a poor man who is ungrateful, unthrifty, discontented, and rebellious, is. . . . a healthy protest."[100]

Given Wilde's incredibly strong antipathy to such self-serving (even tyrannical) altruism in both "A Chinese Sage" and *The Soul of Man*, it is of course possible the ending of "The Star-Child" is intended as an ironic joke to further mock the philanthropic impulse. But there just does not seem to be much if any textual evidence that Wilde's peculiar protagonist is, in his interactions with the Hare and the leper or in his transformative rule as king, replicating the dynamics of a "sentimental dole" or engaging in an "inadequate mode of partial restitution" to assuage his guilt or otherwise make himself feel better. This is a story in which pity not only is central to the plot (it is referenced eleven separate times) but further is seemingly valorized as the key to both individual virtue and social justice. As such, Wilde could be offering his own dangerous and discontented "healthy protest" against unhealthy and exaggerated altruism by endorsing instead a recursive emotional response that encourages both the shared emotional connection and the compassionate action foregrounded by Rousseau and Schopenhauer in their conceptions of pity. Here, the Star-Child's narratable journey endorses, without recourse to a trite moral or happy ending, what Wilde so boldly proclaims in *The Soul of Man*: "The proper aim is to try and reconstruct society on such a basis that poverty will be impossible."[101] Wilde decidedly shows himself to be as thorough a detractor of the charity model of pity as Nietzsche or Shapiro when he goes on to insist, "And the altruistic virtues have really prevented the carrying out of this aim."[102] It is very important, then, not to gloss over the fact that during the Star-Child's brief reign, this goal is actually fully realized ("to the poor he gave bread, and to the naked he gave raiment, and there was peace and plenty in the land"), which in and of itself is perhaps the strongest case for not casting his compassionate pity as simply another version of the ineffectual "altruistic virtues" that otherwise prevent the realization of such a utopia, in Wilde's opinion. My own reading of "The Star-Child" thus positions it as in fact powerfully reinforcing the notion that our "proper aim" should be to "reconstruct" society on such a basis that "poverty"—and the degradation and demoralization of all the marginalized bodies who are denied self-development and self-sufficiency through it—"will be impossible."

In conclusion, though its utopia may not have lasted, its disability-aligned hero nonetheless experiences an extended transformation encouraging active commitment to reciprocity and loving-kindness within interpersonal relationships, but also with an eye toward broader social change. If "The Star-Child" remains undeniably problematic in some of its messages about disability and the emotions it invokes, it also contains elements that deserve reconsideration, if not recuperation. According to Donaldson and Prendergast, "abject bodies and abject emotions can reveal the fault lines of foundational concepts of what the body should be or should do."[103] Wilde's exploration of the constellation of powerful emotional responses evoked through his enfreaked protagonist's narratable journey potentially portrays disability as an undesirable martyrdom, rather than a form of difference that need not preclude the possibility of one's leading a fulfilling life. Yet it also powerfully calls attention to the reality of prejudice against those who appear "less than" to normalized eyes, moving readers, along with the Star-Child, away from disgust and rejection, toward compassion and activism, by endorsing a form of pity that serves not merely as a counter to the aggressive egotism of charity's self-love but further as a catalyst for shared connection and public action leading to fellow feeling and social justice. One may still rightfully reject the offensive pity of the philanthropist and the sentimentalist (with its performative duty and self-righteousness rooted in superiority) while embracing the sort of emotional response that grows out of natural mutuality and generous reciprocity grounded in equality. In the end, the complexities of parsing such complicated possibilities in "The Star-Child" (and in all of the other fairy tales, for that matter) justify the importance of an earnest re-visioning of the decidedly fraught yet ever-evolving relationship between disability and the emotions.

## 4

# "You Are Blind Now...
# So I Will Stay with You Always"

### "The Happy Prince" and the Disability-Aligned
### Protagonist as Utopian Hero

"The Happy Prince" is rivaled only by "The Selfish Giant" for the honor of Wilde's most famous fairy tale, and as such it would represent a logical focus point for any argument engaging with these texts. It is a crucial story for this study in particular, though, given that it offers an even more extensive narration of ongoing activism in the name of social justice than the preceding chapter on "The Star-Child." What is more, as the book's last content chapter, it also fittingly brings us full circle, back to the introduction's initial close reading of "The Selfish Giant" within the context of devoted friendship between a larger-than-life-sized peculiar body and a small companion. In this wonderful work, we are richly afforded the opportunity to witness again how disability-aligned characters do not have to be limited to roles in which they are the unfortunate objects of charitable aid, but rather they may serve as powerful agents who actively promote and effect beneficial social change through compassionate action (and who enrich interpersonal relationships as well). "The Happy Prince" also extends our consideration of peculiar bodies beyond the figure of the freak toward more commonplace conditions such as mobility and vision impairments. At the same time, the story does (through the statue's gradual transformation from stately splendor to unsightly shabbiness) evoke the Star-Child's enfreakment and invoke the intersection of disability and class; it is, after all, a text first and foremost concerned with poverty. Still, given that its titular character opts to become blind in order for others not to starve, any sociopolitical agenda or messaging in the tale is inextricably intertwined with its literary representation of disability, a connection further solidified by the Prince's present embodiment as an immobile statue. In the end, while the story undeniably allows for the damaging suggestion that a disabled existence represents some form of martyrdom, what makes "The Happy Prince" rise above the time's more typical renderings of disability remains how it casts its exceptional protagonist in the role of a hero who is the provider rather than recipient of much-needed succor, on both an individual and a collective level.

As Mary Klages has noted, the nineteenth century saw the start of a shift in the significance of blindness, away from "suffering and dependence" toward "competence and pride."[1] Rodas has thoroughly delineated Dickens's own difficulties in responding to this trajectory, judging by his treatments of Laura Bridgman in *American Notes for General Circulation* and Bertha Plummer in *The Cricket on the Hearth*. The former is a text that seems to reinforce a sense of Dickens as mired in stereotypes when it comes to his views on disabled persons, "unable to break free from existing conventions, to reimagine disability as fully human, as having agency, as a site of potential positivity."[2] Works such as the latter, though, seem to offer instead a writer inviting his audience "to read past . . . pathos and sentimentality toward an understanding of disability as the site of a complex and powerful identity, one not to be easily appropriated, manipulated, or exploited."[3] In some respects, Bertha is an "object of charity" with "limited agency," her epithet itself (Blind Bertha) presenting "an almost absurdly sentimental trope of helpless blind femininity."[4] At the same time, though, while Dickens is "motivated in part by the desire to construct himself as a beneficent mediating agent," his attempts at authorial control, ironically, ultimately provide a "platform from which the disabled subject speaks with a voice and an authority that reject the ministrations of the mediating satellite"—here, the writer himself.[5] Significantly, in the book's last pages, Plummer is referred to simply as Bertha (instead of as Blind Bertha or the Blind Girl, as she is throughout the rest of the narrative), a concession "that the character must now be understood as being and belonging to herself instead of being and belonging to the idea of Blindness."[6]

Certainly, one might question whether Wilde's relationship to the extraordinary bodies around whom his stories revolve relies upon its own sort of satellite control through which he adopts the authorial role of "beneficent mediating agent" to unconsciously "assert his own normative identity,"[7] especially if he felt vulnerable to ridicule or rejection on account of his own physical appearance. Still, whether it be his potential parody of writers' "ministrations" in the service of the maudlin mawkishness or offensive objectification many do still find dominating Dickens's work, or his active creation of disability-aligned characters who represent dynamic identities with "a voice and an authority" to counter more paternalistic or pejorative predecessors owing to his own unrepentant nonnormative view of himself on so many different levels, Wilde in "The Happy Prince" seems dedicated to insisting upon full agency for his titular protagonist and upon positioning disability as a site of positivity and power.

The story opens with an image of the statue of the Happy Prince standing "high above the city, on a tall column."[8] It is a strikingly beautiful sight: "He was gilded all over with thin leaves of fine gold, for eyes he had two bright sapphires, and a large red ruby glowed on his sword-hilt."[9] In the second paragraph, Wilde introduces a central binary within the narrative, bringing together two concerns he already has considered within the context of mainstream society's attempts to define and delimit disability: beauty versus utility. As the first example of how "very much admired" the statue is, readers are treated to a remark by one of the Town Councillors, who observes the Prince "is as beautiful as a weathercock . . . only not quite so useful."[10] Significantly, both sides of these measures of worth and importance are equally fraught ones when contextualized within disability history. Disabled persons have endured for centuries their natural human variation serving as the basis for a dehumanization and, ultimately, an abjection that insists upon casting their difference as unsightly, as unnatural, as ungodly. They also have faced judgment not merely of their value but of their personhood itself, owing to their perceived inability to lead "independent" lives and to "contribute" to society. Traditionally, in other words, disability has been relegated to an undesirable state associated with repulsiveness and worthlessness, the very opposite of both beauty and utility, and this legacy looms large when one attempts to parse the ramifications of Wilde's representation of disability in this particular text, even as, at this stage, readers are unlikely to view the Happy Prince as disabled.

In spite of the Councillor's insinuation, the next few paragraphs suggest the statue actually does hold a truly appreciated utility for the community (even if he is not as useful as a weathercock). A "sensible mother" uses the Prince as an exemplar of her own practical orientation, asking her sobbing little boy "who was crying for the moon" why he cannot "be like the Happy Prince," as she claims the stoic statue "never dreams of crying for anything."[11] Further, a bitter man employs the Prince as a measuring stick for his own disappointment, muttering, "I am glad there is some one in the world who is quite happy," while the Charity Children (though the Mathematical Master disapproves of such fanciful thoughts) see him as the perfect match for the angels of whom they dream.[12] His utility, then, is serving as the personification of, unsurprisingly, Happiness. This happiness, though, tinged as it is with a taste of unrealistic aspirations and tainted by a message reinforcing the age-old mantra regarding the necessity of accepting one's own lot in life, rings as hollow as the statue's chest cavity that contains his leaden heart.

Enter the Swallow, who shortly will become the Prince's messenger and, eventually, his devoted friend. The bird is a bit of a poet, a dreamer who has delayed migrating south to Egypt out of love for a beautiful Reed. Having very belatedly begun this journey, he alights at the base of the statue, only to find himself subject to drops of water from above. Rather than rain, they are tears of sadness from the town's idealized symbol of pure unadulterated joy. "His face was so beautiful in the moonlight," Wilde writes, with his tears "running down his golden cheeks," that the bird becomes "filled with pity" and asks to hear his story.[13] Born thus out of pity, so begins a profound partnership that will bloom beyond the bird's original intent of expressing individual empathetic concern for another into shared compassionate succor for many others. The Prince, it turns out, really was a happy one while human, but as a statue he now realizes to his dismay that this was only because his life of luxury within the walls of "the Palace of Sans-Souci, where sorrow is not allowed to enter," led him to remain ignorant of all of the poverty and suffering surrounding him.[14] He explains, "I never cared to ask what lay beyond it, everything about me was so beautiful," but, he continues, "now that I am dead they have set me up here so high that I can see all the ugliness and all the misery of my city, and though my heart is made of lead yet I cannot choose but weep."[15] We do not know to what extent the Prince might be said to tower over the city simply owing to the tall column upon which the statue has been placed, or if he himself is now a towering figure in the form of a gigantic statue, or both, but he appears to be experiencing a reformation on the scale of that experienced by the selfish Giant, who was so moved by the plight (and, specifically, by the tears) of a special little friend.

Intriguingly, Wilde here is employing a common nineteenth-century trope regarding mobility impairments in that, as Karen Bourrier has documented, such disabilities typically were used as plot devices to reform characters.[16] Here the epiphany, in part, is simply owing to the fact the Prince is now so high up he can see all across the city, but it also is a consequence of his not being able to return to the palace, where he would theoretically be shielded from the ugliness and misery he is now forced to not just notice but live with all day and night long. In this light, there are ways in which Wilde's statue might already be positioned as disability-aligned, unable to retreat from his street view because unable to remove himself from the pedestal upon which he is forced to remain on display for all to see. Wilde's plotline regarding disablement is to a large extent still to be revealed, as it ultimately will extend to blindness, maiming, and ugliness. As already suggested from the introduction's discussion of freak shows and ugly laws, on down through the preceding chapter's documentation of the isolation, stigma, and peril faced by those whose physical appearance was deemed so disgusting it needed to be concealed or otherwise removed from sight, the cultural location of disabled people is fundamentally limited by their nondisabled peers. At this stage of the story, though, the Happy Prince occupies a highly visible, central place (literally and figuratively) in the city's civic life, suggesting the town certainly does not think of him through the lens of impairment.

Nonetheless, Wilde already has deftly deconstructed traditional conceptions of both beauty and utility through the town's suspect appropriation of the stately statue as an object lesson to buttress a status quo that perpetuates inequality, lavishing lives of privilege with a tarnished beauty at the expense of the happiness and health of the rest of society. As we saw in the last chapter, Wilde in *The Soul of Man* decried the notion that the poor (and, arguably, by extension, all lives relegated to the margins of society) should accept their lot in life and strive (if at all) to thrive only within the system as it currently exists. Wilde, contra Andersen and so many other writers, instead praises those who are "ungrateful, discontented, disobedient, and rebellious" in the face of not just inequity but the very real threat of starvation.[17] It is fitting, then, given the aforementioned role of these traditional conceptions of beauty and utility in underpinning long-standing pejorative responses to disability, that this moment provides the pivot for the tale's clear-cut integration of disability into the narrative, a move that will reveal the extent to which the Happy Prince is able to free himself from the exploitation he has been subject to as a motionless monument to the middle-class morality that most fundamentally serves the interests of the rich and powerful.

The Prince wishes to alleviate the suffering he now sees in his city (a wish that, ironically, will soon lead to him no longer being able to see said suffering, or anything else, for that matter), and his attention has fixed first upon "a poor house" where an oppressed seamstress with a "thin and worn" face and "coarse, red hands, all pricked by the needle"[18] is frantically trying to finish "embroidering passion-flowers on a satin gown for the loveliest of the Queen's maids-of-honour to wear at the next Court-ball."[19] The woman's face and hands reveal the debilitating effects of her working conditions and her poverty, and accordingly serve as reminders of how both may lead in time to disability and death. She subjects herself to terrible pain in order to provide pleasure for those who know nothing of her sacrifice and, even more compellingly to the Prince, she lives with a sick child: "her little boy is lying ill" with "a fever, and is asking for oranges," but she "has nothing to give him but river water, so he is crying."[20] The child's tears link the little boy's sadness with the Happy Prince's own newfound sorrow regarding the pain and suffering so many marginalized lives are made to endure owing to generally being considered so unworthy—so unattractive and so useless—that their hardships are not important enough to be noticed.

His new insights into the plight of the poor engender within his leaden heart the selfsame pity that his own tears had provoked for the Swallow, and, notably, this emotion leads both of Wilde's heroes in this story to compassionate action based not on the performative self-righteousness of charity but rather on genuine fellow feeling. While the townspeople we heard from at the opening of the story would seem to prefer the Prince remain the poster boy for what they see as the appropriate response to difficulty and duress (breeding a whole brood of Tiny Tims, cheerful and patient in spite of their devalued and discarded lives), Wilde instead employs the figure of a sickly small child whose tears may recall those of the Giant's special little friend, evoking the Christ-child as disabled God, whose suffering (below the tree and up on the cross) is not to be airbrushed away (as his stigmata signal) but acknowledged as a sign of strength.

Fascinatingly, disability-aligned difference is also intriguingly invoked here toward similar ends by the Prince's previously mentioned predicament as a stationary statue. He wants to supply the seamstress with "the ruby out of [his] sword-hilt," but he needs the bird's help because, as he notes, "my feet are fastened to this pedestal and I cannot move."[21] Since statues as a general rule do not move, it is admittedly a little tenuous to suggest the Happy Prince might serve as a stand-in for someone with a mobility impairment. Still, statues technically do not talk or see, either, yet he does. This is a fantastical fairy tale, after all, not a realistic rendering, so what seems most salient here is that the Prince used to be able to walk and run about but now no longer can, and his current lack of mobility is what is preventing him from engaging in a particular action (namely, going to the poor house himself to give the seamstress his ruby). Thus, while Wilde confronts readers with the regular role poverty plays in the onset and aggravation of illness and injury, he also subtly but significantly allows one to position his would-be benefactor of the poor as disabled, even before he parts with his sapphire eyes and becomes blind.

On the one hand, this typically overlooked aspect of the story may seem merely to reinforce the age-old association of disability with dependency, as the Happy Prince's impairment (his lack of mobility) causes him to need the Swallow's help in the first place, just as his imminent blindness ends up motivating the Swallow's eventual decision to stay with him. But if in fact the Prince is already disabled before he embarks upon his mission to remedy the suffering he sees, this allows one to assign a more agential role to Wilde's disability-aligned hero. This would then mitigate the effect of otherwise understanding disability as an unfortunate consequence of his charitable selflessness, as a sacrifice he must make to right the wrongs of his previous obliviousness to ugliness and misery. That is, if we may posit the Prince as disabled even before his later blindness and his shabbiness, disability is less easily perceived as problematically only relegated to a pejorative state (a once nondisabled character now reduced to his own miserable and, eventually, ugly existence through some sort of masochistic impulse involving maiming). Instead, Wilde's statue represents a dynamic character who, like both the literally stigmatized Christ-child and the enfreaked Star-Child, is not relegated to a passive dependence by any markers of disability-aligned difference but who instead shows how disabled people (no matter the scale of their bodies or the scope of their lives) may serve as actants of change, as providers of aid to others. In this way—regardless of whether or not he can move on his own or, later, see—the Happy Prince is not limited to the role of helpless recipient but rather takes on the empowering mantle of active benefactor.

The Swallow, though, hesitates to do his part, arguably with answers in which intriguingly he first appeals to beauty and then to utility. He initially replies, "I am waited for in Egypt," and proceeds to offer a brief but poetic account of the exotic decadence awaiting him there.[22] After the Prince renews his appeal, the Swallow offers a more pragmatic reason why he should decline to go on the statue's errand: "I don't think I like boys. . . . [because they are] always throwing stones at me."[23] Eventually, though, the bird relents, opting to place the needs of others before his own personal pleasure and practical concerns, and he flies with the Prince's ruby past the cathedral and the palace (two entities that have failed in their responsibility toward the poor—the latter, in particular, it would seem, as he hears "the sound of dancing" there in spite of the people's suffering).[24] In fact, just then, the beautiful maid-of-honour steps out onto a balcony with her lover, effusing about the wonders of love and of the stars, only to end by selfishly complaining about how "lazy" seamstresses are.[25]

The poor house lies across the river, beyond the Jewish Ghetto, which Wilde disturbingly decides to highlight not as a site of segregation, or even simply of community, but rather as a place characterized by "bargaining" and "weighing out money in copper scales."[26] Although these comments are contained within only a single sentence, they nonetheless stand as a stark reminder that any claims for more expansive and sympathetic understanding of the poor and other marginalized members of society such as disabled persons need be qualified by an acknowledgment of the text's regressive elements (here, of reprehensible stereotyping). The description sadly is not the only instance of such prejudice in Wilde's writings—witness his offensive characterization of Mr. Isaacs, the Jewish theatre manager, in *The Picture of Dorian Gray*, or his upsetting claim in *The Soul of Man* not only that enslaved people in America never expressed a desire to be free before the Abolitionist movement but further that after the war "many of them bitterly regretted the new state of things" upon discovering that their freedom merely meant they "were free to starve."[27] Thus, it is essential to point out the hypocrisy of Wilde (without any apparent concern about Jewish lives or commitment to alleviating Jewish suffering) sending his messenger bird to pass over an area of confinement and discrimination historically home to some profound poverty as a result of the ethnically and religiously based hatred that required such segregation.

Having thus passed over the Ghetto with his shallow if not willful ignorance intact, the Swallow alights at the house to find the boy "tossing feverishly" and the seamstress collapsed into sleep out of exhaustion.[28] He deposits the gem and then flies around the sick boy's bed to fan his forehead with his wings (in a gesture reminiscent of the Birds' friendly attentions to the Dwarf in "The Birthday of the Infanta"). Upon returning to the Prince, the little bird observes, "It is curious, ... but I feel quite warm now, although it is so cold," to which the statue replies, "That is because you have done a good action."[29] Together, they have not simply been saddened by and empathized with the plight of the poor but have provided succor through compassionate "good action." Over the next couple of days, the Swallow continues to invoke through lovely poetic lines the warmth and beauty awaiting him in Egypt, but each time finds himself unable to deny the Happy Prince's efforts to direct his attention more to the needs of others than to his own agenda, aiding first a starving student-playwright and then a destitute and abused little match girl, by plucking out both of his rare sapphire eyes for their use. When the Prince at last tells the Swallow he must now fly south before it is too late, the bird refuses, answering, "You are blind now, ... so I will stay with you always."[30]

This scene is another potentially troubling one for any disability studies approach, particularly if it implies in any way that the Swallow's pity toward the sapphire-less statue is based upon a view of the Happy Prince as now nothing but a pathetic object of charity himself. Readers surely experience discomfort over his self-maiming. Further, his blindness in and of itself (the maiming aside), for Victorian readers at least, likely leads to disfiguring views of his person, born out of disgust. After all, as Huff and Stoddard Holmes document, in the nineteenth century, blind persons were stigmatized not just for being sightless but also for being unsightly, and thus they were deemed "unfit to mingle in society," even denigrated as a "separate race of beings"; further, blindness was seen as prohibiting the "full and harmonious development of character."[31] The Swallow's initial pitying response to the Prince's tears certainly can suggest to some that his sudden insistence he will stay with the statue because he has become blind is born out of a sentimental assumption of the role of mediating agent, insisting the Happy

Prince needs company or help now that he no longer can see and thus that it is the bird's obligation or duty to stay as a result. If so, then it may not really matter that the statue's sacrifice comes from the most admirable of motives, if it entails readers will view his blindness through the lens of martyrdom. Wilde, in other words, risks repositioning his active benefactor as a helpless dependent by representing disability as a form of difference cast solely as an unfortunate identity when conceived of through the charity/tragedy model.

The Swallow's subsequent interactions with the Prince, though, seem far from simply obligatory but instead demonstrative of profound personal attachment. Rather than minimal caretaking duties, the bird is bent on offering captivating companionship. Perhaps not surprisingly from a character associated with the figures of both the true lover and the decadent poet, the Swallow attends to his friend by regaling him with exotic tales reminiscent of the stories with which the young Fisherman's Soul tries to tempt him away from the little Mermaid. On the one hand, these narratives effectively evoke the worlds of enchantment and wonder Wilde associates with freakery and its unusual bodies by admiringly cataloging a curiousness mated to marvel, painting in a positive light the attractions of these domains of difference and their varied denizens. Still, as the previous passage mentioning the Ghetto should remind all readers, such accounts also potentially hold within them, whether or not unintentionally, a danger of employing an exoticism tinged with its own prejudicial overtones (here, of orientalism). "All the next day," Wilde writes, the Swallow "sat on the Prince's shoulder, and told him stories of what he had seen in strange lands."[32] He recounts multiple things that blur the boundaries between human and nonhuman animals in ways that portray non-Western peoples through the lens of some sort of primitive bestiality. The Swallow sings to him of the Sphinx and of "the King of the Mountains of the Moon, who is as black as ebony, and worships a large crystal,"[33] but also of "the pygmies who sail over a big lake on large flat leaves, and are always at war with the butterflies."[34] Such portrayals, so suspect when framed by the Soul's ulterior motives, should equally be acknowledged as problematic in their potential xenophobic orientation, even as others might instead laud them for painting difference in a positive, even celebratory light.

Wilde's main point here, however, seems to fall more in line with a critique of the limitations, even failings, of such an exclusively aestheticized orientation. Significantly, the Prince responds by saying, "Dear little

Swallow, . . . you tell me of marvellous things, but more marvellous than anything is the suffering of men and of women. There is no Mystery so great as Misery. Fly over my city, little Swallow, and tell me what you see there."[35] This exchange is crucial in a couple of ways. First, it reestablishes that even though the Happy Prince is now blind, he does not see himself in a dependent position; indeed, he reasserts his role as benefactor, as an active administrator of aid and agent of change. Second, it furthers Wilde's deconstruction of standard notions of beauty and understandings of utility. Indeed, as already noted, many of the fairy tales work together to undermine the gospel of beauty one finds proselytized elsewhere in his oeuvre. This alternative take on the attractions of aestheticism exposes the exploitation upon which luxury and extravagance rely. Straley notes "a conflict between art and ethics" in the story,[36] a tension that Tatar's identification of "two competing regimes," of beauty and suffering, also invokes.[37] While the Swallow may wish to fill the statue's world with wonder, self-indulgent quiescence is as insufficient as the statue's sheltered former existence. Indeed, for Zipes, the Prince "overcomes an art for art's sake position and thereby reveals the social essence of all beauty."[38] Refusing to merely remain some sort of Andersenian monument to the necessity of coming to terms with an unjust society by ultimately accepting and adjusting to the terms and conditions that support the status quo, Wilde's statue shifts reader interest toward boldly embodying the necessity of working to alleviate suffering and inequality with the goal of discovering new social relations that would make injustices such as poverty impossible.

Given the genre within which Wilde has chosen to work, it is not surprising to find his tale awash in the marvelous (even as it insists upon attending to the Mystery of Misery). As Kathryn A. Hoffmann asserts, "there is a marvel that lives in the spaces of connection among fairy tales, fairgrounds, cabinets of curiosities, and medical literature. It crosses limits and melds bodies, makes the boundaries among disciplines unstable, and draws bodies, objects, and tales about them into a web of connections."[39] For Hoffmann, "Marvel is what links pumpkins and carriages, literature and medicine, tales and cabinets, streets and courts,"[40] and accordingly, explorations of literary marvel attuned to "that mix of threads—where anomalous bodies became tellable, collectible, and commercial—" are equally essential to the discovery of "both new directions and new problems."[41] Such an attunement might just allow for the very sort of moment that Vivian, Wilde's spokesperson in "The Decay of Lying," imagines with such anticipation, when "Facts will be regarded as discreditable . . . and Romance, with her temper of wonder, will return to the land."[42] Notably, Vivian's utopia is envisioned as a glorious celebration of extraordinary bodies: "Out of the sea will rise Behemoth and Leviathan. . . . Dragons will wander about the waste places, and the phoenix will soar from her nest of fire into the air. We shall lay our hands upon the basilisk. . . . the Hippogriff will stand in our stalls, and over our heads will float the Blue Bird singing of beautiful and impossible things, of things that are lovely and that never happen, of things that are not and that should be."[43] As Wilde writes in his own voice in *The Soul of Man*, "a map of the world that does not include Utopia is not worth even glancing at. . . . Progress is the realization of Utopias."[44]

Significantly, though, Wilde is interested in giving us neither a classic love story set within the confines of some royal palace nor a travel adventure set in an exotic land. Instead, he insists (through his disability-aligned spokesstatue) that readers continue to confront the pain and sorrow of poverty. For him, marvel and wonder work hand in hand with compassionate action to bring our world closer to the utopian dream of an equal society. So, in response to the Prince's request that the Swallow survey anew the suffering surrounding them, the bird flies all over the city, observing "the rich making merry in their beautiful houses, while the beggars were sitting at the gates."[45] He even ventures "into dark lanes," where he discovers "white faces of starving children looking out listlessly at the black streets."[46] As a testament to the Swallow's own transformation, Wilde redeems the bird's earlier self-concern stemming from the two rude boys who had harried him with rocks, by having him now with sympathetic eyes bear witness to "two little boys [who] were lying in one another's arms to try to keep themselves warm" and suffering from hunger, only to be chased out from "under the archway of a bridge" and into the rain by the city's Watchman.[47] What is precisely so striking about Wilde's deployment of marvel is his attempt to marry it to materiality (even more so than to magic), to the all-too-real misery of so many destitute lives—including how such impoverishment can lead to deteriorating health and other disabling conditions. Wilde's world is indeed a fantastical one, where a dead prince literally lives on in statue form and thereby is afforded the opportunity to atone for his previous beautiful life of blind entitlement (not to mention his best friend is a talking bird), but it also is a world where the very real destitution upon which the luxurious lives of the rich depend is clearly exposed.

Upon hearing the Swallow's report confirming the sad reality of the marvelous Mystery that is human Misery throughout his city, Wilde's blind and immobile hero determines that further compassionate action is required. "I am covered with fine gold," he tells his friend, "you must take it off, leaf by leaf, and give it to my poor."[48] The first-person possessive pronoun adds to the tale's complicated presentation of disability, as it potentially positions the Prince as a superior savior whose motivation stems from an aristocratic noblesse oblige toward perceived pathetic inferiors. At the same time, it also offers readers the option of understanding it as an indication of affiliation, an affirmation of shared identification, even mutual concern. Hollander offers a generative approach to this development as a form of divestment, an "uncloth[ing]" from the "spoils of empire": "Wilde's Happy Prince can only become happy by deconstructing the appearance of happiness—namely, his rich decoration."[49] His beautiful and happy appearance, after all, is precisely what the Town Councillors and citizens use to appropriate and manipulate the Prince into a symbol of the importance of accepting one's lot in life. Even though the new unattractive look leads to the devaluation and ultimately to the destruction of the statue (as it is no longer useful to their agenda of preserving the status quo), it also frees him from the mediating narratives of his anything but well-intentioned satellite controllers.

Regardless, the bird obliges his royal friend's request: "Leaf after leaf of the fine gold the Swallow picked off, till the Happy Prince looked quite dull and grey. Leaf after leaf of the fine gold he brought to the poor, and the children's faces grew rosier, and they laughed and played games in the street. 'We have bread now!' they cried."[50] With this, Wilde further deconstructs the traditional conception of beauty, for without the gold leaf and jewels the statue is no longer resplendent (indeed, now rather quite shabby-looking), but his own transformation artfully has created another in the opposite direction, with the wan "white faces of starving children looking out listlessly" now replaced by children's rosy, laughing faces. With want's sorrow abated, at least for the time being, the work of Wilde's dynamic duo is done, which is particularly lucky for the poor, as winter soon arrives in full force. To the cold is added snow and frost, and tragically, before long, it is too much for the little bird's body to take any longer. In this, Wilde has plotted another inversion of sorts. The dark lanes and black streets have been transformed into thoroughfares that "looked as if they were made of silver, they were so bright and glistening"; more importantly, instead of freezing and hungry children huddled under bridges, "everybody went about in furs, and the little boys wore scarlet caps and skated on the ice."[51] The Swallow, however, once a carefree, decadent dreamer-lover-poet figure, is reduced to the plight of the beggars he had told the statue about, "pick[ing] up crumbs outside the baker's door" and trying "to keep himself warm by flapping his wings."[52]

Eventually, on the point of dying, he "had just strength to fly up to the Prince's shoulder once more" to say goodbye and to request the favor of kissing his hand.[53] The Prince's reply is a significant one, on a number of levels: "you must kiss me on the lips, for I love you."[54] The Swallow does so, only to immediately "[fall] down dead at his feet."[55] Among other things, this shared kiss solidifies how the Swallow's work distributing the statue's finery to the poor and his decision to keep his blind friend company in spite of the dangerous consequences for his own health are motivated by mutual love rather than performative duty. Their intimacy is confirmed by a kiss on the lips rather than merely on the hand. Their final scene together also suggests that this same dynamic informs the pair's response to the poor. In other words, where both poverty and disability are concerned, it is not the charity/tragedy model driving the donations of gems and gold. The Prince and the Swallow devote their friendship to responding to the Mystery of human Misery through compassionate acts of succor demonstrative of true emotional connection. They care about, not just for, the people whose lives they improve, and the aforementioned trajectories of transformation reinforce the ideas of mutuality and reciprocity emphasized in "The Star-Child," blurring boundaries between those in need of pity and those willing and able to supply it. This, then, falls in line very nicely with Zipes's view of the whole collection as Wilde's apt attempt "at altering classical fairy-tale discourse and at provoking readers to contemplate social change."[56]

Still, even if one chooses to cast the pair's efforts to help the poor as rising above the sort of standard sentimental charitable responses, is it still not questionable to what extent their success merely serves as some sort of temporary Band-Aid, not some sort of permanent improvement in the poor's lot? Given the plot developments immediately following the kiss, this certainly seems a valid concern, for the Mayor and the Town Councillors (the official representatives of the unjust sociopolitical system in need of change) appear not only oblivious to the pair's mission but completely unaffected in their attitudes. Early the next morning, they express disdain for "how shabby the Happy Prince looks": "The ruby has fallen out of his sword, his eyes are gone, and he is golden no longer . . . in fact, he is little better than a beggar."[57] Their disgust is only compounded by finding "a dead bird at his feet," so they immediately set about having the statue pulled down and melted in a furnace, with the approval of the Art Professor at the University, who matter-of-factly asserts, "As he is no longer beautiful he is no longer useful."[58] At the same time, though, very few (if any) readers find themselves in agreement with the academic and the politicians, so their stance hardly seems like some sort of litmus test for how efficacious we view this attempt to render poverty impossible.

As with the Swallow shortly before his death, the Prince is presented as having undergone his own dramatic reversal in fortune. Once the epitome of the privileged few who lived carefree lives blind to the misery of others that enables their ease and luxury, the statue finds himself reduced to the status of a beggar. The poor he has aided, meanwhile, at least temporarily, again, seem to be included among the "everybody" who are going about in furs through streets glistening like silver, and in this sense, readers understand how ironically erroneous the remarks of the Art Professor are, for the true beauty of the statue's shabbiness is that it has served a most useful purpose, indeed—a democratization of happiness and health. What is more, the Swallow too in this scene arguably has become inscribed as an ugly, useless, peculiar body in his own right after his decaying remains are discarded as worthless trash, in the end potentially joining his partner, the Happy Prince, as a disability-aligned protagonist. Indeed, for some he may already have been at least (by virtue of his size and the Prince's propensity to address him as "little Swallow") associated with Wilde's other diminutive disability-aligned characters: the Christ-child, the Dwarf, the little Mermaid, and the Star-Child.

Through such resonances, Wilde powerfully portrays the peril ultimately faced not just by the poor but also in particular by all the different bodies devalued in a world where wholeness, utility, and vitality are so privileged. Even as society may not actually have been reconstructed by their efforts, the aforementioned reversals nonetheless suggest that, on some level at least, such a utopian transformation is possible. The statue, once a living embodiment of the "beautiful life" and then a utilitarian reminder of remaining content with one's lot, now through its dull and drab appearance actually displays (to readers, but also potentially to the poor residents, if not the town officials) the very real possibilities of both individual succor and social change, in spite of the fact those in power will not leave it standing in its transformed state. Instead, then, of viewing the pair's compassionate actions as completely useless, as merely beautiful but ineffective gestures, there might also (or, instead?) be a lesson for those who have ears to hear (if not eyes to see) about the essential role of pity and love (rather than charity or duty) in changing marginalized lives for the better, in the here and now, on both personal and collective levels.

It should not surprise us, perhaps, if the Prince's plan might seem to some merely a charming sentiment that is decidedly impractical and thoroughly ineffectual. After all, Wilde anticipates a similar response to his own theorization of the utopian transformation within the very soul of humanity itself, which he insists inevitably would take place under the sort of anarchic individualistic socialism he espouses in *The Soul of Man*. To the objection that any such scheme "is quite unpractical, and goes against human nature," Wilde acknowledges this is in fact "perfectly true," but he follows this admission by asserting, "This is why it is worth carrying out, and that is why one proposes it."[59] "For what is a practical scheme?" he continues. "A practical scheme is either a scheme that is already in existence, or a scheme that could be carried out under existing conditions. But it is exactly the existing conditions that one objects to; and any scheme that could accept these conditions is wrong and foolish."[60] In this, Wilde seems to deconstruct the very binary between the theoretical and the practical itself, allowing fancy and marvel to remain as part of both the philosophical core of his utopian sociopolitical agenda and the actual means of carrying out said agenda through "Lying in Art,"[61] through his own Chuang Tsŭ-inspired "charming" storytelling.

Indeed, those who limit themselves to literal interpretations and practical possibilities are the very readers who are the object of the narrator's deadpan dismissal for overlooking the role of love in the denouement set in motion by the kiss between Wilde's peculiar protagonists. As soon as their lips meet, the Swallow expires, and we are told, "at that moment a curious crack sounded inside the statue, as if something had broken. The fact is that the leaden heart had snapped right in two. It certainly was a dreadfully hard frost."[62] Genuine heartbreak over his partner's demise—owing to their devoted friendship and, yes, true love, not extremely cold temperatures—is, however curiously, actually behind the "broken lead heart" that "will not melt in the furnace" with the rest of the statue and thus is thrown onto the same "dust-heap" where they had disposed of the dead bird.[63] Such compassionate devotion also arguably informs their succor for the poor and, accordingly, offers a model as to how readers might themselves respond to the immobile, blind, shabby Prince and the discarded little Swallow, whose miserable end from hunger and cold matches the fate their good deeds helped others avoid. Thus, though the Mayor and the Town Councillors destroy the statue when they notice it is no longer beautiful, Wilde ends the story with God's declaration that the dead bird's body and the Happy Prince's broken lead heart are "the two most precious things in the city,"[64] a direct divine disputation of the narrow views on beauty and usefulness held by the pragmatic politicians and the pompous professor, a refusal to allow the status quo to stand (as in, say, Andersen).

Markey does not provide any specific precursor texts by Andersen that Wilde is consciously revisiting and revisioning through "The Happy Prince," but she offers Dinah Mulock Craik's *The Little Lame Prince*[65] as one potential source he is bent on refracting, claiming he "eschews Craik's conventional happy ending where virtuous compassion is rewarded in this life."[66] It is still fair, of course, to question if Wilde intended his ending to inspire touching tears akin to those shed by the Prince in the story's opening pages or if he instead was inviting readers to glibly dismiss it as the very sort of maudlin sentimentality he himself spoofed elsewhere. The conclusion, after all, has its troubling aspects. For one, the consolation offered readers for the deaths of Wilde's two utopian dreamers is that God, at least, recognizes and appreciates their efforts. But is this not in fact yet another deferral of justice, to the afterlife? And what if one is not an adherent of the Christian faith, or is someone for whom the very concept of God, much less an anthropomorphic one, is as marvelously unrealistic as living statues and talking birds? Wilde's deus ex machina maneuver to close out his tale (which to some extent we also see in "The Selfish Giant" and "The Fisherman and His Soul") holds some hefty hesitations specifically for a disability studies approach as well. Without the religious framework, the fairy tale reads more as a tragedy than a triumph—especially since, even if one accepts the conclusion's Christian consolation, the ending still holds the potential to reinforce the pervasive nondisabled view of the disabled as "special" messengers from God. Obviously, a different outcome in which poverty itself is erased and in which nonnormative bodies can live long, fulfilling, and valued lives may not have been a particularly realistic option, but fairy tales are far from realist narratives, and so it is more than fair to wish Wilde might have been able to move beyond such a failure to envision for his peculiar protagonists anything but the sort of grim imagined futures Alison Kafer decries as not just profoundly disappointing and damaging but, further, actually inaccurate.[67] This significant concern must be reckoned with rather than dismissed.

Still, Christina Scheuer, building off of the work of Jahan Ramazani, does offer one way to at least somewhat offset the disappointment readers understandably may register at the ultimate excision of all of Wilde's exceptional bodies, insisting as she does that texts which refuse the sort of endings requiring "a 'cure' or consolation for grief" are fundamentally "anti-ableist" in their resistance to such cooptation.[68] Wilde decidedly has shown himself to be averse to the closure of traditional "happily ever after" conclusions, just as he seems absolutely uninterested in maudlin maneuvering to push pathetic pity on minds that do not wish to be disturbed with the very real devastating consequences of inequality. In the end, Wilde's fairy tales provide an impressive preponderance of progressive elements, far more than one might expect from a Victorian writer but also plenty even in comparison to many literary representations of disability being produced today. Their depictions of devoted friends and winning lovers, compassionate community members and dedicated agents of social change, while not outweighing all of the above concerns, nonetheless may be parlayed into offering a genuine opportunity to answer Hingston's question ("Who or what am I in relation to this character?") in the affirmative, finally recognizing ourselves, maybe even the best of ourselves, in Wilde's proud parade of disability-aligned protagonists.

"The Happy Prince" suggests how compassionate action can transform individual lives and begin the process of remedying social injustice—while also showcasing disability-aligned bodies making a difference as active benefactors with a platform and the means to succeed. With its ending's endorsement of the shabby blind immobile statue and the dead ugly useless bird, Wilde also allows for readers to reject the popular view of disability as some sort of divine punishment or unnatural flaw. While on its surface "The Happy Prince" may seem to fit in with the standard sentimental framework of the genre, those who dig deeper past the pathos may find the sort of unconventional approach Rodas wishes Dickens would decide upon, a reimagining of disability "as the site of a complex and powerful identity" and therefore "as a site of potential positivity." Wilde's strong condemnation of the status quo, and of the selfishness and privilege that perpetuate it, problematizes any simplistic reduction of the text to some sort of mawkish moral. In its own way, "The Happy Prince" pushes readers to move beyond mere awareness or even just acceptance toward actual appreciation and affirmation of the peculiar bodies Wilde himself champions across the whole of his fairy tales.

The arc of finishing up the main section of the book focusing on "The Star-Child" and "The Happy Prince" (with their arguably more progressive portrayals of purposeful commitment to a utopian future in which poverty—and all forms of prejudice, including ableism—would become impossible) is, of course, an admittedly artificial one. It, for some, might even smack of the willful illusions of an academic who needs the neatness of a tidy trajectory and some comforting closure, or who wants his literary hero to come across in a positive light (a Victorian version of the Romantic Ideology Jerome J. McGann has been warning us all against for decades now). Then again, I have taken pains from the beginning to stress Wilde's slipperiness as a writer and to stress the difficulty of not just determining his intentions but even simply deciding on a clear, much less definitive, answer where his emphases and his tone are concerned. Wilde's fairy tales are indeed complex conundrums that are beautifully bewildering and opulently opaque, and I have tried to respect that throughout—both by presenting differing options for how one might assess his literary representations of disability and by at times privileging the positing of questions over a decisive delineation of textual truths (which, as Oscar would remind us, are rarely pure and never simple). One thing I do feel confident in assuredly asserting, however, is that the issues and concerns Wilde explores in his fairy tales continue to interest him for the rest of his life, in particular during and after his time in prison, which, as I will show in the conclusion, he experiences as a form of enfreakment and enfoolment which only intensifies his attunement to disability-aligned difference.

CONCLUSION

# "We Are the Zanies of Sorrow"

### Reflections and Refractions in Wilde's Prison Literature

Early on in the long prison letter "Epistola" (now commonly referred to as *De Profundis*), which he wrote during a few of his final months at Reading Gaol, Oscar Wilde recounts a particularly damning moment from his tumultuous relationship with Lord Alfred Douglas. Douglas had come down with a severe case of influenza the first night of their stay at the Grand Hotel in Brighton, so Wilde "tended" to him with "affection, tenderness and love."[1] When Wilde in turn fell ill, however, Douglas left him "entirely alone without care" for days, and when Wilde wrote to remind him of his delinquency, Douglas suddenly showed up to rail "with every hideous word" at what he claimed was Wilde's "selfishness" in sending the note.[2] According to Wilde, such a response originated in "the terrible alchemy of egotism," perversely turning Douglas's "remorse into rage."[3] The next morning, Douglas repeated the scene until, "with brutality of laughter and hysteria of rage," he "moved suddenly towards" Wilde in a threatening manner, frightening the latter enough he felt he needed to flee the room.[4] Wilde then heard nothing for three days, until a letter arrived taunting him for his "ugly moment" in bolting from his sickbed and concluding, "When you are not on your pedestal you are not interesting. The next time you are ill I will go away at once."[5]

Later on in "Epistola," Wilde insists, "I don't regret for a single moment having lived for pleasure," but confesses, "My only mistake was that I confined myself so exclusively to the . . . sun-lit side of the garden."[6] He lists "failure, disgrace, poverty, sorrow, despair, suffering, tears even, the broken words that come from the lips of pain, remorse that makes one walk on thorns, conscience that condemns, self-abasement that punishes, the misery that puts ashes on its head, the anguish that chooses sackcloth for its raiment and into its own drink puts gall" as "things of which [he] was afraid" and "had determined to know nothing of."[7] His prison experience, however, agonizingly but also indispensably taught him how "the other half of the garden had its secrets" worth knowing.[8] Intriguingly, Wilde goes on to claim, "all this is foreshadowed and prefigured in my books," and the first work he mentions as proof of this is "The Happy Prince."[9] Indeed, although typically slotted by critics into completely different categories, the fairy tales and "Epistola" in fact share thematic concerns, tonal qualities, and even some similar language—all of which suggest the value of reading Wilde's last writings through the lens of his earlier engagements with the world of "poverty, sorrow, despair, suffering, tears even" that he published as fairy tales in spite of his fears regarding such things.

While Wilde already was a bona fide celebrity, the appearance in May 1888 of *The Happy Prince and Other Tales* constituted his first true literary triumph and launched his full reign as a real-life Prince of Pleasure. But in May 1895, his conviction for crimes of gross indecency, carrying with it a two-year sentence to hard labor, brought him crashing down from his pedestal of success and laid him far lower than the flu ever could, most seeing the years remaining to him as the pathetic pageant of a broken man of sorrows, all too well acquainted with grief. In his fairy tales, Wilde had proven himself a sympathetic champion of numerous nonnormative bodies, particularly those whose plights were compounded by the pain and suffering of marginalization and poverty. In penning these stories, he might seem a version of his own stately statue, placed on a pedestal of privilege but using his platform to push for sympathetic individual understanding and beneficial broader change. Yet to whatever extent this may have been motivated by a sense of himself, of his body, as markedly different (whether owing to his nationality, his sexuality, or just his larger stature and unusual features), the arc of his life from prison onwards dramatically shifted his status from friend of the freaks to fellow outcast.

Perhaps no single moment more captures the personal cost of his own Prince-like transformation from shiny success to shabby shame than his humiliation on the Clapham Junction train platform while being transferred to Reading. Standing "in convict dress, and handcuffed, for the world to look at,"¹⁰ Wilde recalls, he found himself "surrounded by a jeering mob," on display as an object of disgust and ridicule for thirty minutes.¹¹ Formerly accustomed to reveling with delight in the applause showered upon his plays by adoring audiences, he is devastated by the comic contrast this public spectacle presents as he feels trotted out as sport for the entertainment of the crowds. Notably, Wilde employs first-person plural here to emphasize how the incident speaks to the shared lived experience of all prisoners, not just his own: "our very dress makes us grotesque. We are the zanies of sorrow. We are clowns whose hearts are broken. We are specially designed to appeal to the sense of humour."¹² The scene cannot help but call to mind "The Birthday of the Infanta," with Wilde—describing himself as a clown who was made to be laughed at and who has suffered a broken heart—in a position akin to that of his Dwarf (while also evoking his other brokenhearted disability-aligned protagonists, the young Fisherman and the Happy Prince).

His adoption of the label "zanies," though, suggests Wilde feels broken in mind or spirit as well. "For a year after that was done to me," Wilde relates, "I wept every day at the same hour and for the same space of time."¹³ Eventually, however, he comes "to feel more regret for the people who laughed than for [him]self": "Of course when they saw me I was not on my pedestal, I was in the pillory. But it is a very unimaginative nature that only cares for people on their pedestals," adding, "They should have known also how to interpret sorrow better," for "to mock at a soul in pain is a dreadful thing," and "unbeautiful are their lives who do it."¹⁴ Wilde had experienced derision as a freak from the press before, of course, particularly while in America, but this far more visceral in-person experience of shaming and taunting invited by his physical appearance powerfully stages his ongoing repositioning since the trials from princely pedestal to perverse pillory and fool's parade, a repositioning that again hearkens back to his earlier championing of peculiar bodies in the fairy tales.

Anthony Giffone (in a sketch that may be applied both to Wilde's disability-aligned protagonists from the fairy tales and his real-life confraternity of convicts) situates the Sleary Circus from Dickens's *Hard Times* within the tradition of fools and jesters. As Giffone notes, "the circus members are physically marginalized by deformity" as well as "socially marginalized by their position on the outskirts of town."¹⁵ He reads both Mr. E. W. B. Childers, whom Dickens portrays with limbs "shorter than legs of good proportions," and Master Kidderminster, his "diminutive boy with an old face," as at the very least evocative of some dwarfs.[16] He also mentions Sissy Jupe's father, a clown whose stiff joints from age and injuries require the medicinal nine oils he sends her out for when he absconds with his dog, Merrylegs. Even the integration of horses and dogs as part of the circus family—along with acts like Childers's Huntsman, called by Dickens a "most remarkable sort of Centaur, compounded of the stable and the playhouse"[17]—contributes to the subversion of binaries (male/female, child/adult, human/animal, etc.) that, Giffone notes, historically has been attributed to fools (a subversion, Fiedler insists, applies to the freak tradition as well).

Giffone's focus is productively complemented by Sena Jeter Naslund, who casts Mr. Sleary (the ringleader of Dickens's family of freaks and fools) as a disability-aligned hero in his own right. Sleary's speech impediment, owing to being "troubled with asthma," and his "one fixed eye and one loose eye"[18] render him both aurally and visually exceptional. Yet, according to Naslund, Sleary is nevertheless "the most whole character of a novel strikingly concerned with the question of how we achieve wholeness and interconnectedness in ourselves and in society."[19] She affirms his "centrality to the vison of the novel," to its insistence "the imagination makes it possible to identify with other people . . . and thus to sympathize with them."[20] Powerfully, this is in part accomplished by requiring readers to enact a compelling sort of identification with Sleary as they attempt to translate his asthmatic lisp: "Dickens insures that Sleary's words will not be recognized merely visually," and as they sound out what they see, readers must "speak like Sleary" to "grasp the meaning."[21] Also significantly, as Naslund points out, Sleary's "Ring stands for a kind of brotherhood, a circle of responsiveness to the needs and pain of individuals,"[22] a "human circle of kindness" that is "not a tit-for-tat sort of kindness" but an open responsiveness that shifts wherever necessary as "his moving eye takes [Sleary] to the person in need."[23] In this, Sleary's Ring represents the very opposite of the sort of circle Wilde found himself surrounded by at Clapham; if anything, it more closely resembles the ring in the jailyard where the prisoners tramp together in commiseration and community, an experience which Wilde characterizes (despite their enforced silence) as fundamentally embodying the kindness and responsiveness he advocated for in his fairy tales through his disability-aligned characters.

Dickens's ringmaster offers a number of observations readers may organize under the head of the Sleary Philosophy as a winning alternative to the literally exploded, bankrupt Gradgrind Philosophy with its cold, hard utilitarian emphasis on Facts alone (to the exclusion of Fancy and Feelings alike). The Sleary Philosophy arguably prevails as the novel's privileged perspective, a more balanced vision from the man with the asymmetrical eyes, clearly articulated and persuasively presented by the man with the hard-to-follow speech impediment. One of Sleary's beliefs is that "people mutht be amuthed."[24] In this, he insists there is value to the circus, to what serious society sees as trivial, low entertainment. There is a place for and a purpose to the lives of its freaks and fools. Sleary's request of Gradgrind to "make the betht of uth; not the wurtht"[25] further shows he knows there is stigma around and prejudice toward those who find themselves isolated on the margins of society, where they are so much more imperiled whenever their worth is overshadowed by "the wurtht" assumptions about their difference. Yet another important postulate of the Sleary Philosophy is his somewhat puzzled but still self-possessed pronouncement, "there ith a love in the world, not all Thelf-intereth, after all, but thomething very different."[26] Arguably, Sleary eschews self-interested duty for precisely the sort of fellow feeling we have seen Wilde portray in the fairy tales, where loving-kindness grounded in reciprocity leads to compassionate action within both interpersonal and social contexts.

Indeed, approaching Wilde's final writings with his fairy tales as a frame of reference offers a compelling further lens into his attraction to aberrant others. His conversion into a convict leaves him hung down with the freaks and fools through the physical debilitation and psychological distress he endures, in turn increasing his appreciation for the beauty and value of the lives of those who find themselves variously marginalized or pilloried by society. Prisoners, Wilde writes in "Epistola," "stand in symbolic relation to the very secret of life," as "the secret of life is suffering."[27] Indeed, his own suffering while in jail arguably positions him as a disability-aligned figure in his own right. In his long letter, Wilde only briefly alludes to the extreme toll incarceration took on his physical and mental health. Notably, though, he characterizes his time in prison as "the paralysing immobility of a life" that "seems to circle round one centre of pain,"[28] its "endless privations and restrictions"[29] effecting a debilitating "degradation of the body" through "the plank bed, the loathsome food, the hard ropes shredded into oakum till one's finger-tips grow dull with pain."[30] Wilde was not only "dazed through pain," however; he also felt so "crushed by anguish, bewildered by terror"[31] that he "longed to die" and even "determined to commit suicide" upon release.[32]

Nicholas Frankel has thoroughly delineated how Wilde was pushed to the brink of physical and psychological collapse in jail, filling in the numerous painful details the prisoner did not for many reasons include in "Epistola." The impact of incarceration was almost immediate; within just a couple of weeks, news reports claimed Wilde already had become "violently insane" while at Pentonville.[33] Home Secretary Herbert Asquith himself made enquiries, and Richard Haldane (prominent Gladstone Commission member) actually paid a visit to Wilde. After his transfer to Wandsworth in July, Wilde's decline was all the more precipitous. He had lost thirty-two pounds by mid-September and was "nearing a complete breakdown."[34] The chaplain wrote to Haldane that Wilde was "quite crushed and broken," so much so that he reported, "Some of our most experienced officers openly say they don't think he will be able to go through the whole two years."[35] Frankel relates that by early October, "weakened by sleeplessness, illness, and semi-starvation, Wilde could no longer get out of bed," and after being "threatened with punishment" for "malingering,"[36] he collapsed unconscious to the floor, causing "painful and lasting damage to his ear,"[37] an injury that according to Frankel ultimately led to his death approximately three and a half years after his release.[38]

In 1895, though, officials were far more focused on Wilde's mental state. The Home Office sent two "leading forensic psychologists" to examine him, and while they formally registered no concerns, they nonetheless recommended he be moved to a "country prison" where he might do garden or library work.[39] Thus, Wilde was transferred to Reading, and this was his unsteady state when paraded on the Clapham platform in his shaved head and comic livery, enfreaked and enfooled, to be spat upon and ridiculed. The transfer, though, still did not improve his health; rather, after six more months, his "physical condition was no better" and "psychologically it was far worse."[40] Robbie Ross described Wilde's eyes as "horribly vacant," while Robert Sherard noted he "was nearly breaking down all the time."[41] It was only when the Governor, who had bragged he was "knocking the nonsense out of Wilde,"[42] was replaced near the end of July 1896 that Wilde finally began to recover with more humane treatment (which eventually included the privilege of writing materials for "Epistola").

The standard line has been to read the years after Reading merely as tragic martyrdom, many unable to understand how such extreme mental and physical duress could lead anywhere but to diminishment and death. Frankel's account of Wilde's unrepentant years, however, represents a long overdue reclamation of Wilde's resilience. To cast Wilde as the "passive victim" of either Douglas or Victorian morality is "to rob him of all agency" when, in fact, "imprisonment and exile, paradoxically, had liberated him to pursue an uninhibited life . . . with conversation as its medium and laughter its index."[43] According to Frankel, in spite of ongoing struggles with sadness, suffering, and insecurity, Wilde ultimately persevered, "with bemusement, irony, and self-conviction, unbowed and impervious to the harsh judgments of smaller natures."[44] From this alternative perspective, one may position him in his prison literature as reconsolidating the insights from his fairy tales into a robust formulation of a Wilde Philosophy endorsing (like Sleary's) the importance of fancy and fellow feeling in encouraging the embrace of marginalized bodies and minds with loving-kindness and compassionate action.

Indeed, as "Epistola" itself shows, even before release Wilde is passionately insistent that he earned priceless epiphanies through his experience of abjection. If the lives of those who deride freaks and fools for their physical or mental differences are the "unbeautiful" ones, might there not conversely be a beauty to the lives of the "zanies of sorrow," of the "clowns whose hearts are broken"? Wilde at times sadly reinforces with his words the pejorative perceptions of disability that dominate his day. He uses such framing as a means of drawing Douglas's flaws, referencing his "almost epileptic rage" as reflective of the "mania"[45] he inherits from his father's "mad, bad line."[46] Perhaps most disappointingly, in a passage only a few paragraphs following the account of his own experience of derisive dehumanization at Clapham Junction, he lashes out at Douglas's father in a damning example of body-shaming, mocking the Marquess's "apelike face" while singling out physical traits as signs of not just his ugliness but inferiority: "the stableman's gait and dress, the bowed legs, the twitching hands, the hanging lower lip, the bestial and half-witted grin."[47] Wilde's overall message to Douglas, however, notwithstanding such exceptions, still strikingly resonates with the tenor of his fairy tales, both in their condemnation of egotism and vanity and in their celebration of fellow feeling and ethical action.[48]

At the end of "Epistola," Wilde tells Douglas, "you came to me to learn the pleasure of life and the pleasure of art. Perhaps I am chosen to teach you something much more wonderful—the meaning of sorrow and its beauty."[49] Part of Wilde's disappointment with Douglas stems from how he evinced "the sentimentality of the spectator of a rather pathetic play."[50] As Wilde puts it more bluntly later, "the fact is that you were . . . a typical sentimentalist. For a sentimentalist is simply one who desires to have the luxury of an emotion without paying for it."[51] Jail, on the other hand, engendered in Wilde an even fuller appreciation of the compassion and reciprocal responsiveness he endorses in the fairy tales. He reveals, "Every day I said to myself: 'I must keep love in my heart to-day, else how shall I live through the day.'"[52] He further comes to appreciate how the poor respond to the pain and suffering of others through this same lens; while in the eyes of people of rank, "prison makes a man a pariah," for the poor it is "something that calls for sympathy in others," and thus "they speak of one who is in prison as of one who is 'in trouble' simply," an expression he insists "has the perfect wisdom of love in it."[53]

In marked contrast to his treatment by the cruel crowd at Clapham, Wilde recalls a humble acknowledgment of his humanity through a small gesture of sympathy by Ross when he was at one of his lowest points, a slight hat tip from his friend as he was brought from Wandsworth into the Court of Bankruptcy not long before his collapse. In an assertion showing he processes this poignant expression of a pity that respects his personhood explicitly through the lens of the lived experiences of poverty and disability-aligned difference, Wilde goes on to claim it was in the same "mode of love, that the saints knelt down to wash the feet of the poor, or stooped to kiss the leper on the cheek."[54] Wilde stores this moment in his heart, "a secret debt that I am glad to think I can never possibly repay": "the memory of that little, lovely, silent act of love," he explains, "has unsealed for me all the wells of pity," has "brought me out of the bitterness of lonely exile into harmony with the wounded, broken, and great heart of the world."[55] This pity, again, is not the self-indulgent sort but instead akin to the compassionate fellow feeling that the initially selfish Star-Child comes to practice toward animals, beggars, and lepers or that the initially selfish Giant shows toward the children (and in particular to his special little friend) to whom he gifts his garden.

In fact, the figure of Christ is central to Wilde's insights in prison about the complex relationship between love and sorrow, insights that reinforce the fairy tales' earlier emphasis upon kindness toward and responsiveness to others, particularly marginalized extraordinary bodies. As he previously offered in *The Soul of Man*, Wilde sees Jesus as the consummate artist figure, as the supreme Individualist.[56] Fascinatingly, seemingly as a consequence of his incarceration, in "Epistola" he considers Christ's contribution to his new understanding of pain and suffering as calling for reciprocal pity and sympathetic action by frequently invoking peculiar bodyminds. Indeed, he takes up this topic in the second paragraph immediately following his suggestion that "The Happy Prince" prefigured the lessons he learned in prison. For Wilde, Jesus "realised in the entire sphere of human relations that imaginative sympathy which in the sphere of Art is the sole secret of creation," and it was precisely through his "intense and flamelike imagination" that Christ "understood the leprosy of the leper, the darkness of the blind."[57] In the very next sentence, he requotes Douglas's claim that Wilde was not interesting while off his pedestal when ill, in order to insist such an orientation is as "remote from the true temper of the artist" as it is from "the Secret of Jesus."[58] To realize this secret, one need recognize how fundamental fancy and feeling are to the way this Christ Philosophy approaches and appreciates the difference of others—seeing people, not pariahs. Jesus "wakes in us that temper of wonder to which romance always appeals," by "imagining that he could bear . . . the burden of the entire world," a burden that encompasses not only "the sins of Nero, of Caesar Borgia" but also "the sufferings of those whose names are legion" and "oppressed nationalities, factory children, thieves, people in prison, outcasts, those who are dumb under oppression."[59] Significantly, this strikingly intersectional catalogue of marginalized and exploited lives evokes not error but wonder while invoking his romantic vision of utopia from "The Decay of Lying."

The life of Christ demonstrates how "entirely may sorrow and beauty be made one in their meaning and manifestation,"[60] perhaps suggesting how Tatar's binary contrasting the beautiful with the grotesque need not be understood as requiring a choice after all. According to Wilde, as "the leader of all the lovers," Jesus understood "it was only through love that one could approach either the heart of the leper or the feet of God."[61] Many, he complains, "have tried to make [Christ] out an ordinary philanthropist, like the dreadful philanthropists of the nineteenth century, or ranked him as an altruist with the unscientific and sentimental" merely because he had "pity . . . for the poor, for those who are shut up in prisons, for the lowly, for the wretched."[62] But Wilde's Jesus instead is "the supreme individualist,"[63] a "personality" who "with a width and wonder of imagination . . . took the entire world of the inarticulate, the voiceless world of pain, as his kingdom,"[64] choosing "as his brothers" those "who are dumb under oppression" and seeking to "become eyes to the blind, ears to the deaf, and a cry in the lips of those whose tongues had been tied."[65] The Christ that Wilde champions selects as his own chosen confraternity those on the margins, with particular and consistent emphasis on disability-aligned difference—explicitly acknowledging the blind, deaf, and dumb while granting, through his hallowing of the heart of the leper, their fundamental worth. Continuing to echo the fairy tales' rejection of selfish and self-important sentimentality in favor of a loving embrace of diversity, Wilde celebrates a disabled God who embodies how the "heart of the world" can be both "wounded, broken" and also "great" (indeed, "great" perhaps actually *because* "wounded, broken," not in spite of being so). This Christ "exposed with utter and relentless scorn" any "cold philanthropies" and "ostentatious public charities,"[66] offering instead a morality that is "all sympathy,"[67] for "to Christ imagination was simply a form of love,"[68] which is why "we owe to him the most diverse things and people"—from Hugo's *Les Misérables* and "the note of pity in Russian novels" to Tannhäuser[69] and "the love of children."[70]

As we have seen, Wilde's own love of children certainly inspired his fairy tales, partly in terms of audience but even more so in terms of focus. Small and youthful bodies dominate his attention in all of the stories we have explored together in the preceding chapters—the Giant's special little friend, the Infanta and the Dwarf, the little Mermaid and the young Fisherman, the Star-Child, and the Happy Prince and the Swallow. It is not surprising, then, given the ways in which his emphases in those texts continue to inform his thinking in "Epistola" as he reflects upon his prison experience, to find him still concerned for such figures on his last full day at Reading, when Wilde sends a brief note to Thomas Martin, one of his warders, inquiring after a couple of his fellow inmates. He requests the names, first, of a convict whom he worries has been driven insane and, second, of three little children jailed for snaring rabbits. "I must get them out," Wilde writes of the latter; he asks to have it arranged so he might pay their fine and have Martin inform them "they are to be released tomorrow by a friend,"[71] which happily happens.

On the eve of leaving behind the walls behind which he endured so much personal pain and suffering, Wilde's fancy and feeling, his imagination and pity, lead him to seem more motivated than ever by loving-kindness and responsiveness to others.

Indeed, less than ten days after his release, Wilde publishes his first public words since being incarcerated, in the form of a letter to the editor of the *Daily Chronicle* on the cruelties of prison life, with particular reference to the above individuals. Having learned Martin was dismissed for giving one of the children a biscuit, and remaining upset such little ones had been sent to jail at all, Wilde decides he must speak out. Upon first seeing these "quite small children, the youngest" of whom was "tinier" than any other child he had seen there (so much so "they had evidently been unable to find clothes small enough to fit" him), Wilde had been "utterly distressed" knowing "the treatment in store for them."[72] "The cruelty that is practised by day and night on children in English prisons is incredible," Wilde proclaims, cruelty made all the more "terrible, primarily from people not understanding the peculiar psychology of a child's nature."[73] As case in point, he mentions another small boy, whose cell was directly across from his own in Reading. The child's face "was like a white wedge of sheer terror," and "there was in his eyes the terror of a hunted animal."[74] Crying "for his parents" and "calling to be let out," Wilde notes he was "very poor," requiring "prison socks and shoes," owing to the "bad state" of those he arrived in "if he had any" at all.[75] To make matters worse, he was only on remand, though, Wilde observes, "In the eyes of humanity it should be a horrible thing for him to be there at all."[76] Arguably even more strongly than in the fairy tales themselves, Wilde here demonstrates his disdain for the dehumanizing degradation and demoralization of especially vulnerable marginalized bodyminds.

Wilde goes on to expose "the brutality of the system,"[77] including the hunger and diarrhea owing to "coarse, horrible" food and the "fetid and unwholesome" conditions of the "sanitary arrangements,"[78] but particularly the isolation of the "solitary cellular system," where "every child is confined to its cell for twenty-three hours out of the twenty-four."[79] He rightly observes, "If an individual, parent or guardian, did this to a child," there would be "the utmost detestation of whomsoever had been guilty of such cruelty," but in the jail setting it is somehow tolerated, even condoned.[80] Wilde reiterates, "the only really humanising influence in prison is the influence of the prisoners," "their sympathy for each other, their humility," for "suffering and the community of suffering makes people kind."[81] Wilde's membership in this community of suffering has made him humbler and kinder, and his letter represents an attempt to enact a similar shift in public perception. "It is not the prisoners who need reformation," he continues, for "in this, as in all other things, philanthropists and people of that kind are astray"; rather, "it is the prisons" themselves that must change.[82]

Wilde is not only concerned about the impact of incarceration on "the peculiar psychology of a child's nature," however. He also wishes to "draw attention" also "to another terrible thing" happening "in ordinary gaols" as well as "convict prisons"—"the large number of men who become insane or weak-minded" owing to "the system of silence and cellular confinement."[83] To do so, he devotes the rest of the letter to relating the specific case of the man about whom he had previously asked Martin. This inmate struck Wilde "as being more than usually half-witted on account of his silly grin and idiotic laughter to himself, and the peculiar restlessness of his eternally twitching hands."[84] "At exercise he always seemed hysterical, and used to walk round crying or laughing,"[85] and at chapel he would sit "with tears streaming down his face and an hysterical throbbing in the throat"[86] or "he would grin idiot-like to himself and make faces."[87] In spite of this all, he was "treated as if he was shamming" and flogged, "the prison silence being broken by the most horrible and revolting shrieks, or rather howls."[88] When he appeared next at exercise, walking "in the centre ring along with the old men, the beggars, and the lame people," "his weak, ugly, wretched face [was] bloated by tears and hysteria almost beyond recognition."[89] Wilde's devastating descriptions of his fellow prisoner's manifestations of profound personal suffering powerfully reinforce his vulnerability to the system's brutality while again linking such suffering to poverty and disability through his highlighting of the center ring of this convict circus—with its hoary, hungry, and hobbled members (together with the particularly frightful accounting of the man's own embodiment of qualities quite the opposite of those mainstream society endorses: strength, beauty, and happiness) reminding his readers of the very perilous predicaments in which so many peculiar bodyminds find themselves, especially in jail.

Only days from freedom, Wilde is distressed to see "this poor creature—made once in the image of God—grinning like an ape, and making with his hands the most fantastic gestures" while "hysterical tears" made "soiled runnels on his white swollen face."[90] Employing some of the same language he used to portray his own pain on the platform, Wilde describes how the "hideous and deliberate grace of his gestures" made this fellow prisoner seem "like an antic," "a living grotesque."[91] Wilde worries about irreparable damage, because "prison doctors have no knowledge of mental disease of any kind" or "the pathology of the mind" or even "the difference between idiocy and lunacy," and simply order such inmates "punished again and again," eventually with flogging.[92] Wilde sees in all this a system pitted against and privileged over a person: "The doctor is fighting for a theory. The man is fighting for his life. I am anxious that the man should win."[93] If this is to happen, though, it must be achieved not by the "interfere[ence]" of "the sentimentalist" but "by people of humane feelings who have still some common sense and some pity."[94] Already suggested in "Epistola," what this letter shows is Wilde acting upon his now even fuller sense of the sort of reciprocal pity born out of love and suffering featured in his fairy tales. Still rejecting sentimental philanthropy in favor of a more humanized and humanizing orientation that respects the humanity of those in need, the newly released Wilde here immediately puts himself in the service of another and many others, not just wallowing in his own sorrow but working to defend and to demand justice for vulnerable bodyminds that society's rejection renders at risk.

Around this same time, Wilde further crystallized these ideas in a tour-de-force prison poem, *The Ballad of Reading Gaol*. During July 1896, one of the inmates, Charles Thomas Wooldridge, was executed for the murder of his wife. In spite of the horrific crime, Wilde's pity extended to the former trooper, even as Wooldridge faced his fate "wistfully" and did not "wring his hands" as "witless men" do.[95] The poetic speaker shows the humility, kindness, and compassion Wilde had attributed in "Epistola" to convicts' focus on others' suffering, above and beyond their own: "though I was a soul in pain, / My pain I could not feel."[96] Indeed, "all the souls in pain / Who tramped the other ring" forgot their own predicaments while they "watched with gaze of dull amaze / The man who had to swing."[97] Here is Sleary's Ring as "a kind of brotherhood, a circle of responsiveness to the needs and pain" of others, an embodiment of loving-kindness made possible through fancy's enabling of identification with different experiences. The mutuality and reciprocity represented by this community of suffering stands in direct contrast with the response of the typical warder, who "Must set a lock upon his lips, / And make his face a mask," lest "he might be moved, and try / To comfort and console."[98] Wilde's poetic speaker even goes on to name the missing element where the warders are concerned: "Human Pity."[99] Again, this is precisely the response his fairy tales seem to suggest is required of readers where his disability-aligned protagonists are concerned—compassionate (inter)action grounded in genuine and generous emotional connections.

Wilde also uses the poem as a further means of foregrounding the dehumanizing and debilitating experience of life in jail. Evoking again his experience of being jeered as a vulgar jester at Clapham Junction, he dubs the exercise ring "the Fools' Parade," as with "shaven head and feet of lead" they "make a merry masquerade" until they feel like "The Devil's Own Brigade."[100] Especially with the execution approaching, "in the heart of every man / Terror was lying still."[101] At night, "the empty corridors / Were full of forms of Fear,"[102] but even in their cells, "crooked shapes of Terror crouched" and "each evil sprite that walks by night" went "glid[ing] past" with "loathsome grace."[103] These "damned grotesques made arabesques" and "with flutes of Fear they filled the ear, / As their grisly masque they led,"[104] singing of how "*fettered limbs grow lame.*"[105] Horrifically, "no things of air these antics were," for "to men whose lives were held in gyves," these phantoms "were living things, / Most terrible to see."[106] As Wooldridge's hour of reckoning nears, their hearts begin beating "Like a madman on a drum!"[107] After the execution, "Like ape or clown, in monstrous garb," the warders "kept their herd of brutes" while "Horror stalked before each man, / And Terror crept behind."[108] This merry masquerade not only recalls Clapham but the spectacle of the freak show more generally, both through its peculiar performers and through its intersectional invoking of ape and clown, brute and madman.

Wilde's poetic speaker goes on to elaborate on how such Horror and Terror combines with the fetters and gyves to produce a profoundly disabling impact on these vulnerable bodyminds. Incarceration, he continues, "wastes and withers" all that "is good in Man" by "starv[ing] the little frightened child," "scourg[ing] the weak, and flog[ging] the fool" until "some grow mad, and all grow bad."[109] Again, Wilde links the physical and mental suffering of children with that of disabled persons ("the weak" and "the fool") in a focus reminiscent of the ones featured in his fairy tales. As "every stone one lifts by day / Becomes one's heart at night," under the "pitiless" eyes of their warders, the inmates are condemned to "rot and rot, / With soul and body marred."[110] Without the loving-kindness and compassionate acts of "Human Pity," the convicts—and especially those who are frail and feeble in size, strength, or sense—seem doomed to be further impoverished, if not to perish, owing to their susceptibility to stigma, isolation, and peril. Wilde's poem is not totally bleak, however, and the hopeful note he strikes in the stanzas following the hanging both further echoes the fairy tales and draws upon "Epistola," among other things by suggesting Christ's centrality to an understanding of how imaginative love might redeem the pain and sorrow of abject bodies and minds. Wilde's fairy tales certainly prepare for this possibility through their various versions of Eiesland's disabled God, whose similarly "marred" body manifests love more than suffering while not merely embracing but incorporating disability-aligned difference into its embodiment of divinity. This process is complemented by the procession of stigmatized and traumatized prisoners and protagonists, whose disposability pushes readers to confront how such lives demand dignity, freedom, love, and, most fundamentally, the right to life itself.

Indeed, Wilde invokes both "The Selfish Giant" and "The Fisherman and His Soul" when he mentions Wooldridge's prison-yard grave. He writes, "For three long years the unblessed spot / Will sterile be and bare," for "They think a murderer's heart would taint" any seeds they might sow there.[111] Wilde's poetic speaker, however, insists "the red rose would but blow more red, / The white rose whiter blow" if planted there, for "who can say by what strange way / Christ brings His will to light,"—as evidenced by how Tannhäuser's "barren staff" was said to have "Bloomed in the great Pope's sight."[112] "Out of his mouth a red, red rose! / Out of his heart a white!"[113] Wilde avers, but the chaplain, doctor, and governor will not allow it, "So never will wine-red rose or white" bloom above "that stretch of mud" to "tell the men who tramp the yard / That God's Son died for all."[114] For Wilde, prisons are "bound with bars lest Christ should see / How men their brothers maim,"[115] but, thankfully, "God's eternal Laws are kind / And break the heart of stone."[116] "How else but through a broken heart / May Lord Christ enter in?"[117] Wilde's speaker asks, perhaps recalling the final moments of his young Fisherman after his costly mistake. Not only Wooldridge but "every human heart that breaks, / In prison-cell or yard" will be welcomed into Paradise like the "Thief" at Golgotha.[118] Each such heart, he proclaims, is like "that broken box" referenced in the Gospel of Mark, which, according to the poetic speaker, "filled the unclean leper's house / With the scent of costliest nard."[119] Brokenness and uncleanliness, the maimed and the diseased, are in Wilde's powerful prison poem, as in the fairy tales, not merely sympathetically rendered but valorized (including by God's very own endorsement)—and, as in "Epistola," the figure of Christ and the figure of the leper are aligned as equally appropriate and respected representatives of the "wounded, broken, and great heart of the world."

While *The Ballad of Reading Gaol* is the only new literary work Wilde published after prison, he did send another letter to the *Daily Chronicle* shortly after the poem's appearance. His last public words reinforce how incarceration helped him realize the fairy tales' messages about love and pity as necessary responses to suffering and injustice are more relevant than ever. Writing in support of the Home Secretary's Prison Reform Bill, he reiterates how jail's "three permanent punishments"—hunger, insomnia, and disease—destroy the minds and bodies of its inmates.[120] The diet of weak gruel and suet leads inevitably to "disease in the form of incessant diarrhoea [sic]," a "most weakening, depressing, and humiliating malady" that causes "foul air" so "sickening and unwholesome" even warders become "violently" ill upon entering cells and that "ultimately with most prisoners becomes a permanent disease."[121] Equally troubling, "the present prison system seems almost to have for its aim the wrecking and the destruction of the mental faculties," and accordingly, "the production of insanity is, if not its object, certainly its result."[122] Wilde's confraternity of convicts are, in other words, once again presented as members of a more comprehensive Victorian menagerie of misfits, all those who live with mental disability, physical disability, illness, or a combination thereof. Significantly, this writer who so self-consciously embraces contradiction and irony and triviality in so many of his other works, remains doggedly consistent in his rejection of altruism, charity, philanthropy, and sentimentality with their self-interested Band-Aid "cures" that do not address the systemic perpetuation of isolation, stigma, and peril. Wilde clarifies that the last thing he wants to do is "excite any momentary sentimental interest," yet he feels obligated to expose how inmates are "isolated from every humane and humanising influence," "treated like an unintelligent animal," and "brutalised below the level of any of the brute-creation."[123]

Notably, one of the specific ways, Wilde goes on to document, that incarceration brutalizes and dehumanizes inmates is "the mode at present in vogue of exhibiting a prisoner to his friends."[124] His word choice in representing the experience of official visits as one of being exhibited is very telling and once again evokes his personal humiliation at Clapham as well as similar, more general settings like freak show exhibitions and zoos. Not only is one allowed visits just "four times a year, for twenty minutes each time," but, even worse, "the prisoner is either locked up in a large iron cage or in a large wooden box, with a small aperture, covered with wire netting," with the visitors "in a similar cage, some three or four feet distant."[125] Wilde ends this section of the letter by reiterating these visits' "intensification of humiliation and mental distress" as akin to being subject to exploitation for the purpose of others' interest, if not entertainment: "to be exhibited, like an ape in a cage," is a "horrible degradation."[126] Finally, for his last point in the letter, Wilde returns to his concern with inmates' mental and physical well-being as he takes another swipe at prison doctors, who are "brutal in manner, coarse in temperament, and utterly indifferent to the health of the prisoners."[127] With his concluding sentence, Wilde identifies that "the first, and perhaps most difficult task" required for reform to take root is "to humanise the governors of prisons, to civilise the warders and to Christianise the chaplains."[128] All of the above brutality and degradation, so detrimental to the well-being of the prisoners and so dehumanizing in its employment of both exhibition and isolation, is absolutely abhorrent to Wilde, and it demands direct action in the form of not just individual empathy but broader social change in order to reform the whole prison system along with all of its separate human cogs. This letter, then, as does every single other published piece of writing in the wake of his conviction for gross indecency, testifies to the extent to which Wilde's own enfreakment and enfoolment in jail exposed him to profound personal experiences of mental and physical illness, moving him to champion anew and all the more compellingly the selfsame reciprocal pity and responsive action he features in his fairy tales as so foundational to happy and healthy lives.

Wilde's exploration of affective response in relation to the peculiar protagonists of his fairy tales truly provides a productive frame for new approaches to the whole of Wilde's life and work, especially as we have seen is the case where his last half-dozen or so years are concerned. This study on the one hand hopefully invites more consideration of what lies between the appearance of *The Happy Prince and Other Tales* in 1888 and the above letter from 1898. For instance, might there be links with disability-aligned embodiment (perhaps in line with Tatar's grotesque aesthetic) in the bestiality, monstrosity, and ugliness Wilde presents across other genres in the intense decadence of works like *The Picture of Dorian Gray, Salome,* and *The Sphinx*? Would it in any way augment standard readings of his portrayal of High Society in the famous comedies to inflect these plays' critiques of the privileged classes' self-absorption through the prism of the sort of satirical minstrelsy mimicry Mendelssohn identifies, if he in fact learns to employ this as a means of turning the gaze under which freaks and other marginalized figures are made the subject of stigmatizing spectacle back upon those who benefit the most from its exclusions? Then, what about the before and the beyond? Might we extend this consideration of Wilde's interest in peculiar bodies to his 1881 *Poems*, to his American lectures in 1882, to his failed early plays, or to his journalism?[129] Should we transport these tales even further forward in time, beyond the end of Wilde's life to our own day, and apply a disability studies lens to contemporary engagements with Wilde—such as films like Clio Barnard's 2013 *The Selfish Giant* and Rupert Everett's 2018 *The Happy Prince*—so as to reinforce the value of, here and now, and in each future potential audience member's own place and time, continuing the conversation about intersectional disability and emotional response that the fairy tales prompt? These are questions outside of my scope here, but by way of wrapping things up where my own focus is concerned, before I offer my three-paragraph closing to this conclusion, I want to suggest how my approach might further fit with the four stories I did not select for close reading: "The Remarkable Rocket," "The Nightingale and the Rose," "The Young King," and "The Devoted Friend."

"The Remarkable Rocket" begins with a very lighthearted comic setting: a royal court in preparations for the nuptials of its crown prince and a beautiful Russian princess. The festivities' grand finale is scheduled to be a fireworks show, and so, soon enough we are introduced to the pyrotechnics performers themselves as they sit around waiting for their headlining role in the spectacle-to-come. Standing out among a crowd of explosive personalities is a tall and very supercilious Rocket, who believes he always is (and should be) the center of attention, ascribing to himself an importance at least equal to that of the Prince and Princess themselves. Indeed, he eventually works himself up to the point of tears over an imagined scenario in which the royal couple's future would be forever ruined if something should happen to him and they then were to suffer the disappointment of never getting to watch him go off. By the time it is his turn to be lit later that night, he in fact is too wet after all of his weeping, and so the next day one of the workers throws him over a wall into a ditch. After more revealing conversations with a Frog, a Dragon-fly, and a Duck, in which he continues to show himself to be haughty and rude (and in total self-denial about his circumstances and his worth), two boys approach and decide to use him as firewood for their kettle. By now, the Rocket has dried off enough to explode up into the air, but the boys have decided to take a nap until the pot boils, so they are asleep and nobody sees or hears his belated big bang.

If in "The Birthday of the Infanta" we are unsure if we are meant to laugh or to cry when it comes to the humble Dwarf, the choice in "The Remarkable Rocket" would seem to be either to laugh at or to decry its pompous protagonist. The real crux is what to make of the fact that the Rocket also may, like the Dwarf, be glossed as disability-aligned, since his tears (affected or no) literally disable him, rendering him useless. The Rocket's insistence others must think only of him if they can be considered to have a sympathetic nature might suggest there is a fine line between self-serving sympathy and conceited self-centeredness. He also makes a spectacle of himself (rather than being turned into one owing to exploitation by others), which might just reveal how entrenched ableism so informs standard assumptions about self-worth that he understands on some level how he must preserve at all costs the illusion of his utility, vitality, and wholeness (and also his superiority). Further, given that the Rocket's egotism precedes his disablement, it seems most likely Wilde's critique of his obnoxious character is not insinuating that what he is most "remarkable" for is his inability to perform (that is, it is his prior self-centeredness that determines reader response to his character).

Some have assumed the Rocket is a wicked wink at James MacNeill Whistler, that magnificent maestro of making enemies, but Wilde also could be spoofing himself, playfully identifying with the self-centered and self-important protagonist. Whistler and Wilde both were social sensations, in large part owing to their abilities as glorious and notorious talkers, but Wilde actually looks even more the part here in that at the time he wrote this tale, he still had not really done anything of consequence in terms of his writing to justify his fame. Regardless of whether or not Wilde was engaging in his own private joke by caricaturing himself precisely along the lines that his detractors had been using for years, it is notable that the Rocket is the only one of Wilde's disability-aligned protagonists who seems to invite downright disdain. His haughtiness and hypocrisy—and, above all, his unsympathetic selfishness—have more in common with the sentimentalists and altruists whose performative charity Wilde so despised than with his other main characters, who present as poignant rather than as poisonous. In sharp contrast to their emotional response at the end of "The Birthday of the Infanta," since readers are likely only too happy to have the Rocket expire, perhaps the more appropriate reaction to the tale's anticlimactic conclusion is either dampened spirits of depressing disappointment or lighthearted laughs of studied triviality. Overall, "The Remarkable Rocket" serves to remind readers not only that Wilde's representation of disability-aligned protagonists is predictably far from progressive in places but also that he simply may not take himself or his stories as seriously as some of the other ones might seem to suggest.

"The Nightingale and the Rose" opens with its titular songbird pitying a poor weeping student whose love interest has promised she would dance with him at the royal ball, but only if he could bring her a red rose during the dead of winter. She decides compassionate action on her part is required and, believing the Student's life and love to be more important than her own, she seeks out the terrible secret of how she might procure such a flower from the Rose-tree beneath his window, whose branches have been broken and all its buds nipped by the wintry weather. She discovers she must be willing to pay with her own heart's blood to produce the rose, by singing all night long as she presses her breast deeper and deeper against a thorn. She tries to convey her plan to the Student, explaining all she asks of him is that he will be a true lover, but he of course only hears warbling and dismisses her as a selfish creature that thinks only of its own purposeless music. Undeterred, though, she follows through with her sacrifice, creating the most beautiful of roses, only to fall down dead in the grass as she finishes. The Student blissfully discovers the rose (though without any idea of his bird-benefactor's role), yet when he presents it to the girl he loves, she tells him he is too late, as another suitor has sent her jewels instead. The story ends with the scornful Student throwing the flower away (into a street gutter, where it gets crushed) and then returning to his study with a dismissive comment about the uselessness of love.

Though a short simple story, this tale offers complex inflections that cast a more critical eye both on the disturbing dynamics of too superficial a representation of the Fisherman's self-maiming and on the dodgy dangers of too naive a romanticization of the love he shares with the Mermaid. The Nightingale's decision to willingly suffer the wounds of Love not only resonates with the Fisherman, who opts to cut away his own soul, but also with the Christ-child, who gave his life in the name of love and has the scars to prove it. What is more, since both the Dwarf and the Fisherman literally die owing to broken hearts from a love that society deemed unacceptable, the Nightingale's imminent self-sacrifice encourages readers to align her fate with these characters (and the little Mermaid, if not also the selfish Giant and possibly even the little Infanta). What is the heart of a bird worth, after all, if the Student can so snidely disregard her (and discard her lovingly made creation) as useless (as useless as a self-centered firework too damp to go off)? Her singing as she presses the thorn into her breast also evokes those same three tales through a wounding Love perfected by Death. The story's highlighting of how the emotional if not physical self-injury many endure in the name of love sometimes is far more disturbing and destructive than praiseworthy and productive.

What is more, it also reinforces how such tragedies seem the more predictable fate for so many different sorts of bodies deemed by society as "less than," as unfit for and unworthy of love. It is worth considering the extent to which she has internalized that her life is somehow "less than" compared to that of the Student, and to weigh whether or not one should extend the potential to see her self-abnegation as problematic to the humility practiced by the likes of the Star-Child and the Happy Prince. To add insult to (self-)injury, unlike for the Fisherman or the Giant, there are no flowers from God sanctifying the Nightingale's love and devotion; indeed, her death is not acknowledged at all. Like little Jenny Wren's subordination to Lizzie and Eugene's love story, the Nightingale's own denigration and devaluation (even if essential to plot resolution) appears compulsory. It further raises for readers the possibility that the Fisherman's self-mutilation might entail a similarly disturbing version of self-sacrificing love, one worthy more of suspicious sympathy, problematic pity, or disgusted abjection. The fate of Wilde's Nightingale certainly serves as a powerful reminder of the dangers of glorifying the spirit of self-sacrifice and blithely insisting love redeems all. Still, there do remain some valid ways to insist upon other empowering elements, for as readers reject the Student's rudeness, even if they cannot revere the bird's romanticization of love, they surely at least refute humanity's disregard for her ostensibly unimportant little life.

"The Young King" centers on its titular character's coming to grips with the consequences of his new royal life of privilege. As the illegitimate child of the old king's now dead daughter, he had been raised as a lowly goatherd, unaware of his lordly lineage, only revealed to be the heir to the throne after his grandfather's passing. Almost immediately, he develops an extremely decadent obsession with all of the beautiful things he now possesses, and he becomes particularly fixated on plans for his coronation attire. However, he has three dreams that change him utterly. First, he sees a factory of weavers being worked to death to produce his new robe. Then, he witnesses the drowning of an enslaved young diver from a galley ship out to secure the pearl for his sceptre. In the last dream, he watches as Avarice and Death barter over the lives of laborers seeking rubies for his crown, until the whole multitude are wiped out by Ague, Plague, and Fever. Upon waking, he dons his humble old outfit for the coronation instead of his beautiful garments, much to the chagrin of not only the Bishop and the courtiers but even the common people. At the church, though, a glorious light shines down upon him, and his shepherd's staff bursts into bloom, leading all to acknowledge his rule is a divinely sanctioned one (even if he refuses to dress like a king).

This story serves as an appropriate coda to "The Star-Child" in that it too presents us with a youthful monarch who becomes committed to reconstructing society on such a basis that the degradation and demoralization of poverty (and other forms of exploitation of the marginalized) will be impossible. The only one of Wilde's tales across both volumes that does not demand the death of the hero(es), it is also arguably the one with perhaps the weakest case for suggesting the main character might be positioned as disability-aligned—which is troubling if he is also the only one to survive. Nonetheless, the tale does share a number of generative points of intersection with the other stories. The King's young age in and of itself links him to most of the other peculiar protagonists, he hails from a humble forest home as do the Star-Child and the Dwarf, and divine favor for his alternative (com)passion is signaled by a miraculous flourish of fantastic flowers as with the Giant and with the Fisherman and the Mermaid. On top of this, the people and places destroyed in order to provide for his pleasure evoke notions of the foreign and exotic that underwrite so many Victorian constructions of freakery. His emotional response to such suffering leads him to decide upon his own far, far better thing to do—not a literal martyrdom like Carton's but a substitution that rises above private interpersonal motivation and instead represents a public act of compassion for his people, a refusal to allow their further exploitation and extermination.

On a more fundamental level, though, his decision to don the dress from his lowly goatherd days not only challenges assumptions about the extent to which outward appearances reflect inner reality, but his commitment to both individual virtue and social justice embodies both compassionate pity and public action. The links we already have seen between a beggarly state and disability further strengthen his character's potential alignment with all those othered on the basis of their physical appearance. Indeed, the Bishop's reaction even more explicitly identifies how the suffering the young King's wealth requires of the poor is inextricably bound up with the lived experience of disability. His two specific examples of those who do not belong in the King's world are beggars and lepers, the same two disability-aligned figures Wilde features in the final pages of "The Star-Child." The Bishop even goes so far as to conceptually link the young King to the leper and the beggar by family ties, asking him to imagine them eating and sleeping together. Again, it is how he looks that seems to determine if he will be granted respect, and notably it is disability-aligned difference that yet again is trotted out as the opposite of, as the Other to, normative notions of dignity and deference. In the end, though, the young King successfully eschews the ableism and classism of paternalistic condescension or hypocritical sentimentality toward lepers and beggars, workers and the enslaved, in favor of an egalitarian refusal to accept poverty and discrimination as inevitable, instead envisioning a world where marginalized lives are affirmed as worthy of respect.

Finally, "The Devoted Friend" begins with the frame of a Linnet telling the story of poor little Hans and big Hugh the Miller to a curmudgeonly Water-rat. The two men are devoted friends despite their class differences, though it soon becomes obvious Hugh's real devotion is to himself, as he takes advantage of Hans's selflessness for increasingly larger favors without ever providing anything in return other than the promise of gifting him a broken wheelbarrow. Hans loses both valuable time and resources in the bargain, only eventually to die trying to fetch a doctor for Hugh's son during a terrible storm. In the return to the frame, with the Water-rat only expressing sympathy for Hugh, the Linnet remarks that he is missing the moral of the story. At this, the Water-rat becomes furious, angrily retorting he would never have listened in the first place if he had known there was a moral. Then, when the Duck paddles up and observes it is indeed a very dangerous thing to tell a tale with a moral, Wilde reveals a heretofore hidden extra frame, within which the talking animals' narrative is nested, with a metanarrator materializing out of nowhere to proclaim agreement with the Duck.

This is a story that clearly invokes the concern with scale. Wilde's use of the adjective "little" in and of itself connects Hans to most of his other peculiar protagonists, and given Wilde also refers to Hugh as "big," together this allows one to view the pair as an ironic contrast to the selfish Giant and the selfless Christ-child. Wilde also would seem to be contrasting his dynamic duo of devoted friends in "The Happy Prince" with a much more depressing, even cynical, version. This pathetic pair of partners reinforces rather than transcends class differences, confronting its audience with a distressing delineation of how disability-aligned difference can be cruelly exploited under the guise of friendship and compassion. The story thus serves as a stark reminder of the selfishness that can frustrate compassionate action at so many turns, particularly when difference (here, littleness, as well as class) is assumed to indicate inferiority and its status as "less than" is in turn used to justify being taken advantage of by more powerful others. The Miller joins the ranks of the Rocket and the Student as the embodiment of such selfishness. In fact, in a way, his character more powerfully represents the threat such selfishness holds for peculiar bodies in that Hugh is consciously aware of the exploitation he engages in. In the end, though, many readers remain unsure whether to admire the kindhearted protagonist with the diminutive moniker or cast him as a patsy whose disappointing spinelessness deserves more mockery than pity.

As a nested narrative where a farcical frame provides crucial context for the interior story, "The Devoted Friend" also encourages readers to acknowledge the role of sentimental pity in preserving paternalistic posturing, even on the part of the most sympathetic readers. The tongue-in-beak delivery of Wilde's bird-bard leaves the Linnet's listeners pulled in different directions, torn between wanting to take the tale at face value as an indictment of selfishness, and being unable to take seriously any notion one should be expecting anything even remotely close to a neatly wrapped moral. Wilde's return to the frame at story's end only leaves a litany of new questions: Does this metanarrator speak as or for the author? Is Wilde himself at yet another remove? If the metanarrator's agreement with the Duck is at all in earnest, then are the Linnet's moralizing intentions equally dangerous, potentially serving as their own form of egocentrism and bullying? Can we take any of this seriously at all, particularly if we entertain the notion the metanarrator speaks in jest? Or, are we merely hearing the voice of a paternalistic moralizer? Do we lump the metanarrator together with the Water-rat and the Miller and the Duck? Are all of them equally manipulative mediating agents attempting to assert their own authority and normative identity? Is Wilde? Regardless of what answers one might assign to which questions, "The Devoted Friend" reminds us how Wilde's disability-aligned characters are not always admirably active benefactors modeling a more humane response to stigmatization and marginalization but sometimes still may be relegated to the role of the vulnerable, helpless victim.

With all of the fairy tales now at least briefly addressed, it is time to bring this book to a close. Wilde's epiphanies in the prison writing about his own positioning relative to his peculiar protagonists (and to all those who live and die in pain and sorrow) show him there is still a world of wonder awaiting him beyond those jail walls. His final years are full of hardship and humiliation, rejection and remorse, but they also bring with such undeniable difficulty a deeper understanding of himself and of his relationship to both fellow downtrodden individuals and oppressed communities. Seeing his last days through the lens of his disability-aligned characters like the Happy Prince allows him (and us) to understand how a life on the margins may still be one of value—of value to oneself and of value to others—with moments of true joy, even under decidedly diminished and disheartening circumstances. Who decides what makes a life worth living? Surely such lives, those of both his fairy-tale and real-life confraternities of outcasts and other have-nots, are as worthy of our attention and respect as the fictitious and real-life High Society haves whose moments of outrageous shallowness provided so much pleasure to him and to his West End audiences before prison.

Wilde's fairy tales are beautiful and ugly, comic and tragic, complex yet simple, engaging and enraging, personal and political texts. They stand out as fantastical reflections on the Victorian abjection of peculiar bodies that he later refracts through the lens of his own experiences of first discipline and punishment and then ostracization and depletion. This set of stories (as well as his prison literature)—with their exposure of the ill treatment of and the damage done to disability-aligned bodyminds, but also with their emphasis upon an emotional response of loving-kindness and compassionate action in the face of sorrow and suffering—remain a truly moving series of interventions in the name of all those who find themselves relegated to the margins of society. While it is crucial never to forget the isolation, stigma, and peril faced by all such lives, it also remains absolutely essential to equally emphasize the very real (as well as the many other still perhaps for now only utopian) possibilities disabled persons may point to as promising great rather than grim imagined futures characterized instead by appreciation, community, and prosperity.

Thus, though Wilde himself (given the difficulty and disappointment and death that dominate the disposable lives of his disability-aligned protagonists) likely might have insisted on nominating the time he was forced to endure that jeering mob on the Clapham Junction platform as the most fitting final image of the fate that awaits even fairy tale freaks and fools, risking his disapproval, I dare to dream up a more redemptive picture to serve as this study's last will and testament, McGann's Romantic Ideology be damned! I wish to offer instead my own perhaps paltry and pitiful but sincerely pity-full and deeply respectful attempt at a hat tip to my beloved Oscar, one still far from the realm of happily-ever-after endings but nonetheless filled with the sort of community and appreciation (if not yet prosperity) that Sleary's circus circle and the Ring at Reading present to us and for us. So, I conjure up Tod Browning's iconic 1932 cinematic representation of disability, *Freaks,* in order to re-vision and transmogrify its famous Wedding Feast scene into a true instance of triumph and celebration.[130] I ask you to imagine with me all of Wilde's disability-aligned protagonists from the fairy tales lovingly surrounding their enchanted creator, wholeheartedly welcoming him into their ranks while enthusiastically chanting, "We accept him. One of us!" Wilde's prison experience and its aftermath show not only that these stories stayed with him all those years, but further, that they came to resonate even more profoundly with a writer who still calls to us from out of the depths of self-reflection; who embraces the lessons he has learned about sorrow and suffering, love and pity, kindness and compassionate action; and who with the help of his own captivating characters asks us to realize together with him, perhaps for the first time in our lives, the vital Importance of Being Different.

# NOTES

## Introduction

1. Throughout this book I will be using the term *dwarf* rather than *little person*, even as the former popularly tends to be glossed nowadays as an outdated, pejorative label. Not only is Wilde's character called the Dwarf, but in disability studies scholarship, recourse to *dwarf* and *dwarfism* is the norm. From Leslie Fiedler's foundational critical work *Freaks*, to Betty M. Adelson's more recent definitive history, *The Lives of Dwarfs*, and down through the 2020 special issue of *Journal of Literary & Cultural Disability Studies* on dwarfism, academic work in this area typically retains *dwarf* and *dwarfism* as its standard terminology.
2. Amanda Hollander, for instance, writing on "The Happy Prince," asserts Wilde "reimagined for the reader—especially the child reader—what it might mean to make mistaken assumptions about the sexual and class values we attribute to certain types of clothing and decoration." Hollander, "Politics of Dress and Decoration," 123. The similar focus on judgements of character or identity based on outward appearance in "The Young King" allows articulation with the ableist values that underwrite the disgust and discrimination directed toward disabled bodies.
3. Readers familiar with disability rights and disability studies likely already are aware of the conflicting opinions among various communities regarding whether to use person-first language or disability- and identity-first language. Briefly, many advocates worked tirelessly over the last quarter of the previous century to reverse stigma by attempting to foreground the personhood of individuals with disabilities through the former. Nonetheless, many others ultimately decided it was more important for disabled

persons to indicate that their difference is a fundamental aspect of their identity. For them, person-first language positions disability as an appendage, something separable from one's person and, most disturbingly, something they themselves worry somehow qualifies their ability to achieve or experience full personhood and a desirable quality of life. As my sentence indicates, while I remain sensitive to the arguments of both sides, I opt to employ disability-first constructions in my writing.

4. In Schaffer's critical orientation, such reparative reading "is not to erase, but to think deeply about the usability of an older, inherited mode: to think about what it offered . . . [and] what can be maintained or transformed for later use." In advancing her own notion of reparative reading, she draws on previous work by Sara Ahmed, Eli Clare, Steven Jackson, and Eve Kosofsky Sedgwick. Schaffer, *Communities of Care*, 4, 3–5.
5. Wilde purportedly wore a reddish-bronze coat to the celebrated opening of London's Grosvenor Gallery in 1877. When seen from behind, the back of the coat supposedly "resembled the outline of a cello." Ellmann, *Oscar Wilde*, 79.
6. Straley, "Evolution of Lying," 159.
7. Ibid., 160. "Decay of Lying" is a brilliant essay presented as a dialogue between two personalities named for Wilde's children (though one with a slightly different spelling) that playfully toes a line between earnest argument and trivial spoof while advancing the premise that lying is the proper aim of art.
8. Tatar, "Aesthetics of Altruism," 148, 153.
9. Markey, *Oscar Wilde's Fairy Tales*, 107.
10. Zipes, *Fairy Tales*, 89, 107, 123.
11. Yenika-Agbaw, "Reading Disability in Children's Literature," 95.
12. Nodelman, "Young Know Everything," 195–96.
13. Kooistra, "Wilde's Legacy," 90. Kooistra singles out Laurence Housman as a notable Wildean protégé in this regard, while Hollander nominates Evelyn Sharp.
14. Nodelman, "Young Know Everything," 197.
15. Markey, *Oscar Wilde's Fairy Tales*, 4.
16. Tatar, "Aesthetics of Altruism," 153.
17. Killeen, *Fairy Tales of Oscar Wilde*, 1.
18. Ibid., 15.
19. Ibid., 17.
20. Markey, *Oscar Wilde's Fairy Tales*, 12.
21. Bristow, "Introduction," 22.

22. Wilde to John Ruskin, 16 Tite Street, [June 1888], in *Complete Letters*, 349; Wilde to W. E. Gladstone, 16 Tite Street, [June 1888], in *Complete Letters*, 350; Wilde to G. H. Kersley, 16 Tite Street, [June 15, 1888], in *Complete Letters*, 352.
23. Wilde to G. H. Kersley, 16 Tite Street, [June 15, 1888], in *Complete Letters*, 352; Wilde to Amelie Rives Chanler, 16 Tite Street, [January 1889], in *Complete Letters*, 388.
24. Wilde to the Editor of the *Pall Mall Gazette*, 29 Boulevard des Capucines, [early December 1891], in *Complete Letters*, 503.
25. Killeen, *Fairy Tales of Oscar Wilde*, 10.
26. Markey, *Oscar Wilde's Fairy Tales*, 201.
27. Nodelman, "Young Know Everything," 183.
28. Ibid., 198.
29. Killeen, *Fairy Tales of Oscar Wilde*, 171.
30. Ibid., 17.
31. Ibid., 32.
32. Huff and Stoddard Holmes, "Introduction," 8.
33. Ibid.
34. Ibid., 10.
35. Longmore, "Cultural Framing of Disability," 505.
36. Ibid., 505–6.
37. Huff and Stoddard Holmes, "Introduction," 1–2.
38. Ibid., 2.
39. Stoddard Holmes, "Queering the Marriage Plot," 241.
40. Huff and Stoddard Holmes, "Introduction," 2.
41. Ibid. Huff and Stoddard Holmes go on to cite the work of Erin O'Connor in order to emphasize how it is not merely in the relative prominence of what we now regard as the pseudosciences of phrenology and physiognomy but also in the prevailing thought of leading figures in numerous more respectable fields that such principles were promulgated: "in works as diverse as Acton and Greg's studies of prostitution, Chadwick's sanitary reports, Galton's eugenics, Lombroso's criminal anthropology, Maudsley's psychology, Mayhew's urban profiles, and Spencer's sociology we see the same sorts of ideas at work again and again." O'Connor, *Raw Material*, 14.
42. Qtd. in Huff and Stoddard Holmes, "Introduction," 5.
43. Ibid.
44. Huff and Stoddard Holmes, "Introduction," 11.
45. Ibid.
46. Ibid., 12.

47. Yenika-Agbaw, "Reading Disability in Children's Literature," 95.
48. Huff and Stoddard Holmes, "Introduction," 1.
49. Garland-Thomson, "Cultural Logic of Euthanasia," 780.
50. Ibid.
51. Hingston, *Articulating Bodies*, 169.
52. Ibid., 12.
53. Ibid., 18.
54. Ibid., 6.
55. Durbach, "Atypical Bodies," 23.
56. Durbach, *Spectacle of Deformity*, 1.
57. Durbach, "Atypical Bodies," 24, 25.
58. Durbach, *Spectacle of Deformity*, 16.
59. Ibid., 28.
60. Ibid.
61. Garland Thomson, "Introduction," 1. As a point of clarification, Garland-Thomson's name is most often hyphenated, but some of her early works, including *Extraordinary Bodies* and *Freakery*, list her name without a hyphen, so I do not include a hyphen when referring to words and ideas from these texts.
62. Ibid., 5.
63. Ibid., 10.
64. Tromp, "Introduction," 8.
65. Stoddard Holmes, "Queering the Marriage Plot," 252.
66. Free, "Freaks That Matter," 278.
67. See McRuer's chapter in the celebrated edited collection *The Disability Studies Reader*, "Compulsory Able-Bodiedness and Queer/Disabled Existence"; for a more extended treatment, consult his important monograph, *Crip Theory*.
68. Fiedler, *Freaks*, 273.
69. Ibid., 27.
70. Ibid., 28.
71. Ibid., 34.
72. Ibid., 269.
73. Killeen, *Fairy Tales of Oscar Wilde*, 137.
74. Ibid. "Dr. Quilp" refers to the character of Daniel Quilp from Charles Dickens's *The Old Curiosity Shop*, an evil dwarf who persecutes the sentimentalized heroine, Little Nell. In the next chapter, I discuss both of these diminutive Dickensian characters in relation to Wilde's "The Birthday of the Infanta."

75. Ibid., 61.
76. Ibid.
77. Fiedler, *Freaks*, 105.
78. Wilde also surely would have been familiar with the controversy surrounding the Cardiff Giant over in America and the subsequent feud between George Hull and P. T. Barnum over whose version, if either, was the authentic one. See Scott Tribble's *A Colossal Hoax*.
79. Mitchell and Snyder, *Narrative Prosthesis*, 1.
80. Mendelssohn, *Making Oscar Wilde*, 3.
81. Ibid., 6.
82. Ibid., 51–58.
83. Ibid., 191.
84. Ibid., 91. Such rhetoric constitutes a powerful example of the extent to which a blurring of the lines between *this* and *that* was employed to fully abject as other those whose anomalous bodies dredged up feelings of discomfort, disgust, and disdain (as opposed to the sort of self-identification with freak figures that I will argue Wilde's texts allow, even encourage)—i.e., how Rodas's question often was answered with a pejorative rather than an affirmative response.
85. Ibid., 92.
86. Ibid., 95.
87. Qtd. in ibid., 95.
88. Qtd. in ibid., 4.
89. Ibid., 122.
90. Ibid., 150–56.
91. Ibid., 160–64.
92. Ibid., 102.
93. Ibid., 109.
94. While Mendelssohn notes an incident in Atlanta where Wilde attempted to take a stand against segregated arrangements for his black valet, in general he tended "to defend his own whiteness" by denigrating African Americans. And it is not merely his predilection for positing similarities between the Confederate cause and Irish republicanism (an affiliation he attempted to solidify through a side pilgrimage to see Jefferson Davis) that is damning in this respect. As Mendelssohn documents, the admittedly scant evidence we have regarding Wilde's comments about the black servants whom he relied on throughout his tour testifies to his own racism. Ibid., 211, 208, 118.
95. Stoddard Holmes, *Fictions of Affliction*, 3, 2.

96. Davidson, "Universal Design," 120.
97. Stoddard Holmes, *Fictions of Affliction*, 5.
98. Donaldson and Prendergast, "Introduction," 132.
99. Sklar, "What the Hell," 138.
100. Chrisman, "Reflection," 174.
101. Shapiro actually barely mentions pity in his book (the index only lists one page for its entry), but the sort of pity his title alludes to is a form of oppression aligned with paternalistic charity and identified as the privileged response to the telethon poster child—the pity most feel for Tim.
102. Kristjánsson, *Virtuous Emotions*, 76, 75. I discuss Kristjánsson's approach to this "conceptual parish" and its potential applications for Wilde's fairy tales later on in the book, specifically in relation to "The Star-Child."
103. Ibid., 77, 78.
104. Ibid., 80.
105. Sklar, "What the Hell," 139, 152.
106. Chrisman, "Reflection," 183.
107. Ibid.
108. Like Ireland, Cornwall has numerous notable connections to giants, including the real-life Cornish Giant from the English Civil War (Anthony Payne) as well as the mythological figures of Bolster and Gogmagog, which likely informed Wilde's decision to choose the county as the site of the Selfish Giant's visit.
109. Wilde, "Selfish Giant," 25.
110. Ibid.
111. Ibid., 25, 26.
112. Hodgkins, "White Blossoms," 42.
113. Markey, *Oscar Wilde's Fairy Tales*, 118.
114. Bristow, "Introduction," 5.
115. Killeen, *Fairy Tales of Oscar Wilde*, 64.
116. Wilde, "Selfish Giant," 27.
117. Ibid.
118. Ibid.
119. Ibid.
120. Ibid., 27–28.
121. Ibid., 28.
122. Ibid.
123. Ibid.
124. Ibid., 29.

125. Ibid.
126. Ibid.
127. Ibid.
128. Ibid.
129. Qtd. in Beckson, *Oscar Wilde Encyclopedia*, 154.
130. Markey, *Oscar Wilde's Fairy Tales*, 120.
131. Nodelman, "Young Know Everything," 189.
132. Eiesland, *Disabled God*, 101.
133. Ibid., 100, 107.
134. Ibid., 116.
135. Tatar, "Aesthetics of Altruism," 152.
136. Ibid.
137. For approaches to this tale through the lens of alternative sexualities, see the work of John-Charles Duffy, Michael Kotzin, and Naomi Wood.
138. Nodelman, "Young Know Everything," 186.
139. Ibid., 187.
140. Bristow, "Introduction," 1.
141. These texts are (in order of appearance) "The Birthday of the Infanta," "The Fisherman and His Soul," "The Star-Child," and "The Happy Prince." Originally, I envisioned pairing each of these main focus points with its own partner from one of the remaining four tales and offering a coda section to its chapter exploring how the second text complemented or complicated the emphases of the matched story. These less obvious or developed disability-aligned tales ("The Remarkable Rocket," "The Nightingale and the Rose," "The Young King," and "The Devoted Friend") now are discussed together briefly in the conclusion, without fully fleshed-out close readings of their own.
142. Theorizations and articulations of the concept of *bodymind* refuse the mind/body binary in positing the two as in fact intimately integrated and interdependent. For a more detailed sense of how this has been developed and delineated within a disability studies context, see Price's "The Bodymind Problem and the Possibilities of Pain"—as well as her landmark *Mad at School*—and then Clare's *Brilliant Imperfection* and Schalk's *Bodyminds Reimagined* for substantial intersectional extensions of this focus, with particular attention to gender, race, and sexuality.
143. McCormack, "Wilde's Fiction(s)," 102.

## 1. "The Birthday of the Infanta"

1. Qtd. in Ellmann, *Oscar Wilde*, 469.
2. For those readers who may not have read the introduction before this chapter, I will clarify here as well that throughout this book I will be using the term *dwarf* rather than *little person*, even as the former popularly tends to be glossed nowadays as an outdated, pejorative label. Not only is Wilde's character called the Dwarf, but in disability studies scholarship, recourse to *dwarf* and *dwarfism* is the norm. From Leslie Fiedler's foundational critical work *Freaks* to Betty M. Adelson's more recent definitive history, *The Lives of Dwarfs*, and down through the 2020 special issue of *Journal of Literary & Cultural Disability Studies* on dwarfism, academic work in this area typically retains *dwarf* and *dwarfism* as its standard terminology.
3. Craton, *Victorian Freak Show*, 51.
4. Ibid., 43.
5. Ibid., 42, 44.
6. Ibid., 58.
7. Ibid., 54.
8. Ibid., 51.
9. Ibid., 51–52.
10. Ibid., 59.
11. In his chapter on dwarfs in *Freaks*, Fiedler notes the distinction between achondroplastic dwarfs (characterized as having disproportionately short legs and large heads) and hypopituitary midgets (represented as small but proportioned) by citing the dark goblin Quilp and the miniature elf-child Nell as, respectively, representative literary types of each. Fiedler, *Freaks*, 43.
12. Wilde, "Birthday," 123, 124, 125, 123.
13. Ibid., 124.
14. Ibid.
15. Ibid., 125.
16. Ibid.
17. Ibid.
18. Ibid., 126.
19. Ibid., 128.
20. Ibid.
21. Craton, *Victorian Freak Show*, 44.
22. Wilde, "Birthday," 128.
23. Ibid., 129.

24. Ibid.
25. Ibid.
26. See Garland Thomson's notable delineation of this distinction in *Freakery*. Garland Thomson, "Introduction," 10.
27. Wilde, "Birthday," 123.
28. Ibid., 124.
29. Ibid., 128–29.
30. Ibid., 129.
31. Killeen, *Fairy Tales of Oscar Wilde*, 137.
32. Wilde, "Birthday," 129.
33. Ibid., 130.
34. Ibid.
35. Ibid.
36. Ibid.
37. Ibid.
38. Ibid., 131.
39. Ibid.
40. Ibid.
41. Ibid.
42. Ibid.
43. Ibid.
44. Ibid.
45. Ibid., 132.
46. Ibid.
47. Ibid.
48. McDonagh, "Learning Difficulties," 136.
49. Ibid., 145.
50. Wilde, "Birthday," 133.
51. Ibid., 132.
52. Ibid., 133.
53. Ibid.
54. Ibid., 136.
55. Ibid.
56. Ibid.
57. Ibid.
58. Ibid.
59. Ibid., 137.
60. Ibid.
61. Ibid.

62. Ibid.
63. Ibid.
64. Ibid.
65. Ibid.
66. Ibid.
67. Ibid., 138.
68. Ibid.
69. Ibid.
70. Ibid.
71. Markey, *Oscar Wilde's Fairy Tales*, 164–66; Killeen, *Fairy Tales of Oscar Wilde*, 137–38.
72. Adelson, *Lives of Dwarfs*, 208.
73. Ibid.
74. Markey, *Oscar Wilde's Fairy Tales*, 165.
75. Zipes, *Fairy Tales*, 123.
76. Killeen, *Fairy Tales of Oscar Wilde*, 125.
77. Markey, *Oscar Wilde's Fairy Tales*, 161.
78. Ibid., 160.
79. Mitchell and Snyder, *Narrative Prosthesis*, 1.
80. Ibid., 3, 8.
81. Ibid., 8.

## 2. "The Fisherman and His Soul"

1. To clarify, while Craton's insights (regarding authorial manipulation, readerly complicity, and sentimentality) will not be totally abandoned across the rest of the book, the point of the Dickensian touchstones is to find fresh angles within each chapter that are more specifically relevant to the focus of each new tale, so in this chapter my focus will turn primarily toward romance plotlines and the roles they allow for disability-aligned protagonists, while continuing to contextualize this discussion in relation to freakery.
2. Qtd. in Free, "Freaks That Matter," 261.
3. Free, "Freaks That Matter," 259.
4. Ibid., 268.
5. Ibid., 269.
6. Ibid.
7. Ibid., 259.
8. Ibid.

9. Ibid., 278.
10. Wilde capitalizes *Soul* when referring to the separate character he becomes after the amputation. Accordingly, I follow suit, using lower case when referring to the Fisherman's soul (or any souls) more generically and using upper case when specifically referencing said separate character.
11. Wilde, "Fisherman," 139.
12. Ibid.
13. Ibid.
14. Ibid.
15. Ibid.
16. Ibid., 140.
17. Ibid.
18. Ibid.
19. Ibid.
20. Ibid., 140–41.
21. Ibid., 141.
22. Killeen, *Fairy Tales of Oscar Wilde*, 149.
23. Wilde, "Fisherman," 141.
24. Ibid.
25. Ibid.
26. Ibid., 142.
27. Ibid.
28. As we saw in the previous chapter, dwarfs also were stigmatized during the nineteenth century by descriptions of them as lacking a soul.
29. Wilde, "Fisherman," 142.
30. Ibid., 143.
31. Ibid.
32. Ibid.
33. Ibid., 144.
34. Mark 8:36 (King James Version).
35. Ibid., 144.
36. Ibid.
37. Free, "Freaks That Matter," 278.
38. Wilde, "Fisherman," 144.
39. Wilde, *Picture of Dorian Gray*, 183.
40. Ibid., 187.
41. Ibid., 183.
42. Wilde, *Soul of Man*, 266.
43. Ibid.

44. Ibid., 267.
45. Ibid., 263.
46. Ibid., 264.
47. Ibid., 263–64.
48. Ibid., 264.
49. Wilde, "Fisherman," 146.
50. Ibid., 147.
51. Ibid., 146.
52. Ibid.
53. Ibid.
54. Ibid., 150.
55. Ibid.
56. Ibid., 151.
57. Ibid.
58. Ibid., 152.
59. Ibid.
60. Ibid.
61. Ibid.
62. Ibid.
63. Ibid., 153.
64. Ibid.
65. Ibid., 155.
66. Markey, *Oscar Wilde's Fairy Tales*, 180.
67. Wilde, "Fisherman," 156.
68. Ibid.
69. Ibid., 157.
70. Ibid., 160.
71. Ibid., 161.
72. Ibid., 163.
73. Ibid., 164.
74. Ibid., 165.
75. Ibid.
76. Ibid., 166.
77. Ibid., 168.
78. Ibid., 169.
79. Ibid.
80. Ibid., 169–70.
81. Ibid., 170.
82. Ibid., 171.

83. Ibid.
84. Ibid.
85. Ibid.
86. Ibid., 172.
87. Ibid.
88. Ibid.
89. Ibid.
90. Ibid.
91. Ibid., 173.
92. Ibid.
93. Wilde, "Birthday," 125.
94. Ibid., 124.
95. Zipes, *Fairy Tales*, 124.
96. Wilde, "Fisherman," 173.
97. Ibid.
98. Ibid.
99. Ibid.
100. Ibid., 174.
101. Ibid.
102. Ibid.
103. Ibid.
104. Ibid.
105. Ibid.
106. Free, "Freaks That Matter," 259, 278.

## 3. "The Star-Child"

1. Zipes, *Fairy Tales*, 123, 124.
2. Markey, *Oscar Wilde's Fairy Tales*, 191, 190.
3. Dickens, *Tale of Two Cities*, 404.
4. Qtd. in Bonfiglio, "Sentimental Transport," 264.
5. Bonfiglio, "Sentimental Transport," 265.
6. Dickens, *Tale of Two Cities*, 1.
7. Bonfiglio, "Sentimental Transport," 277.
8. Dickens, *Tale of Two Cities*, 388.
9. Ibid., 403–4.
10. Ibid., 396.
11. Bonfiglio, "Sentimental Transport," 265.
12. Wilde, "Star-Child," 175.

13. Ibid., 176.
14. Ibid., 177.
15. Ibid.
16. Ibid., 181.
17. Ibid., 178.
18. Ibid., 179.
19. Markey, *Oscar Wilde's Fairy Tales*, 183.
20. Smith, "Play[ing] Narcissus," 56, 50, 56.
21. McDonagh, "Learning Difficulties," 136.
22. Wilde, "Star-Child," 179.
23. Ibid., 179.
24. Ibid.
25. Ibid.
26. Ibid.
27. Ibid., 180.
28. Ibid.
29. Ibid.
30. Ibid.
31. Ibid.
32. Ibid.
33. Ibid., 181.
34. Ibid., 182.
35. Hingston, *Articulating Bodies*, 166.
36. Wilde, "Star-Child," 182.
37. Ibid.
38. Ibid., 183.
39. Prendergast, "And Now," 243, 242.
40. Kristjánsson, *Virtuous Emotions*, 76, 77.
41. Ibid., 78.
42. Ibid., 80.
43. Warner, *Rousseau*, 60, 60–61.
44. Ibid., 61.
45. Ibid., 64.
46. Qtd. in Sprigge, "Is Pity the Basis of Ethics?" 103.
47. Sprigge, "Is Pity the Basis of Ethics?" 106.
48. Ibid., 104.
49. Wilde, "Star-Child," 183.
50. Ibid.
51. Ibid., 184.

52. Ibid.
53. Ibid.
54. Ibid.
55. Ibid.
56. Ibid., 184, 185.
57. Nodelman, "Young Know Everything," 192.
58. Wilde, "Star-Child," 185.
59. Ibid., 186.
60. Ibid., 187.
61. Ibid., 188.
62. Ibid.
63. Ibid.
64. Ibid.
65. Warner, *Rousseau*, 64.
66. Wilde, "Star-Child," 188.
67. Killeen, *Fairy Tales of Oscar Wilde*, 162.
68. Wilde, "Star-Child," 189.
69. Ibid.
70. Ibid., 190.
71. Ibid.
72. Ibid.
73. Ibid., 191.
74. Ibid.
75. Ibid.
76. Ibid., 192.
77. Prendergast, "And Now," 240.
78. Wilde, "Star-Child," 192–93.
79. Ibid., 193.
80. Killeen, *Fairy Tales of Oscar Wilde*, 165.
81. Ibid., 166.
82. Ibid., 170.
83. Ibid.
84. Markey, *Oscar Wilde's Fairy Tales*, 189.
85. Ibid., 180.
86. Ibid., 190.
87. Ibid., 181.
88. Wilde, "Chinese Sage," 237, 238.
89. Ibid., 238–39.
90. Ibid., 239.

91. Ibid., 240–41.
92. Ibid., 241.
93. Ibid., 242.
94. Perhaps the most extended example of this is his tribute to Thomas Griffiths Wainewright in "Pen, Pencil and Poison" (originally published in 1889, then revised and reprinted for *Intentions* in 1891).
95. Wilde, "Chinese Sage," 242.
96. Wilde, *Soul of Man*, 231.
97. Ibid., 232.
98. Ibid., 234.
99. Ibid.
100. Ibid., 235.
101. Ibid., 232.
102. Ibid.
103. Donaldson and Prendergast, "Introduction," 130.

## 4. "The Happy Prince"

1. Klages, *Woeful Afflictions*, 115.
2. Rodas, "Tiny Tim," 65.
3. Ibid., 52.
4. Ibid., 71, 75.
5. Ibid., 52.
6. Ibid., 78.
7. Ibid., 52.
8. Wilde, "Happy Prince," 13.
9. Ibid.
10. Ibid.
11. Ibid.
12. Ibid.
13. Ibid., 14.
14. Ibid.
15. Ibid. Wilde again does not provide a sense of the age of the Prince, as he is depicted in statue form, but this comment suggests he likely did not live into adulthood, as then he surely would have had at least some experience with the world beyond the palace walls. Walter Crane's illustration for the volume's first edition would seem to corroborate that Wilde is conceiving of him as a youth, if not a child.
16. Bourrier, "Mobility Impairment," 57–58.

17. Wilde, *Soul of Man*, 235.
18. Wilde, "Happy Prince," 14.
19. Ibid., 14–15.
20. Ibid., 15.
21. Ibid.
22. Ibid.
23. Ibid.
24. Ibid.
25. Ibid.
26. Ibid.
27. Wilde, *Soul of Man*, 236.
28. Wilde, "Happy Prince," 15.
29. Ibid., 15, 16.
30. Ibid., 17.
31. Huff and Stoddard Holmes, "Introduction," 6, 5, 3.
32. Wilde, "Happy Prince," 17.
33. Ibid.
34. Ibid., 18.
35. Ibid.
36. Straley, "Oscar Wilde's Fairy Tales," 166.
37. Tatar, "Aesthetics of Altruism," 151.
38. Zipes, *Fairy Tales*, 121.
39. Hoffmann, "Of Monkey Girls," 67.
40. Ibid., 81.
41. Ibid., 82.
42. Wilde, "Decay of Lying," 101.
43. Ibid., 101–2.
44. Wilde, *Soul of Man*, 247.
45. Wilde, "Happy Prince," 18.
46. Ibid.
47. Ibid.
48. Ibid.
49. Hollander, "Oscar Wilde," 137, 138.
50. Wilde, "Happy Prince," 18.
51. Ibid.
52. Ibid.
53. Ibid.
54. Ibid.
55. Ibid.

56. Zipes, *Fairy Tales*, 121.
57. Wilde, "Happy Prince," 19.
58. Ibid.
59. Wilde, *Soul of Man*, 262.
60. Ibid.
61. Wilde, "Decay of Lying," 101.
62. Wilde, "Happy Prince," 18.
63. Ibid., 19.
64. Ibid.
65. Coincidentally, Hingston posits this text is a crucial one for analyzing how Victorian writers articulate disability-aligned bodies. Hingston, *Articulating Bodies*, 139–60.
66. Markey, *Oscar Wilde's Fairy Tales*, 99.
67. Kafer, *Feminist, Queer, Crip*, 1–3.
68. Scheuer, "Bodily Compositions," 158.

## Conclusion

1. Wilde, "Epistola," 52. To clarify, in Ian Small's definitive edition, from which I am citing, he uses "Epistola: In Carcere et Vinculis" (Wilde's original title) for the authoritative full text of this document, and he employs the more popularly known title of *De Profundis* to reference the partial version originally published by Robbie Ross in 1905. Following Small, I will be referring to the full work as "Epistola" rather than as *De Profundis*. I would also like to indicate here that since this authoritative edition of "Epistola" is a base-text derived from multiple versions, Small utilizes square brackets to identify words omitted from the typescript but present in the manuscript; in the interest of avoiding confusion about the nature of any such brackets in material I am quoting, I have made the editorial decision not to include any such brackets, just the words themselves. Consequently, any brackets appearing in quotations from "Epistola" are my own, not Small's.
2. Ibid., 53.
3. Ibid.
4. Ibid., 54.
5. Ibid., 55, 56.
6. Ibid., 109, 108.
7. Ibid., 108.
8. Ibid., 109.

9. Ibid.
10. Ibid., 127–28.
11. Ibid., 128.
12. Ibid., 127.
13. Ibid., 128.
14. Ibid.
15. Giffone, "Sleary Circus," 397.
16. Dickens, *Hard Times*, 30.
17. Ibid.
18. Ibid., 36.
19. Naslund, "Mr. Sleary's Lisp," 42.
20. Ibid., 43.
21. Ibid.
22. Ibid., 44.
23. Ibid., 45.
24. Dickens, *Hard Times*, 41.
25. Ibid.
26. Ibid., 259.
27. Wilde, "Epistola," 106.
28. Ibid., 82.
29. Ibid., 108.
30. Ibid., 99.
31. Ibid., 75.
32. Ibid., 103.
33. Frankel, *Oscar Wilde*, 41.
34. Ibid., 46.
35. Qtd. in Frankel, *Oscar Wilde*, 46.
36. Frankel, *Oscar Wilde*, 46.
37. Ibid., 47.
38. Ibid., 277–78.
39. Ibid., 48–49.
40. Ibid., 53.
41. Ibid., 53; qtd. in Frankel, *Oscar Wilde*, 54.
42. Qtd. in Frankel, *Oscar Wilde*, 54.
43. Frankel, *Oscar Wilde*, 297, 298, 303.
44. Ibid., 303.
45. Wilde, "Epistola," 42.
46. Ibid., 50.
47. Ibid., 129.

48. This also extends to the four stories not covered in the content chapters, where we meet both selfless agents of others' happiness (like little Hans, the young King, and the Nightingale) as well as selfish purveyors of suffering and death (such as Hugh the Miller, the Remarkable Rocket, and the young Student).
49. Wilde, "Epistola," 155.
50. Ibid., 71.
51. Ibid., 140.
52. Ibid., 75.
53. Ibid., 93.
54. Ibid., 85.
55. Ibid.
56. Wilde, *Soul of Man*, 240–43.
57. Wilde, "Epistola," 110.
58. Ibid.
59. Ibid., 111.
60. Ibid., 112.
61. Ibid.
62. Ibid., 113.
63. Ibid.
64. Ibid., 114.
65. Ibid., 115.
66. Ibid., 121.
67. Ibid., 120.
68. Ibid., 119.
69. Ibid., 116.
70. Ibid., 117.
71. Wilde to Thomas Martin, HM Prison Reading, [May 17, 1897], in *Complete Letters*, 831.
72. Wilde to the Editor of the *Daily Chronicle*, Dieppe, May 27, [1897], in *Complete Letters*, 848.
73. Ibid.
74. Ibid., 849.
75. Ibid.
76. Ibid.
77. Ibid., 848.
78. Ibid., 850.
79. Ibid., 849.
80. Ibid.

81. Ibid., 851.
82. Ibid., 852.
83. Ibid.
84. Ibid.
85. Ibid.
86. Ibid., 852–53.
87. Ibid., 853.
88. Ibid.
89. Ibid.
90. Ibid.
91. Ibid.
92. Ibid., 854.
93. Ibid.
94. Ibid.
95. Wilde, *Ballad of Reading Gaol,* 198, lines 102, 109, 110.
96. Ibid., 195, lines 29–30.
97. Ibid., 198, lines 121–22, 125–26.
98. Ibid., 201, lines 203–4, 205–6.
99. Ibid., 201, line 207.
100. Ibid., 201, lines 12, 15, 16, 14.
101. Ibid., 202, lines 226–27.
102. Ibid., 203, lines 247–48.
103. Ibid., 204, lines 285, 287, 289, 293.
104. Ibid., 204, lines 299, 303–4.
105. Ibid., 205, line 308.
106. Ibid., 205, lines 313, 315, 317–18.
107. Ibid., 207, line 378.
108. Ibid., 209, lines 433, 446, 443–44.
109. Ibid., 213, lines 562, 561, 565, 567, 569.
110. Ibid., 214, lines 587–88, 598, 599–600.
111. Ibid., 210, lines 471–72, 475.
112. Ibid., 210, lines 479–80, 483–84, 485, 486.
113. Ibid., 210, lines 481–82.
114. Ibid., 211, lines 493, 495, 497–98.
115. Ibid., 213, lines 551–52.
116. Ibid., 215, lines 605–6.
117. Ibid., 215, lines 617–18.
118. Ibid., 215, lines 607–8, 622.

119. Ibid., 215, lines 609, 611–12. The Biblical passage Wilde references is Mark 14:3–9.
120. Wilde to the Editor of the *Daily Chronicle,* Paris, March 23, [1898], in *Complete Letters,* 1045.
121. Ibid., 1046.
122. Ibid., 1047.
123. Ibid.
124. Ibid.
125. Ibid.
126. Ibid., 1048.
127. Ibid., 1049.
128. Ibid.
129. Wilde's first play, *Vera,* was completed by 1880, and the following year he arranged for a London debut that ended up never coming to fruition. When it did at last open, it was in New York, and its run there only lasted one week. Wilde also wrote a second play, *The Duchess of Padua,* in 1882–83, and it eventually had a short stint of twenty-one performances in New York in 1891. Regarding his journalism, Wilde wrote hundreds of pieces, both signed and unsigned, between the years 1885 and 1890.
130. Browning's controversial film is seen today as a compassionate antieugenicist representation of a "family" of freaks who live and work for a carnival sideshow, even as it is generally still classified as a horror movie. The scene in question takes place at the dinner to mark the wedding between Hans, a dwarf, and Cleopatra, a nondisabled trapeze performer. Cleopatra is only marrying Hans to get her hands on his inheritance, and so when the group begins chanting that they accept her as one of them (that is, as a freak), she becomes so upset at the notion that she angrily denounces them all and cruelly humiliates Hans.

# BIBLIOGRAPHY

Adelson, Betty M. *The Lives of Dwarfs: Their Journey from Public Curiosity toward Social Liberation.* New Brunswick, NJ: Rutgers University Press, 2005.
Barnard, Clio, dir. *The Selfish Giant.* IFC Films, 2013.
Baynton, Douglas C. *Defectives in the Land: Disability and Immigration in the Age of Eugenics.* Chicago: University of Chicago Press, 2016.
Beckson, Karl. *The Oscar Wilde Encyclopedia.* New York: AMS, 1998.
Bolt, David. "Aesthetic Blindness: Symbolism, Realism, and Reality." *Mosaic* 46, no. 3 (2013): 93–108.
Bonfiglio, Richard. "Sentimental Transport and Stoic Sacrifice in *A Tale of Two Cities*." *Dickens Quarterly* 37, no. 3 (2020): 264–84.
Bourrier, Karen. "Mobility Impairment: From the Bath Chair to the Wheelchair." In Huff and Stoddard Holmes, *Cultural History,* 43–60.
Bristow, Joseph. "Introduction: Oscar Wilde and the Cultures of Childhood." In Bristow, *Oscar Wilde,* 1–39.
Bristow, Joseph, ed. *Oscar Wilde and the Cultures of Childhood.* London: Palgrave, 2017.
Browning, Tod, dir. *Freaks.* MGM, 1932.
Chrisman, Wendy L. "A Reflection on Inspiration: A Recuperative Call for Emotion in Disability Studies." *Journal of Literary & Cultural Disability Studies* 5, no. 2 (2011): 173–84.
Clare, Eli. *Brilliant Imperfection: Grappling with Cure.* Durham, NC: Duke University Press, 2017.
Craton, Lillian. *The Victorian Freak Show: The Significance of Disability and Physical Differences in 19th-Century Fiction.* Amherst, NY: Cambria, 2009.

Davidson, Michael. "The Rage of Caliban: Disabling Bodies in Modernist Aesthetics." *Modernism/Modernity* 22, no. 4 (2015): 609–25.

———. "Universal Design: The Work of Disability in an Age of Globalization." In *The Disability Studies Reader*, 2nd ed., edited by Lennard Davis, 117–28. New York: Routledge, 2006.

Dickens, Charles. *American Notes and Pictures from Italy*. London: Oxford University Press, 1970.

———. *Christmas Books*. London: Oxford University Press, 1968.

———. *Hard Times*. Edited by Jeff Nunokawa and Gage C. McWeeny. New York: Pearson Longman, 2004.

———. *The Old Curiosity Shop*. New York: Knopf Everyman's Library, 1995.

———. *Our Mutual Friend*. New York: Knopf Everyman's Library, 1994.

———. *A Tale of Two Cities*. New York: Knopf Everyman's Library, 1993.

Donaldson, Elizabeth J., and Catherine Prendergast. "Introduction: Disability and Emotion—'There's No Crying in Disability Studies!'" *Journal of Literary & Cultural Disability Studies* 5, no. 2 (2011): 129–35.

Duffy, John-Charles. "Gay-Related Themes in the Fairy Tales of Oscar Wilde." *Victorian Literature and Culture* 29, no. 2 (2001): 327–49.

Durbach, Nadja. "Atypical Bodies: The Cultural Work of the Nineteenth-Century Freak Show." In Huff and Stoddard Holmes, *Cultural History*, 23–42.

———. *The Spectacle of Deformity: Freak Shows and Modern British Culture*. Berkeley: University of California Press, 2009.

Eiesland, Nancy L. *The Disabled God: Toward a Liberatory Theology of Disability*. Nashville: Abingdon Press, 1994.

Ellmann, Richard. *Oscar Wilde*. New York: Vintage, 1988.

Everett, Rupert, dir. *The Happy Prince*. Sony, 2018.

Fiedler, Leslie. *Freaks: Myths and Images of the Secret Self*. New York: Simon and Schuster, 1978.

Frankel, Nicholas. *Oscar Wilde: The Unrepentant Years*. Cambridge, MA: Harvard University Press, 2017.

Free, Melissa. "Freaks That Matter: The Dolls' Dressmaker, the Doctor's Assistant, and the Limits of Difference." In Tromp, *Victorian Freaks*, 259–82.

Garland-Thomson, Rosemarie. "The Cultural Logic of Euthanasia: 'Sad Fancyings' in Herman Melville's 'Bartleby.'" *American Literature* 76, no. 4 (2004): 777–806.

Garland Thomson, Rosemarie. *Extraordinary Bodies: Figuring Physical Disability in American Culture and Literature*. New York: Columbia University Press, 1997.

———. "Introduction: From Wonder to Error—A Genealogy of Freak Discourse in Modernity." In *Freakery: Cultural Spectacles of the Extraordinary Body*, edited by Rosemarie Garland Thomson, 1–19. New York: New York University Press, 1996.

Giffone, Anthony. "The Sleary Circus." In *Fools and Jesters in Literature, Art, and History: A Bio-bibliographical Sourcebook*, edited by Vicki K. Janik, 395–99. Westport, CT: Greenwood Press, 1998.

Hingston, Kylee-Anne. *Articulating Bodies: The Narrative Form of Disability and Illness in Victorian Fiction*. Liverpool: Liverpool University Press, 2019.

Hodgkins, Hope Howell. "White Blossoms and Snozzcumbers: Alternative Sentimentalities in the Giants of Oscar Wilde and Roald Dahl." *CEA Critic* 65, no. 1 (2002): 41–49.

Hoffmann, Kathryn A. "Of Monkey Girls and a Hog-Faced Gentlewoman: Marvel in Fairy Tales, Fairgrounds, and Cabinets of Curiosities." *Marvels & Tales* 19, no. 1 (2005): 67–85.

Hollander, Amanda. "Oscar Wilde, Evelyn Sharp, and the Politics of Dress and Decoration in the Fin-de-Siècle Fairy Tale." In Bristow, *Oscar Wilde*, 119–44.

*The Holy Bible*. Grand Rapids, MI: Zondervan, 1990.

Huff, Joyce L., and Martha Stoddard Holmes, eds. *A Cultural History of Disability in the Long Nineteenth Century*. New York: Bloomsbury, 2024.

———. "Introduction: Negotiating Normalcy in the Long Nineteenth Century." In Huff and Stoddard Holmes, *Cultural History*, 1–21.

Kafer, Alison. *Feminist, Queer, Crip*. Bloomington: Indiana University Press, 2013.

Killeen, Jarleth. *The Fairy Tales of Oscar Wilde*. Aldershot: Ashgate, 2007.

Klages, Mary. *Woeful Afflictions: Disability and Sentimentality in Victorian America*. Philadelphia: University of Pennsylvania Press, 1999.

Kooistra, Lorraine Janzen. "Wilde's Legacy: Fairy Tales, Laurence Housman, and the Expression of 'Beautiful Untrue Things.'" In Bristow, *Oscar Wilde*, 89–118.

Kotzin, Michael. "'The Selfish Giant' as Literary Fairy Tale." *Studies in Short Fiction* 16, no. 4 (1979): 301–9.

Kristjánsson, Kristján. *Virtuous Emotions*. Oxford: Oxford University Press, 2018.

Longmore, Paul K. "The Cultural Framing of Disability: Telethons as a Case Study." *PMLA* 120, no. 2 (2005): 502–8.

Lukács, Georg. *The Historical Novel*. Translated by Hannah Mitchell and Stanley Mitchell. Lincoln: University of Nebraska Press, 1983.

Markey, Anne. *Oscar Wilde's Fairy Tales: Origins and Contexts.* Dublin: Irish Academic Press, 2011.

McCormack, Jerusha. "Wilde's Fiction(s)." In *The Cambridge Companion to Oscar Wilde,* edited by Peter Raby, 96–115. Cambridge: Cambridge University Press, 1997.

McDonagh, Patrick. "Learning Difficulties: The Transformation of 'Idiocy' in the Nineteenth Century." In Huff and Stoddard Holmes, *Cultural History,* 129–48.

McGann, Jerome J. *The Romantic Ideology: A Critical Investigation.* Chicago: University of Chicago Press, 1983.

McRuer, Robert. "Compulsory Able-Bodiedness and Queer/Disabled Existence." In *The Disability Studies Reader,* 4th ed., edited by Lennard Davis, 369–80. New York: Routledge, 2013.

———. *Crip Theory: Cultural Signs of Queerness and Disability.* New York: New York University Press, 2006.

Mendelssohn, Michèle. *Making Oscar Wilde.* Oxford: Oxford University Press, 2018.

Mitchell, David T., and Sharon L. Snyder. *Narrative Prosthesis: Disability and the Dependencies of Discourse.* Ann Arbor: University of Michigan Press, 2000.

Mossman, Mark. *Disability, Representation and the Body in Irish Writing: 1800–1922.* New York: Palgrave, 2009.

Naslund, Sena Jeter. "Mr. Sleary's Lisp: A Note on *Hard Times.*" *Dickens Studies Newsletter* 12, no. 2 (1981): 42–46.

Nodelman, Perry. "The Young Know Everything: Oscar Wilde's Fairy Tales as Children's Literature." In Bristow, *Oscar Wilde,* 181–202.

O'Connor, Erin. *Raw Material: Producing Pathology in Victorian Culture.* Durham, NC: Duke University Press, 2000.

Prendergast, Catherine. "And Now, a Necessarily Pathetic Response: A Response to Susan Schweik." *ALH* 20, nos. 1–2 (2008): 238–44.

Price, Margaret. "The Bodymind Problem and the Possibilities of Pain." *Hypatia* 30, no. 1 (2015): 268–84.

———. *Mad at School: Rhetorics of Mental Disability and Academic Life.* Ann Arbor: University of Michigan Press, 2011.

Rodas, Julia Miele. "Tiny Tim, Blind Bertha, and the Resistance of Miss Mowcher: Charles Dickens and the Uses of Disability." *Dickens Studies Annual,* no. 34 (2004): 51–97.

Schaffer, Talia. *Communities of Care: The Social Ethics of Victorian Fiction.* Princeton, NJ: Princeton University Press, 2021.

Schalk, Sami. *Bodyminds Reimagined: (Dis)ability, Race, and Gender in Black Women's Speculative Fiction.* Durham, NC: Duke University Press, 2018.

Scheuer, Christina. "Bodily Compositions: The Disability Poetics of Karen Fiser and Laurie Clements Lambeth." *Journal of Literary & Cultural Disability Studies* 5, no. 2 (2011): 155–72.

Shapiro, Joseph P. *No Pity: People with Disabilities Forging a New Civil Rights Movement.* New York: Times Books, 1993.

Sklar, Howard. "'What the Hell Happened to Maggie?': Stereotype, Sympathy, and Disability in Toni Morrison's 'Recitatif.'" *Journal of Literary & Cultural Disability Studies* 5, no. 2 (2011): 137–54.

Smith, Lindsay. "'Play[ing] Narcissus to a Photograph': Oscar Wilde and the Image of the Child." In Bristow, *Oscar Wilde*, 41–68.

Sprigge, T. L. S. "Is Pity the Basis of Ethics? Nietzsche versus Schopenhauer." In *The Bases of Ethics*, edited by William Sweet, 103–25. Milwaukee, WI: Marquette University Press, 2001.

Stetz, Margaret D. "Greater than the Mystery of Death: Rewriting Oscar Wilde for Young Audiences." In Bristow, *Oscar Wilde*, 203–20.

Stoddard Holmes, Martha. *Fictions of Affliction: Physical Disability in Victorian Culture.* Ann Arbor: University of Michigan Press, 2004.

———. "Queering the Marriage Plot: Wilkie Collins's *The Law and the Lady*." In Tromp, *Victorian Freaks*, 237–58.

Straley, Jessica. "Oscar Wilde's Fairy Tales and the Evolution of Lying." In Bristow, *Oscar Wilde*, 159–80.

Tatar, Maria. "The Aesthetics of Altruism in Oscar Wilde's Fairy Tales." In Bristow, *Oscar Wilde*, 145–57.

Tribble, Scott. *A Colossal Hoax: The Giant from Cardiff That Fooled America.* Lanham, MD: Rowman and Littlefield, 2008.

Tromp, Marlene, ed. *Victorian Freaks: The Social Context of Freakery in Britain.* Columbus: Ohio State University Press, 2008.

Tromp, Marlene, with Karyn Valerius. "Introduction: Toward Situating the Victorian Freak." In Tromp, *Victorian Freaks*, 1–18.

Warner, John M. *Rousseau and the Problem of Human Relations.* University Park: Pennsylvania State University Press, 2015.

Wilde, Oscar. *The Ballad of Reading Gaol.* In *Poems and Poems in Prose*, edited by Bobby Fong and Karl Beckson, 195–216. Vol. 1 of *The Complete Works of Oscar Wilde*, edited by Ian Small. Oxford: Oxford University Press, 2000.

———. "The Birthday of the Infanta." In Wilde, *Short Fiction*, 123–38.

———. "A Chinese Sage." In *Journalism Part 2*, edited by John Stokes and Mark W. Turner, 237–43. Vol. 7 of *The Complete Works of Oscar Wilde*, edited by Ian Small. Oxford: Oxford University Press, 2013.

———. *The Complete Letters of Oscar Wilde*. Edited by Merlin Holland and Rupert Hart-Davis. New York: Holt, 2000.

———. *Criticism: Historical Criticism, Intentions, The Soul of Man*. Edited by Josephine Guy. Vol. 4 of *The Complete Works of Oscar Wilde*, edited by Ian Small. Oxford: Oxford University Press, 2007.

———. "The Decay of Lying." In Wilde, *Criticism*, 72–103.

———. "The Devoted Friend." In Wilde, *Short Fiction*, 30–38.

———. *The Duchess of Padua*. In *Plays 1*, edited by Joseph Donohue, 97–192. Vol. 5 of *The Complete Works of Oscar Wilde*, edited by Ian Small. Oxford: Oxford University Press, 2013.

———. "Epistola: In Carcere et Vinculis." In *De Profundis 'Epistola: In Carcere et Vinculis,'* edited by Ian Small, 35–155. Vol. 2 of *The Complete Works of Oscar Wilde*, edited by Ian Small. Oxford: Oxford University Press, 2005.

———. "The Fisherman and His Soul." In Wilde, *Short Fiction*, 139–74.

———. "The Happy Prince." In Wilde, *Short Fiction*, 13–19.

———. "The Nightingale and the Rose." In Wilde, *Short Fiction*, 20–24.

———. "Pen, Pencil and Poison." In Wilde, *Criticism*, 104–22.

———. *The Picture of Dorian Gray*. In *The Picture of Dorian Gray*, edited by Joseph Bristow, 165–357. Vol. 3 of *The Complete Works of Oscar Wilde*, edited by Ian Small. Oxford: Oxford University Press, 2005. Originally published in 1891.

———. "The Remarkable Rocket." In Wilde, *Short Fiction*, 39–47.

———. *Salome*. In *Plays 1*, edited by Joseph Donohue, 703–31. Vol. 5 of *The Complete Works of Oscar Wilde*, edited by Ian Small. Oxford: Oxford University Press, 2013.

———. "The Selfish Giant." In Wilde, *Short Fiction*, 25–29.

———. *The Short Fiction*, edited by Ian Small. Vol. 8 of *The Complete Works of Oscar Wilde*, edited by Ian Small. Oxford: Oxford University Press, 2017.

———. *The Soul of Man*. In Wilde, *Criticism*, 229–68.

———. *The Sphinx*. In *Poems and Poems in Prose*, edited by Bobby Fong and Karl Beckson, 180–94. Vol. 1 of *The Complete Works of Oscar Wilde*, edited by Ian Small. Oxford: Oxford University Press, 2000.

———. "The Star-Child." In Wilde, *Short Fiction*, 175–93.

———. *Vera; or, the Nihilist*. In *Plays 4*, edited by Josephine Guy, 161–201. Vol. 11 of *The Complete Works of Oscar Wilde*, edited by Ian Small. Oxford: Oxford University Press, 2021.

———. "The Young King." In Wilde, *Short Fiction*, 113–22.

Wood, Naomi. "Creating the Sensual Child: Paterian Aesthetics, Pederasty, and Oscar Wilde's Fairy Tales." *Marvels & Tales* 16, no. 2 (2002): 156–70.

Yenika-Agbaw, Vivian. "Reading Disability in Children's Literature: Hans Christian Andersen's Tales." *Journal of Literary & Cultural Disability Studies* 5, no. 1 (2011): 91–108.

Zipes, Jack. *Fairy Tales and the Art of Subversion: The Classical Genre for Children and the Process of Civilization*. New York: Routledge Classics, 2015.

# INDEX

ableism, 7, 12, 52, 70–71, 74, 76–77, 116
Adelson, Betty M., 50, 143n1, 150n2
aestheticism, 6, 18–19, 108
agency, 33, 98, 100, 104, 108, 115, 162n48
Ahmed, Sara, 144n4
altruism, 85, 93–96, 126, 132. *See also* charity; philanthropy
Andersen, Hans Christian, 7, 76, 102, 108, 114; "The Little Mermaid," 54, 56, 64, 71–72; "Thumbelina," 13; "The Ugly Duckling," 13, 51
animality, 17; in relation to "The Birthday of the Infanta," 40, 42; in relation to "The Fisherman and His Soul," 54, 57, 59, 63, 65, 68, 70; in relation to "The Happy Prince," 107; in relation to "The Star-Child," 82, 92, 95; in relation to Wilde's prison literature, 120, 123, 127, 132–33
Aristotle, 21
Asquith, Herbert, 122
Auerbach, Nina, 58

*Ballad of Reading Gaol, The* (Wilde), 31, 129–32
Barnard, Clio: *The Selfish Giant*, 134
Barnum, P. T., 14, 18–19, 147n78
Baudelaire, Charles, 50

Baynton, Douglas, 12
beauty, 2, 7; in relation to "The Birthday of the Infanta," 35–37, 40, 43–44, 50–51; in relation to "The Fisherman and His Soul," 57, 62, 65, 68, 70; in relation to "The Happy Prince," 100–103, 105, 108–10, 112–14; in relation to "The Selfish Giant," 27–28; in relation to "The Star-Child," 80–81, 83, 91–93; in relation to Wilde's prison literature, 121, 123–25, 128
beggar, figure of: in relation to "The Fisherman and His Soul," 69; in relation to "The Happy Prince," 109, 111–12; in relation to "The Star-Child," 82–84, 86–87, 91; in relation to Wilde's prison literature, 128; in relation to "The Young King," 139
benefactor, role of, 33; in relation to "The Birthday of the Infanta," 44; in relation to "The Happy Prince," 104–5, 107–8, 115; in relation to "The Selfish Giant," 25, 35; in relation to "The Star-Child," 79, 88–90
bestiality. *See* animality
"Birthday of the Infanta, The" (Wilde), 3–4, 6, 29–30, 35–53; in relation to "The Fisherman and His Soul," 54,

"Birthday of the Infanta, The" (*continued*) in relation to "The Fisherman and His Soul," 56–59, 69–71, 73–74; in relation to "The Happy Prince," 106, 112; in relation to "The Nightingale and the Rose," 137; in relation to "The Remarkable Rocket," 32, 135–36; in relation to "The Star-Child," 80–81, 83, 88, 91–92; in relation to Wilde's prison literature, 119, 126; in relation to "The Young King," 138

blindness, 3, 6, 12; in relation to "The Birthday of the Infanta," 39; in relation to "The Fisherman and His Soul," 66, 71; in relation to "The Happy Prince," 98–99, 102, 104, 106–8, 115; in relation to "The Star-Child," 81–82, 87, 89; in relation to Wilde's prison literature, 125–26

bodymind, 32, 71, 83, 125, 127–30, 149n142

Bolster, 148n108

Bolt, David, 6

Bonfiglio, Richard, 77–78, 85–86, 92

Bourrier, Karen, 102

Bristow, Joseph, 8–9, 23, 29

Browning, Tod: *Freaks*, 142, 164n130

Carroll, Lewis, 17

Catholicism, 8, 10, 28. *See also* Christianity

changeling, 79–80

charity, 10–11, 21, 25, 148n101; in relation to "The Birthday of the Infanta," 44; in relation to "A Chinese Sage," 93–94; in relation to "The Happy Prince," 98, 103–4, 106–7, 111; in relation to *Soul of Man*, 95–96; in relation to "The Star-Child," 79, 81, 84–85, 87, 90–93, 96; in relation to Wilde's prison literature, 132. *See also* altruism; philanthropy

child, figure of, 10–11, 16–17, 55, 120, 148n101; in relation to "The Birthday of the Infanta," 36–39, 41, 45, 49; in relation to "The Fisherman and His Soul," 57, 67; in relation to "The Happy Prince," 103, 109–11, 158n15; in relation to "The Selfish Giant," 23–27, 35; in relation to "The Star-Child," 76, 80, 87, 94; in relation to Wilde's prison literature, 125–28, 130. *See also* littleness

childhood culture, 8–10, 16–17, 20

child reader, 9–10, 71–72, 126, 143n2

children's literature, 1, 8–10, 16–17, 20, 26

"Chinese Sage, A" (Wilde), 93–95, 113

Chrisman, Wendy L., 21–22, 52

Christ, figure of, 27, 50, 60, 92, 125–26, 131–32. *See also* Christ-child, figure of

Christ-child, figure of, 25–27, 35, 60, 72–73, 91, 103–4, 112. *See also* Christ, figure of

Christianity, 10, 28; in relation to "The Fisherman and His Soul," 60–63, 65, 67, 72–73; in relation to "The Happy Prince," 103, 114; in relation to "The Selfish Giant," 26–28; in relation to "The Star-Child," 82, 87, 92; in relation to Wilde's prison literature, 125–26, 131–33. *See also* Catholicism

Chuang Tsŭ, 93–94, 113

Cinderella, 55

Clare, Eli, 31–32, 144n4, 149n142

class, 6–7, 10–13, 16, 18, 20, 32, 134; in relation to "The Birthday of the Infanta," 38, 42–46, 50–51, 53; in relation to "The Devoted Friend," 139–40; in relation to "The Fisherman and His Soul," 69; in relation to "The Happy Prince," 98, 101–6, 108–16, 143n2; in relation to "The Nightingale and the Rose," 136; in relation to "The Selfish Giant," 22–23; in relation to "The Star-Child," 75–90, 92, 95–96; in relation

to Wilde's prison literature, 118, 124, 126–28, 133; in relation to "The Young King," 138–39. *See also* disability, in relation to poverty
Collins, Wilkie, 15–16, 61
colonized other, figure of. *See* racism and ethnocentrism
compassion and compassionate action, 21–22, 141–42; in relation to "The Birthday of the Infanta," 47–48, 51–52; in relation to "The Devoted Friend," 140; in relation to "The Fisherman and His Soul," 56, 71; in relation to "The Happy Prince," 98, 101, 103, 106, 109–12, 114–15; in relation to "The Nightingale and the Rose," 136; in relation to "The Selfish Giant," 26; in relation to "The Star-Child," 75–77, 79–80, 82–88, 90, 92, 94, 96; in relation to Wilde's prison literature, 123–24, 129–31; in relation to "The Young King," 139. *See also* pity
compulsory able-bodiedness, 16, 146n67
conditioned disgust, 12, 14, 147n84; in relation to "The Birthday of the Infanta," 36, 38, 43, 52; in relation to "The Fisherman and His Soul," 73; in relation to "The Happy Prince," 106, 112; in relation to "The Selfish Giant," 24; in relation to "The Star-Child," 81, 83–84; in relation to Wilde's prison literature, 119
Craik, Dinah Mulock, 114
Crane, Stephen, 91
Crane, Walter, 158n15
Craton, Lillian, 36–37, 40, 47, 192n1
Cú Chulainn, 18
Currier and Ives, 19

*Daily Chronicle*, 127, 132
d'Aulnoy, Madame (Marie-Catherine Le Jumel de Barneville), 51

Davidson, Michael, 6, 20
Davis, Jefferson, 147n94
"Decay of Lying, The" (Wilde), 6, 109, 113, 125, 144n7
*De Profundis* (Wilde). *See* "Epistola" (Wilde)
"Devoted Friend, The" (Wilde), 2, 6–7, 32, 139–41, 162n48
Dickens, Charles, 20, 29, 35–36, 55, 61, 99–100, 115. *See also* Dickens, Charles, works of
Dickens, Charles, works of: *American Notes*, 99; *A Christmas Carol*, 11, 20, 22, 24, 27, 35–36, 51, 77, 103, 148n101; *The Cricket on the Hearth*, 31, 99; *Hard Times*, 31, 119–21, 129, 142; *The Old Curiosity Shop*, 17, 30, 35–37, 39, 41, 44, 48–49, 51–52, 55, 77, 146n74, 150n11; *Our Mutual Friend*, 30, 55–56, 64–65, 77, 137; *A Tale of Two Cities*, 30, 77–78, 83, 86, 138
disability
—developmental, intellectual, mental, neurological, or other invisible, 11–13, 31–32, 45, 116, 149n142; in relation to "The Star-Child," 55, 71, 77–78, 80, 83; in relation to Wilde's prison literature, 122, 125, 130, 132–33, 141
—emotional response to, 20–22, 24, 32, 36, 52, 141; in relation to "The Star-Child," 75–76, 81, 84–86, 89, 96–97
—as martyrdom, 96, 99, 106
—nineteenth-century constructions of, 3–4, 10–14, 20
—as punishment, 27, 66, 86–87, 91, 115
—in relation to freakery, 4, 14–16 (*see also* freakery and freaks)
—in relation to gender and sexuality, 4–5, 12–13, 15–17, 28, 38; in relation to "The Fisherman and His Soul," 55–58, 61–63, 65, 67–69, 71, 74

disability (continued)
—in relation to intersectionality, 1–2, 4–5,
—in relation to intersectionality, 12–13, 15–16, 20, 28, 32, 71, 81, 105, 139 (see also intersectionality)
—in relation to poverty, 2, 11, 13, 38, 124, 128, 139; in relation to "The Star-Child," 81, 83, 89; in relation to "The Happy Prince," 98, 103, 109, 111 (see also class)
—in relation to work, 10–11
disability-aligned characters, use of, 3–4, 13
disability-first language (identity-first language), 143n3
disability studies and Wilde, 3–6
disabled god: in relation to "The Fisherman and His Soul," 60, 72–73; in relation to "The Happy Prince," 103; in relation to "The Selfish Giant," 27–28; in relation to "The Star-Child," 91–92; in relation to Wilde's prison literature, 126, 131
disfigurement. See ugliness
Donaldson, Elizabeth J., 20–21, 96
Douglas, Alfred "Bosie," 29, 117, 123–25
*Duchess of Padua, The* (Wilde), 164n129
Duffy, John-Charles, 149n137
Durbach, Nadja, 14–15, 65
dwarfism and dwarfs, 3–4, 15, 29, 55, 80, 146n74, 150n11, 153n28; in relation to "The Birthday of the Infanta," 35–53; in relation to the Irish, 17; in relation to William Wilde, 17; use of, 143n1. See also littleness

Eiesland, Nancy L., 27, 92, 131
emotional response. See under disability
empathy, 21, 26, 133; in relation to "The Birthday of the Infanta," 37, 52; in relation to "The Star-Child," 75, 77, 79, 84
enfoolment, 116, 122, 133. See also disability: developmental, intellectual, mental, neurological, or other invisible
enfreakment. See disability: in relation to freakery; freakery and freaks
"Epistola" (Wilde), 31, 50, 117–26, 129–32, 160n1
ethnic other, figure of. See racism and ethnocentrism
eugenics, 38, 42, 44, 145n41
Everett, Rupert: *The Happy Prince*, 134
extraordinary, use of as adjective, 4

fellow feelings, 21, 26, 32; in relation to "The Happy Prince," 103; in relation to "The Star-Child," 76–80, 84–85, 90, 92, 96; in relation to Wilde's prison literature, 121, 123–24
Fiedler, Leslie, 16–18, 54, 120, 143n1, 150n11
"Fisherman and His Soul, The" (Wilde), 2–4, 30, 54–74; in relation to "The Happy Prince," 107, 112, 114; in relation to "The Nightingale and the Rose," 32, 136–37; in relation to "The Star-Child," 75, 82, 91–92; in relation to Wilde's prison literature, 119, 126, 131; in relation to "The Young King," 138
Fomori, 18
foreign other, figure of. See racism and ethnocentrism
Frankel, Nicholas, 122–23
freakery and freaks, 4, 6, 14–17, 19–20, 142, 147n84, 151n26, 164n130; in relation to "The Birthday of the Infanta," 36–37, 39–40, 42, 50–53; in relation to "The Fisherman and His Soul," 54–55, 57–58, 60–61, 63–66, 71–74; in relation to "The Happy Prince," 98, 102, 107, 116; in relation to "The Selfish Giant," 22, 24, 26–27; in relation to "The Star-Child," 76, 86–88, 91; in relation to Wilde's prison literature,

118–21, 123, 130, 133–34. *See also* disability: in relation to freakery
Free, Melissa, 16, 55–56, 61, 64–65, 74

Garland-Thomson, Rosemarie (Rosemarie Garland Thomson), 4, 13, 15, 54, 65, 79, 146n61, 151n26
gender and sexuality, 4–5, 12–13, 15–17, 28, 38; in relation to "The Fisherman and His Soul," 55–58, 61–63, 65, 67–69, 71, 74
Giffone, Anthony, 119–20
gigantism and giants, 3–4, 15, 17; famous giants, 147n78, 148n108; in relation to the Irish, 17–18; in relation to Jane Wilde, 17; in relation to Oscar Wilde, 17; in relation to "The Selfish Giant," 22–28
Gogmagog, 148n108
Gower, George Leveson, 29
grotesque. *See* ugliness

Haldane, Richard, 122
"Happy Prince, The" (Wilde), 3, 31, 98–116, 158n15; in relation to "The Devoted Friend," 32, 140; in relation to "The Nightingale and the Rose," 137; in relation to "The Star-Child," 92; in relation to Wilde's prison literature, 118–19, 125–26, 141; in relation to "The Young King," 143n2
*Happy Prince and Other Tales, The* (Wilde), 1–2, 9, 118, 133
*Harper's Weekly*, 18
Hauser, Caspar, 80
Hingston, Kylee-Anne, 14, 36, 83–84, 86, 115, 160n65
Hodgkins, Hope Howell, 23
Hoffmann, Kathryn A., 108
Hollander, Amanda, 8, 110, 143n2, 144n13
*House of Pomegranates, A* (Wilde), 1–2, 9, 62, 93–94

Housman, Laurence, 144n13
Huff, Joyce L., 10–13, 74, 106, 145n41
Hugo, Victor, 126
Hull, George, 147n78
hybridity, 15, 54, 57, 61, 65, 71, 80

immigrant, figure of. *See* racism and ethnocentrism
infantilization, 2, 10–11
intersectionality, 5, 10, 12–13, 15–16, 20, 28–29, 149n142; in relation to "The Birthday of the Infanta," 38, 44; in relation to "The Fisherman and His Soul," 56, 58, 70; in relation to "The Happy Prince," 98; in relation to "The Star-Child," 79, 81–82; in relation to Wilde's prison literature, 125, 130, 134. *See also* disability: in relation to intersectionality
Ireland and the Irish, 5, 8, 10, 17–19, 147n94; in relation to "The Selfish Giant," 23, 28
irony, 6–7; in relation to "The Birthday of the Infanta," 40, 43, 48; in relation to "The Fisherman and His Soul," 70, 74; in relation to "The Happy Prince," 99, 103, 112; in relation to "The Selfish Giant," 26; in relation to "The Star-Child," 81, 86, 93, 95; in relation to Wilde's prison literature, 123, 132
isolation, 13, 142; in relation to "The Fisherman and His Soul," 60, 71; in relation to "The Happy Prince," 102; in relation to "The Selfish Giant," 25; in relation to "The Star-Child," 75, 77; in relation to Wilde's prison literature, 121, 127, 131–33

Jackson, Steven, 144n4
James, Henry, 55
Jesus. *See* Christ, figure of

Kafer, Alison, 115
Killeen, Jarleth, 8–10, 17; in relation to "The Birthday of the Infanta," 42, 50–51; in relation to "The Fisherman and His Soul," 58; in relation to "The Selfish Giant," 23, 28; in relation to "The Star-Child," 89, 92–93
Klages, Mary, 99
Kooistra, Lorraine Janzen, 7, 8, 144n13
Kotzin, Michael, 149n137
Kristjánsson, Kristján, 21–22, 76, 84–85

Lear, Edward, 17
leper, figure of: in relation to "The Fisherman and His Soul," 69–70; in relation to "The Star-Child," 82, 86–87, 89–91, 95; in relation to Wilde's prison literature, 124–25, 131–32, 139
littleness, 10, 17, 143n1; in relation to "The Birthday of the Infanta," 35, 37–40; in relation to "The Devoted Friend," 139–40; in relation to "The Fisherman and His Soul," 54–56, 67, 73; in relation to "The Happy Prince," 103, 106, 107–9, 112; in relation to "The Nightingale and the Rose," 137; in relation to "The Selfish Giant," 23–25, 27; in relation to "The Star-Child," 82, 87–88; in relation to Wilde's prison literature, 120, 126, 130. *See also* child, figure of; dwarfism and dwarfs
Longmore, Paul K., 11, 24–25
love: in relation to "The Birthday of the Infanta," 39, 42, 46–47; in relation to "The Fisherman and His Soul," 54, 56–57, 59–74; in relation to "The Happy Prince," 101, 105, 109, 111, 113; in relation to "The Nightingale and the Rose," 136–37; in relation to "The Selfish Giant," 25, 27–28; in relation to "The Star-Child," 75–82, 84–88, 92, 96; in relation to Wilde's prison literature, 117, 121, 124–26, 129, 131–32, 142
loving-kindness: in relation to "The Star-Child," 76, 80, 86–87, 90, 92, 96; in relation to Wilde's prison literature, 121, 123, 127, 129, 131, 141
Lukács, Georg, 77

mac Cumhaill, Fionn, 18
MacRitchie, David, 17
madness, 13, 149n142; in relation to "The Birthday of the Infanta," 38; in relation to "The Fisherman and His Soul," 60, 70–71; in relation to "The Star-Child," 83, 89; in relation to Wilde's prison literature, 123, 130. *See also* disability: developmental, intellectual, mental, neurological, or other invisible
Maeterlinck, Maurice, 6
Markey, Anne, 7–9; in relation to "The Birthday of the Infanta," 50–51; in relation to "The Fisherman and His Soul," 65; in relation to "The Happy Prince," 114; in relation to "The Selfish Giant," 23, 26, 28; in relation to "The Star-Child," 76, 80, 92–93, 95
Martin, Thomas, 126–28
marvel: in relation to "The Birthday of the Infanta," 45; in relation to "The Fisherman and His Soul," 57–59, 65, 67, 73; in relation to "The Happy Prince," 107–10, 113–14. *See also* wonder
McCormack, Jerusha, 32
McDonagh, Patrick, 45, 80
McGann, Jerome J., 116, 142
McRuer, Robert, 16, 146n67
medievalism, 61–62, 64, 71, 74
melodrama, 20, 29, 52, 88
Mendelssohn, Michèle, 18–19, 36, 134, 147n94
mer-creatures and mermaids, 3–4, 15, 17,

92, 137; in relation to "The Fisherman and His Soul," 54–74
Mitchell, David T., 18, 51
*mitleid*, 85
mobility (impairment), 12, 31; in relation to "The Happy Prince," 3, 98–99, 102–4, 114–15
moralizing, 6, 8, 26, 62, 71, 103, 140–41
morals, in fairy tales, 6–7, 37, 73, 91, 96, 116, 139–40
Mossman, Mark, 5–6
mutuality, 76, 85, 89–90, 97, 110–11, 129. *See also* reciprocity

Naslund, Sena Jeter, 120
Nietzsche, Friedrich, 21, 85, 96
"Nightingale and the Rose, The" (Wilde), 28, 32, 136–37, 140, 162n48
Nodelman, Perry, 7–8, 10, 26, 28, 87–88

O'Connor, Erin, 145n41

*Pall Mall Gazette*, 9
paternalism, 29, 148n101; in relation to "Birthday of the Infanta," 35, 46, 51; in relation to "The Devoted Friend," 140–41; in relation to "The Happy Prince," 100; in relation to "The Selfish Giant," 23; in relation to "The Star-Child," 82, 85, 93, 95; in relation to "The Young King," 139
*Patience* (Gilbert and Sullivan), 18
Payne, Anthony, 148n108
peculiar, use of as adjective, 4
"Pen, Pencil and Poison" (Wilde), 158n94
peril, 13, 15, 19, 142; in relation to "The Fisherman and His Soul," 58, 71, 73; in relation to "The Happy Prince," 102, 112; in relation to "The Star-Child," 75, 77; in relation to Wilde's prison literature, 128, 131–32
person-first language, 143n3

philanthropy, 85, 93–97, 125–29, 132. *See also* altruism; charity
physiognomy, 19, 35, 40, 86, 145n41
*Picture of Dorian Gray, The* (Wilde), 6, 61–62, 105, 134
pity, 7, 20–22, 137, 140, 142, 148n101; in relation to "The Birthday of the Infanta," 36, 46, 48–49, 51–52; in relation to "The Happy Prince," 101–3, 106, 111, 113, 115; in relation to "The Selfish Giant," 24–25, 27–28; in relation to "The Star-Child," 77–79, 81–97; in relation to Wilde's prison literature, 124–27, 129–33. *See also* compassion and compassionate action
*Poems* (Wilde), 134
poor, the. *See* class
Poor Law Amendment Act of 1834, 11
poverty. *See* class
Prendergast, Catherine, 20–21, 84, 91, 96
Price, Margaret, 32, 149n142

Queensberry, 9th Marquess of (John Sholto Douglas), 123
queer, use of term, 4–5

racism and ethnocentrism, 2, 10, 12–13, 15–20, 32, 147n94, 149n142; in relation to "The Birthday of the Infanta," 38–40, 42, 44; in relation to "The Fisherman and His Soul," 54–58, 61, 64–66, 71; in relation to "The Happy Prince," 105–7; in relation to "The Young King," 138
Ramazani, Jahan, 115
reciprocity: in relation to "The Happy Prince," 111; in relation to "The Star-Child," 76, 85–86, 88, 91–92, 96–97; in relation to Wilde's prison literature, 121, 124–25, 129, 133. *See also* mutuality

religion. *See* Christianity
"Remarkable Rocket, The" (Wilde), 32, 134–36, 140, 162n48
reparative reading, 5, 53, 144n4
Rodas, Julia Miele, 14–15, 99–100, 115, 147n84
Ross, Robert "Robbie," 122, 124, 160n1
Rousseau, Jean-Jacques, 21, 85, 89, 92–93, 95

*Salome* (Wilde), 134
Schaffer, Talia, 5, 53, 144n4
Schalk, Sami, 31–32, 149n142
Scheuer, Christina, 115
Schopenhauer, Arthur, 21, 85–86, 93, 95
Sedgwick, Eve Kosofsky, 144n4
self-injury and self-maiming, 12; in relation to "The Fisherman and His Soul," 64, 66; in relation to "The Happy Prince," 102, 104, 106; in relation to "The Nightingale and the Rose," 2, 32, 136–37
"Selfish Giant, The" (Wilde), 3–4, 17, 22–28, 148n108; in relation to "The Birthday of the Infanta," 35–36, 38, 44; in relation to "The Devoted Friend," 32, 140; in relation to "The Fisherman and His Soul," 56, 60, 72–73; in relation to "The Happy Prince," 98, 102–4, 112, 114; in relation to "The Nightingale and the Rose," 137; in relation to "The Star-Child," 87, 91; in relation to Wilde's prison literature, 124, 126, 131; in relation to "The Young King," 138
selfishness, 162n48; in relation to "The Birthday of the Infanta," 35–37; in relation to "The Devoted Friend," 140; in relation to "The Fisherman and His Soul," 62, 67; in relation to "The Happy Prince," 116; in relation to "The Remarkable Rocket," 32, 136; in relation to "The Selfish Giant," 23, 26; in relation to "The Star-Child," 75, 80, 82, 85; in relation to Wilde's prison literature, 117, 124, 126
selflessness, 162n48; in relation to "The Birthday of the Infanta," 36, 46; in relation to "The Devoted Friend," 32, 139–40; in relation to "The Fisherman and His Soul," 61; in relation to "The Happy Prince," 104; in relation to "The Selfish Giant," 26; in relation to "The Star-Child," 87, 90
sentimentality, 7, 11; in relation to "The Birthday of the Infanta," 35–36, 45, 47, 50, 52; in relation to "The Devoted Friend," 140; in relation to "The Fisherman and His Soul," 55; in relation to "The Happy Prince," 99, 106, 111, 114–15; in relation to "The Remarkable Rocket," 136; in relation to "The Selfish Giant," 22, 25–26; in relation to "The Star-Child," 76–77, 80, 84–85, 89, 92–93, 95, 97; in relation to Wilde's prison literature, 124, 126, 129, 132; in relation to "The Young King," 139
sexuality. *See* gender and sexuality
Shapiro, Joseph P., 21, 52, 96, 148n101
Sharp, Evelyn, 144n13
Shaw, George Bernard, 17
Shelley, Mary: *Frankenstein*, 13
Sherard, Robert, 122
Sklar, Howard, 21–22, 52
Small, Ian, 160n1
Smith, Lindsay, 80
Snyder, Sharon L., 18, 51
social change. *See* class
social justice. *See* class
*Soul of Man, The* (Wilde): in relation to "The Fisherman and His Soul," 62, 69–70; in relation to "The Happy

Prince," 102, 105, 109, 113; in relation to "The Star-Child," 94–96; in relation to Wilde's prison literature, 125
Spencer, Herbert, 93, 145n41
Speranza. *See* Wilde, Jane
*Sphinx, The* (Wilde), 134
Sprigge, T. L. S., 85–86
"Star-Child, The" (Wilde), 2–3, 30, 75–97; in relation to "The Happy Prince," 98, 104, 111–12, 116, 137; in relation to Wilde's prison literature, 124, 126; in relation to "The Young King," 32, 138–39
Stephen, James Fitzjames, 77
Stetz, Margaret D., 9–10
Stevenson, Robert Louis: *Strange Case of Dr. Jekyll and Mr. Hyde*, 14
stigma, 4, 10, 13, 15, 18–19, 21; in relation to "The Birthday of the Infanta," 38, 40, 50; in relation to "The Devoted Friend," 141; in relation to "The Fisherman and His Soul," 56, 60–61, 64, 71, 74; in relation to "The Happy Prince," 102, 104, 106; in relation to "The Selfish Giant," 23, 28; in relation to "The Star-Child," 75–77; in relation to Wilde's prison literature, 121, 131–32, 134, 142
Stoddard Holmes, Martha, 10–13, 15–16, 20, 74, 106, 145n41
Straley, Jessica, 6, 8, 108
suffering, 15, 21, 141–42; in relation to "The Birthday of the Infanta," 36; in relation to "The Fisherman and His Soul," 61, 71; in relation to "The Happy Prince," 99, 101, 103–5, 108–9; in relation to "The Selfish Giant," 28; in relation to "The Star-Child," 76, 78, 84–89, 92–93; in relation to Wilde's prison literature, 117–18, 121, 123–25, 127–32; in relation to "The Young King," 138–39

sympathy, 7, 17, 21–22; in relation to "The Birthday of the Infanta," 35, 42–43, 48, 50, 52; in relation to "The Devoted Friend," 139; in relation to "The Fisherman and His Soul," 60, 73; in relation to "The Happy Prince," 105, 109; in relation to "The Nightingale and the Rose," 137; in relation to "The Remarkable Rocket," 135; in relation to "The Star-Child," 75, 84–85; in relation to Wilde's prison literature, 118, 120, 124–27

Tannhäuser, 126, 131
Tatar, Maria, 7–8, 27–28, 40, 50, 108, 125, 133
telethon culture and telethons, 11, 148n101
Travers, Mary, 17
Tribble, Scott, 147n78
Tromp, Marlene, 15

ugliness, 4, 12–13; in relation to "The Birthday of the Infanta," 35–37, 40, 42–44, 47–48, 50–51; in relation to "The Happy Prince," 98, 100–102, 104, 106, 112, 115; in relation to "The Selfish Giant," 23, 27–28; in relation to "The Star-Child," 76–79, 83–84, 86–87, 89, 91, 95; in relation to Wilde's prison literature, 119, 123, 125, 128–29, 130, 133–34
ugly laws, 12, 102
utility, 12, 32; in relation to "The Fisherman and His Soul," 74; in relation to "The Happy Prince," 100–103, 105, 108, 110, 112–15; in relation to "The Nightingale and the Rose," 137; in relation to "The Remarkable Rocket," 135; in relation to "The Star-Child," 81, 89
utopianism and utopias, 71, 92, 96, 109, 112–14, 116, 125, 142

Velázquez, Diego: *Las Meninas*, 6
*Vera; or, the Nihilist* (Wilde), 164n129
Victor ("the Wild Boy of Aveyron"), 45, 80

Wainewright, Thomas Griffiths, 158n94
Warner, John M., 85, 92
*Washington Post*, 18–19
Whistler, James MacNeill, 50, 135
wild child. *See* changeling
Wilde, Jane "Speranza" (mother of Oscar Wilde), 17
Wilde, Oscar: American tour, 18–19; fairy tales taken as a whole, 1–4, 6–10, 22, 28–29, 32–33, 116, 141–42; prison experience, 118–19, 121–24; views on prison reform, 126–33; work's relationship to disability studies, 3–6
Wilde, Oscar, works of: *The Ballad of Reading Gaol*, 31, 129–32; "The Birthday of the Infanta," 3–4, 6, 29–30, 32, 35–54, 56–59, 69–71, 73–74, 80–81, 83, 88, 91–92, 106, 112, 119, 126, 135–38; "A Chinese Sage," 93–95, 113; "The Decay of Lying," 6, 109, 113, 125, 144n7; "The Devoted Friend," 2, 6–7, 32, 139–41, 162n48; *The Duchess of Padua*, 164n129; "Epistola," 31, 50, 117–26, 129–32, 160n1; "The Fisherman and His Soul," 2–4, 30, 32, 54–75, 82, 91–92, 107, 112, 114, 119, 126, 131, 136–38; "The Happy Prince," 3, 31–32, 98–116, 118–19, 125–26, 137, 140–41, 143n2, 158n15; *The Happy Prince and Other Tales*, 1–2, 9, 118, 133; *A House of Pomegranates*, 1–2, 9, 62, 93–94; letters to the *Daily Chronicle*, 127–29, 132–33; "The Nightingale and the Rose," 28, 32, 136–37, 140, 162n48; "Pen, Pencil and Poison," 158n94; *The Picture of Dorian Gray*, 6, 61–62, 105, 134; *Poems*, 134; "The Remarkable Rocket," 32, 134–36, 140, 162n48; *Salome*, 134; "The Selfish Giant," 3–4, 17, 22–28, 32, 35–36, 38, 44, 56, 60, 72–73, 87, 91, 98, 102–4, 112, 114, 124, 126, 131, 136–38, 140, 148n108; *The Soul of Man*, 62, 69–70, 94–96, 102, 105, 109, 113, 125; *The Sphinx*, 134; "The Star-Child," 2–3, 30, 32, 75–98, 104, 111–12, 116, 124, 126, 137–39; *Vera; or, the Nihilist*, 164n129; "The Young King," 2, 32, 80, 138–39, 143n2, 162n48
Wilde, William (father of Oscar Wilde), 17
wonder, 9, 15, 28–29, 33; in relation to "The Fisherman and His Soul," 57–59, 65–66, 73; in relation to "The Happy Prince," 107–9, 113; in relation to Wilde's prison literature, 125–26, 141. *See also* marvel
Wood, Naomi, 149n137
Wooldridge, Charles Thomas, 129–31
working class other, figure of. *See* class; disability: in relation to poverty

Yenika-Agbaw, Vivian, 7, 13
"Young King, The" (Wilde), 2, 32, 80, 138–39, 143n2, 162n48

Zemlinsky, Alexander von: *Der Zwerg*, 6
Zhuang Zhou. *See* Chuang Tsŭ
Zhuangzi. *See* Chuang Tsŭ
Zipes, Jack, 7, 23, 51–52, 71, 76, 108, 111

## PECULIAR BODIES: STORIES AND HISTORIES

*They Run with Surprising Swiftness:*
*The Woman Athletes of Early Modern Britain*
Peter Radford

*Melville's Other Lives: Bodies on Trial in "The Piazza Tales"*
Christopher Sten

*Lame Captains and Left-Handed Admirals:*
*Amputee Officers in Nelson's Navy*
Teresa Michals

*Beyond the Moulin Rouge: The Life and Legacy of La Goulue*
Will Visconti

*Sapphic Crossings: Cross-Dressing Women in*
*Eighteenth-Century British Literature*
Ula Lukszo Klein

*Sight Correction: Vision and Blindness in Eighteenth-Century Britain*
Chris Mounsey

www.ingramcontent.com/pod-product-compliance
Lightning Source LLC
Chambersburg PA
CBHW021734220426
43662CB00008B/855